T0065775

A Special Mission: Hitler's Secret Plot to Sieze the Vatican and Kidnap Pope Pius XII

Disaster!: The Great San Francisco Earthquake and Fire of 1906

Soldier of Peace: The Life of Yitzhak Rabin

Blood and Water: Sabotaging Hitler's Bomb

Left to Die: The Tragedy of the USS Juneau

Fatal Voyage: The Sinking of the USS Indianapolis

A Killing Wind: Inside Union Carbide and the Bhopal Catastrophe

Day of the Bomb: Countdown to Hiroshima

Ben-Gurion: Prophet of Fire

Miracle of November: Madrid's Epic Stand, 1936

The Bravest Battle: The 28 Days of the Warsaw Ghetto Uprising

The Race for Rome

Genesis 1948: The First Arab-Israeli War

Santo Domingo: Revolt of the Damned

Subversion of the Innocents

Kishi and Japan: The Search for the Sun

No Greater Glory

No
Greater
Glory

THE FOUR IMMORTAL CHAPLAINS AND THE
SINKING OF THE DORCHESTER IN WORLD WAR II

Dan Kurzman

RANDOM HOUSE TRADE PAPERBACKS | NEW YORK

2005 Random House Trade Paperback Edition

Copyright © 2004 by Dan Kurzman
Map copyright © 2004 by Jeffrey L. Ward

Published in the United States by Random House Trade Paperbacks,
an imprint of The Random House Publishing Group,
a division of Random House, Inc., New York.

RANDOM HOUSE TRADE PAPERBACKS and colophon are
registered trademarks of Random House, Inc.

Originally published in hardcover in the United States
by Random House, an imprint of The Random House Publishing Group,
a division of Random House, Inc., in 2004.

Grateful acknowledgment is made to the Immortal Chaplains Foundation
(www.ImmortalChaplains.org) for permission to reprint excerpts from letters,
video transcripts, and all photos, unless otherwise credited.

LIBRARY OF CONGRESS CATALOGING-IN-PUBLICATION DATA
Kurzman, Dan.
No greater glory: the four immortal chaplains and the sinking of the Dorchester
in World War II / by Dan Kurzman.
p.   cm.
Includes bibliographical references and index.
ISBN 0-8129-6609-0
1. Fox, George Lansing, 1900–1943.   2. Poling, Clark Vandersall, 1910–1943.
3. Washington, John P. (John Patrick), 1908–1943.   4. Goode, Alexander D.
(Alexander David), 1911–1943.   5. *Dorchester* (Ship).   6. Chaplains, Military—
United States—Biography.   7. World War, 1939–1945—Chaplains—United
States—Biography.   I. Title.
D774.D56K87 2004   940.54'293—dc22 [B]   2003060313

www.atrandom.com

To the memory of the Four Immortal Chaplains
and the other men of the Dorchester
who died; to the brave survivors
and their rescuers; and to my
dear wife, Florence, who put
so much of herself into
helping me bring these
heroes to life

PREFACE

As a reporter and author, I have encountered many extraordinarily heroic people while conducting research for my articles and books. But I have never come upon an act more glorious or more selfless than that of four chaplains of different faiths who, during World War II, became an immortal symbol of brotherhood. As their torpedoed troopship, the USAT *Dorchester,* plunged into the depths of the North Atlantic, these men—a priest, a rabbi, and two ministers of diverse denominations— gave up their life jackets to passengers who didn't have one, then, arm in arm, joined in prayer as they sank together into eternity.

Complementing the personal drama of these chaplains is the largely untold story of the relatively few men who, with incredible will and fortitude, managed to survive one of the worst sea disasters of the war; men who drifted for hours piled up like living corpses in leaky lifeboats and on battered rafts that lurched precariously from wave to wave in the glaciated sea near Greenland. They were the lucky ones. More than two-thirds of the nine hundred men aboard the *Dorchester,* those who could not find room on the floating mountains of flesh, froze to death in a vast watery graveyard studded with Christmas-like blinking red lights that were attached to life jackets to attract rescuers.

Why did so many men die? In part, because of an incomprehensible command decision delaying their rescue. But even more would have perished if not for the selfless actions of the four chaplains, who prodded terrified passengers to leap from the sinking ship into a forbidding black void while surrendering their own means of survival.

I have long wanted to explore the lives of these heroes, to understand the shaping of character that would permit such supreme altruism—especially since they were representatives of three great religions bound together by love for a common God and for one another. In a sense, their actions enthrallingly signified a repudiation of all the prejudice and hate that over the centuries have led to so many crimes, even genocide, in the name of God—hate that tragically still pollutes the psyche of many people in the world, to which the horrors of September 11, 2001, bear witness.

Shortly after that catastrophe, Bob Loomis, my editor at Random House, agreed that the full story of the four chaplains and their shipmates would have special meaning. So I finally embarked on a work that I hope will contribute to the feeling of interfaith harmony that pervaded this country and much of the world when the Twin Towers crumbled, to the sense of national unity that can meet the challenge of those who claim that God wants them to hate and kill those who do not practice their means of worshiping Him.

In researching this book, I personally interviewed dozens of people and was given access to many videotaped interviews. I also perused thousands of documents, including diaries and memoirs, and consulted countless relevant books. (A full accounting of sources can be found in the Acknowledgments and Bibliography.) Nothing in this book is fictionalized. Indeed, this is a story that does not need fictional embroidery. For no imaginary figures could emerge with greater glory than did the four chaplains, who died together hoping to guide humanity into a new era of peace based on democratic and enlightened spiritual values.

—DAN KURZMAN

ACKNOWLEDGMENTS

I am deeply indebted to my wife, Florence, who contributed her exceptional rewriting talent to this book, finding the right word, the descriptive phrase, the measured nuance in depicting character and atmosphere. She also helped conduct the research and ferret out information from people we interviewed. And she displayed enormous patience in transcribing more than thirty videotapes of interviews given by *Dorchester* passengers and relatives of the four chaplains, many of whom are now deceased.

I am also grateful to Bob Loomis, one of America's great editors, who offered me invaluable editorial guidance.

My thanks go as well to David Fox, a nephew of Chaplain George Fox and the cofounder, with the late Rosalie Goode Fried, of the Immortal Chaplains Foundation, for his insights and his help in contacting key individuals and making available to me the above-mentioned videotapes of interviews, which he had conducted over the years.

And what a joy to meet Theresa Goode Kaplan, the lovely, indomitable widow of Chaplain Alexander Goode, who spoke with my wife and me for many hours and permitted us to examine a whole cabinetful of documents related to her husband and his times, including hundreds of treasured personal letters from him.

Thanks also to Laura Linder, registrar of the Schenectady Museum and an official of the Dutch Reformed Church in that city, who provided me with a great deal of material on the life of Chaplain Clark Poling; Monsignor Michael J. Desmond of St. Stephen's Church in Kearny, New Jersey, who opened his file on Chaplain John Washington to me; Paul Fried, Chaplain Goode's son-in-law, for making available a number of tapes; Stan Kruger of the New York Public Library; Dennis Ambrose, Random House associate copy chief; and Bonnie Thompson, copyeditor.

My gratitude is also due my agent, Elaine Markson, and my literary consultant, Gladys Justin Carr, former vice president of Harper-Collins, for their advice, encouragement, and friendship.

And I'm indebted to Jeanette Kronick, a technical wizard who, on several occasions, saved many of these pages when, to my horror, whole chapters suddenly disappeared from my computer screen (making me pine for my old Olivetti portable). She also helped with the research.

Others whose assistance I greatly appreciate include:

Richard Boylan, archivist, National Records and Archives, College Park, Maryland
Robert Browning, chief historian, U.S. Coast Guard, Washington, D.C.
Rita Chesney, secretary, St. Stephen's Church, Kearney, N.J.
Peggy DeMaio, secretary, St. Stephen's Church, Kearney, N.J.
Mike Gay, photographer, Taunton (Mass.) *Daily Gazette*
Klee Dugan, niece of Clark Poling
Mary Haynes, archivist, U.S. Army Center of Military History, Washington, D.C.
Reverend Christopher Keenan, pastor, New York Fire Department
Claire Knopf, researcher
Fred Knopf, contributor of ideas
Judy McCloskey, official, Catholic War Veterans
Patrick R. Osborn, archivist, National Archives and Records Administration
Dawn Patterson, archivist, United Methodist Church, General Commission on Archives and History
Daniel Poling Jr., brother of Clark Poling
Vernon R. Smith, archivist, National Records and Archives

Jonathan Stayer, archivist, Pennsylvania State Archives
John Taylor, archivist, National Records and Archives
Anke Voss-Hubbard, archivist, Special Collections Library, Illinois Wesleyan University
Barry Zerby, archivist, National Records and Archives

I wish to express my gratitude to the following people for agreeing to be interviewed:

Norma Bernstein, member of Alexander Goode's temple
Daniel Blank, husband of Elaine Sevel Blank
Elaine Sevel Blank, student of Alexander Goode
Mildred M. Boeckholt, widow of Walter Boeckholt, *Dorchester* survivor
Joanne Schwoebel Brunetti, niece of John Washington
Gerhard Buske, first officer, *U-223*
Robin Chaffee, family friend of Clark Poling
Edward Chicowski, student of John Washington
Theresa Jordan Corcoran, friend of John Washington
Franklyn E. Dailey Jr., naval expert
James Eardley, *Dorchester* survivor
Benjamin Epstein, *Dorchester* survivor
Miriam Epstein, wife of Benjamin Epstein
Peter Ten Eyck, parishioner, Clark Poling's church
Betty Forner, student of Alexander Goode
Herschel Forner, friend of Alexander Goode
David P. Fox, nephew of George Fox
Edna M. Fox, daughter-in-law of George Fox
Siglinda Fox, sister-in-law of George Fox
Wyatt Fox Jr., grandson of George Fox
Alexander D. Fried, grandson of Alexander Goode
Paul Fried, son-in-law of Alexander Goode
Joseph Henry L. Geoguen, *Dorchester* survivor
Frederick S. Gillespie Sr., army personnel officer
Erwin Goldenberg, rabbi in Alexander Goode's temple
Gaylord T. Gunhus, chief of chaplains
Betty Hirschfield, member of Alexander Goode's temple
Bryna Jaman, niece of Alexander Goode

Theresa Goode Kaplan, widow of Alexander Goode

Marge Kolosek, sister-in-law of John Washington

William Kramer, *Dorchester* survivor

David J. Labadie, *Dorchester* survivor

Irma Long, student of Clark Poling

Elliot Miller, member of Alexander Goode's temple

Michael J. Nowins, *Dorchester* survivor

Daniel O'Keeffe, *Dorchester* survivor

Raymond F. O'Malley, one of two *Escanaba* survivors

John Pearse, member of *Tampa* crew

Edward Pinsky, nephew of Alexander Goode

Clark Poling Jr., son of Clark Poling

Victor Prevosti, secretary, United Staten Island Veterans Organization

Katherine Scranton Rozendaal, friend of Clark Poling

Louis Saporito, priest, student of John Washington

Paul Shalvoy, friend of John Washington

John S. Stamford, editor, *Greenland Patrol: 1940–45*

Edwin Sullivan, monsignor, colleague of John Washington

Earl B. Summers, brother of Roy Summers

Roy Nicholas Summers, *Dorchester* survivor

Richard N. Swanson, member of *Comanche* crew

Michael Warish, *Dorchester* survivor

Grace Fox Wiest, sister of George Fox

CONTENTS

CONTENTS

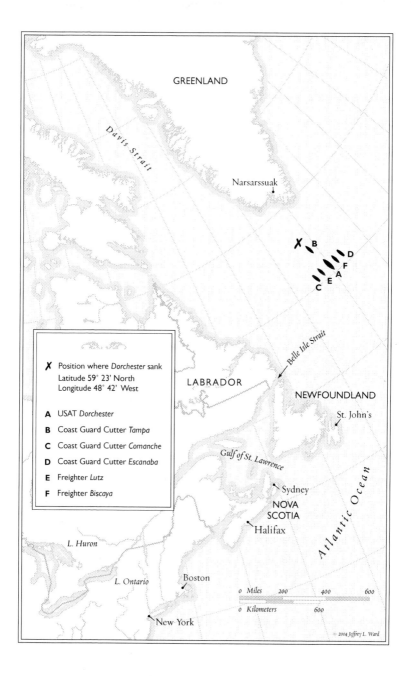

GREENLAND

Davis Strait

Narsarssuak

X B
      D
    F
   A
  E
C

Belle Isle Strait

LABRADOR

NEWFOUNDLAND

St. John's

✗ Position where *Dorchester* sank
   Latitude 59° 23' North
   Longitude 48° 42' West

A USAT *Dorchester*

B Coast Guard Cutter *Tampa*

C Coast Guard Cutter *Comanche*

D Coast Guard Cutter *Escanaba*

E Freighter *Lutz*

F Freighter *Biscaya*

Gulf of St. Lawrence

Sydney

NOVA
SCOTIA

Halifax

Atlantic Ocean

L. Huron

L. Ontario

Boston

New York

o Miles   200   400   600

o Kilometers   600

© 2004 Jeffrey L. Ward

No Greater Glory

CHAPTER I

THE SUICIDE SHIP

1

"Sergeant Warish! Sergeant Warish! Wake up!"

First Sergeant Michael Warish did not respond to the pleas of the shadowy figure hovering over his ravaged body, which, shortly before dawn on February 4, 1943, lay crumpled on a stretcher spread on the snow-blanketed dock in Narsarssuak, a port town near the southern tip of Greenland. He had just been carried from the Coast Guard cutter *Comanche,* together with scores of other wounded and dying men who were awaiting an ambulance from a nearby hospital.

They had been pulled out of the freezing waters of the North Atlantic about one hundred miles south of Greenland after a German U-boat torpedoed the USAT *Dorchester,* a troop carrier crammed with nine hundred men, most of whom died aboard the ship when it went down or froze to death in the icy currents. The sinking was one of the worst sea disasters in World War II.

Finally, the figure crouching over Michael shook him by the shoulders and saw his eyelids flutter, then open slightly. Michael glimpsed the dark form of someone etched against the slightly lighter sky.

"Where am I?" he muttered.

"Greenland," replied the fuzzy image. "How ya doin'?"

Michael didn't recognize the commander of the United States Army unit he was returning to after a leave at home. Greenland? Was that another name for heaven? Was he alive? Michael wasn't sure. He couldn't even remember his name, who he was. But he vaguely recalled stepping off the sinking ship into a black, foaming, ice-strewn infinity. Then the agonized cry that had resonated in the night and lingered in the frosty air, a cry that now echoed mercilessly in his mind: "Mother! Mother! Please save me!"

And gradually all those hundreds of little red lights that had speckled the ocean began flickering again. Almost like Christmas, he thought. Except that these lights reflected not a merry affirmation of life but a cynical celebration of death. Attached to life jackets so that the glitter could attract rescuers, they marked the graves of men like himself who were either dead or dying. No one, he had heard, could live more than twenty minutes in freezing water, and there was no time, he was sure, for rescue ships to come.

As Michael bounced in his life jacket from wave to wave, he resigned himself to death and suddenly, to his surprise, felt relaxed. He thought about his mother and his deceased sister, whom he would soon join, and about his fourth-grade teacher, who had given him a cookie every day. Yes, he was dying, but he could feel nothing—other than the burning in his throat from the salt and oil he swallowed as he drifted through the slick polluting the sea around the stricken ship. His body, nearly frozen, was numb. He simply felt sleepy, but once he fell asleep, he knew, he would not wake. Actually, an easy way to die.

Yet instinct forced him to refrain from shutting his eyes as long as possible, at least until the full twenty minutes medically allotted to life in the icy ocean was up. . . . What happened after that? He didn't remember. He must have died . . . and so, it seemed, he was in heaven . . .

Some hours later, Michael, conscious but with his mind still muddled, was carried along with other survivors to an ambulance that sped to a nearby barracks serving as a hospital, where doctors put him to bed and treated his leg, head, and back wounds. Soon, he drifted again into a deep sleep, though this time he would wake in the morning without prodding. He could remember his name now, and he realized that Greenland, where he was based, was not heaven.

Though the numbness was partially gone and the pain from his wounds was intensifying, Michael got up, deeply depressed, and, ignoring the advice of his doctors, hobbled to the barracks housing his unit a few hundred yards away to see his old comrades. Perhaps they could help rid him of his depression and put the horrors he had endured behind him.

But the reunion didn't work. His friends greeted him with joy, but also with endless questions about the disaster. In desperation, Michael locked himself in the barracks boiler room and sat on a stool. He wanted to ease his pain in the warmth—and to be alone; to drain his soul of the torment inflicted by fragmented memory, to still the echo of that maddening cry for help. But he knew this was impossible without first unblocking all the horrific details festering in the inner recesses of his mind.

Gradually, Michael relived the catastrophe. He could see himself getting wounded in the explosion, trapped in his quarters, then escaping and crawling to the deck, where, as the ship was going down, he witnessed a scene of an almost biblical nature. He had never been religious, but he felt strangely exalted now in the presence of four familiar figures in the tableau. Unable to imagine a more sacred moment, he began mumbling the half-forgotten words of the Lord's Prayer and, climbing over the railing of the swiftly sinking ship, stepped into the arctic sea.

2

Michael Warish had not been eager to leave home after his furlough and return to Greenland, with its icy weather, its bare, snow-covered fields, its overwhelming desolation and dreariness of life. But worst of all, as a North Atlantic veteran he knew the dangers lurking along the route to Greenland. German U-boats in so-called wolf packs infested the Strait of Belle Isle, aptly referred to as Torpedo Junction, between Labrador and Newfoundland Island. They had already sunk scores of Allied ships in these swirling waters.

Still, Michael, an eleven-year army enlistee who was now a member of an artillery company assigned to protect bases and construction crews in Greenland, was consoled by the thought that he would be rejoining his buddies, with whom he had tightly bonded in seeking to ease the bleakness of almost total isolation. Besides, he was scheduled to be back in the United States soon. He had first been sent to this vast arctic desert, the world's largest island, in 1941, and this was his sixth trip there. He had come home on furlough this time to attend his sister's funeral, and now, two weeks later, he was returning, one of the few passengers on the *Dorchester* who was sure where it was headed.

On the afternoon of January 22, 1943, Michael stepped off the train from Camp Miles Standish in Taunton, Massachusetts, with a "casual," or temporary, company of about three hundred other men, mostly green recruits, and onto Pier 11 in Staten Island, New York. Some who had never sailed on a large ship before gaped at the sight of the *Dorchester*. Despite its rather shabby, gray exterior, it had the sleek and graceful lines of a luxury liner rather than the forbidding, fortlike appearance of a warship. The men were excited as they mounted the gangplank.

In fact, the *Dorchester,* 367 feet long and weighing a relatively light 5,680 tons, had been launched in 1926 as a luxury passenger ship by the Merchant and Miners Transportation Company of Baltimore, Maryland. It could provide 314 vacationers with comfortable cabins, suites, and public rooms that advertisements claimed matched the magnificence of the "finest hotel." It was alive every night with laughter, bright lights, and soothing dance music.

Also aboard was a large, dazzling casino, where patrons could gamble as the ship cruised up the East Coast from Florida to New York, with stops in between at various ports. But in March 1942, with the war under way, the vessel metamorphosed into a troop carrier and the slot machines gave way to cannons. German U-boats were sinking ship after Allied ship, and the United States, caught unprepared for a full-scale sea war, had to bring every available vessel into service, no matter how old or dilapidated.

Soon bases were sprouting in the white, windy, arctic wilderness of Greenland as American engineers and military personnel poured in—those who were lucky enough to survive the U-boat attacks on troop transports taking them there. One *Dorchester* crew member, Chester J. Szymczak, who had sailed several times on the ship, later said:

"Breaking down in the middle of the North Atlantic, or being lost for days in the fog, seeing a ship disappear from a convoy, was nothing new for the *Dorchester*. If the ship made a trip without a mishap, it was considered lucky. There were many reports that the *Dorchester* was sunk."

In fact, one of the *Dorchester*'s two sister ships, the *Chatham*, was the first American troopship sunk in the war. After two uneventful round-trips to Newfoundland and Greenland from New York and Boston, its luck ran out. On August 27, 1942, the USAT *Chatham* was torpedoed and sent to the bottom of the Strait of Belle Isle. Fortunately, escorts were able to save all but twenty-six of the 569 people aboard. Would the *Dorchester*'s luck run out, too, perhaps with much deadlier results?

Anyway, many soldiers saw before them a ship whose weather-stained exterior still offered the impression of a luxury liner, if a rather decrepit one, and some felt they might be embarking on a more pleasant cruise than they had anticipated. And they wouldn't need a casino to carry on their crap games.

As James McAtamney, one of the soldiers, said of this first impression, "All the kids, at least of my generation, had the same idea: One of these days I'm gonna make enough money to take one of those luxury trans-Atlantic cruises. In those days it was the *Queen Mary* or the *Mauritania*, et cetera."

Still, stevedores and others on the dock warned, "You'll be sorry, you'll be sorry," and one soldier, an undertaker from Long Island—perhaps influenced by the end product of his civilian occupation—ominously predicted, "This damn thing is never gonna make it!" Indeed, some who had earlier sailed on the *Dorchester* called it "the suicide ship" because it seldom exceeded a speed of twelve knots, though, at least theoretically, it was capable of fourteen and a half knots.

Another man could not imagine enjoying a pleasant cruise, but for a less portentous reason. He was so prone to seasickness that he felt nauseated even *before* he boarded the ship—while marching on the slightly swaying dock leading to the gangplank. Nor did his misery abate when he vomited into a barrel of water nearby, for his false teeth fell into the barrel! How could he go overseas without his teeth? How could he eat? His buddies tipped the barrel over, and the embarrassed soldier retrieved his teeth—though, considering the condition of his stomach, he didn't expect to have much use for them while at sea. He couldn't imagine any greater horror awaiting him.

3

Pfc Benjamin Epstein, a twenty-two-year-old Army Air Forces soldier who was among the recruits and would keep personnel records, was an optimist by nature who seldom worried about anything. But now he, too, worried about his stomach—even though it had managed to survive ravaging by the rich eastern European food his doting parents, immigrants from Russia, had fed him at home. It had not even rebelled when his father had inculcated in him, only too effectively, the worthy but stress-ridden principle of hard work and refusal to accept failure—a formula that had helped Ben's father become a successful businessman and realize the American dream.

Hoping to avoid the torture of seasickness, Ben cautiously asked the purser, who looked twice his own age and wore stripes that revealed his experience, "I wonder if you can help me. I've got a problem."

"Sure," the purser answered. "What is it?"

"I have never been on a boat of this size," the young man said. "In fact, the only boat I've ever been on is a small rowboat that one uses on the lake. I know I'm gonna be a miserable passenger on this ship. I just have a feeling. I was just wondering if you could recommend some food that will prevent me from getting ill."

"Son," the purser replied, "I've got just the food for you."

"You do? What is it?"

"I want you to eat a lot of strawberry jam."

"Strawberry jam?" Ben said in astonishment. "How come?"

"Because it'll taste twice as good coming up as it did going down!"

Nausea gripped Ben prematurely. What was the antidote for strawberry jam? He could hardly wait to reach wherever the ship was going.

4

The *Dorchester* was sailing the ice-packed North Atlantic waters with 900 passengers and crewmen: 597 military men, who would replace those based in Greenland since Pearl Harbor; 171 civilians, mostly engineers and Danish workers under contract to the Department of War; and 132 crewmen. The ship also carried one thousand tons of engineering equipment, food, and other cargo. Most of the people aboard would help maintain and improve two airfields in southwestern Greenland—bulldozing, tarring roads, scanning blueprints—or would operate weather stations to determine the best time for air attacks on Nazi forces in Europe. Weather was most accurately predicted in the arctic region.

Though the *Dorchester* functioned under army orders, it was commanded by a merchant marine officer, Captain Hans Danielsen, whose voice barked over the loudspeaker system. But Michael, as first sergeant, would serve as an important troop leader under Captain Preston S. Krecker Jr. of the U.S. Army.

Michael was a slender, dark-haired man with a docile demeanor and a soft voice that belied his toughness. Born in Greensburg, Pennsylvania, in 1912, the son of a poor coal miner who had emigrated from Czechoslovakia, he was hardened by rough times at an early age. The Warishes moved to Pittsburgh when Michael was sixteen, and he left high school to work part-time in order to help support his family.

As the Depression deepened, Michael tried to find a steady job, but to no avail. He thought of joining the army, but so did hundreds of others; they formed a line to the recruiting office that snaked for more than a block, only to learn that the army didn't need them. Then, one day in 1932 an aching tooth landed Michael in a dentist's chair, and he moaned about more than the ache. He was in financial straits. The soft-hearted dentist not only agreed to insert a filling for one dollar but also called a friend in the recruiting office on his patient's behalf.

The next day, Michael, on the recruiter's advice, entered the office by the back door so he could bypass the long line of applicants and, with a certain sense of guilt, was soon donning his army uniform. He served in Panama until May 1941, when he joined an artillery unit based in Greenland to protect engineers who were building and maintaining runways there. Now, new engineers would be relieving those grown weary in that white wilderness, and they were about to sail there on the *Dorchester*.

As the passengers climbed aboard the ship, four officers stood by the gangplank watching them approach and occasionally crying out, "Welcome aboard!" Three of them wore on their lapels a cross, and one, Hebrew tablets under a Star of David. The four chaplains, each of a different faith or denomination, were welcoming aboard their common flock.

CHAPTER II

A RARE KIND OF LOVE

I

Senior Chaplain George Lansing Fox, whose mild manner, baby face, and short stature masked the steeliness of a committed warrior, grasped more clearly than most men the horrific banality of young, mentally unprepared soldiers marching off like sacrificial lambs to what could be violent death. For he was a badly wounded, highly decorated veteran of World War I, a lucky survivor.

Nevertheless, George decided to volunteer again when he had digested the shocking radio report he heard one Sunday in December 1941 while sitting at home in Gilman, Vermont. The Japanese had bombed Pearl Harbor.

He suddenly jumped up and, his wife, Isadore, later related, "paced the floor of our living room, pounding his fist into his hand. 'Now we will go after them!' he exclaimed. In that moment more than ever, I began to realize what his country meant to him. From that day on, he began telling me that he was going to apply for commission in the Chaplains Corps of the United States."

Yet it wasn't easy taking this step. The minister and his wife had struggled fiercely to make ends meet ever since they married in 1924, moving from town to town, from one Methodist church to another, existing on a salary of less than a thousand dollars a year. Their son,

Wyatt, would one day tell them, "You need not expect me to be a minister. I would not put my family through what we have to go through."

George and his wife were shattered, not because he wouldn't choose the clergy but because these words laid bare the hardships their children had to endure. No, they could never abandon their vow to serve God. But was it necessary for George to serve God on the battlefield, Isadore asked herself—if indeed the services accepted him? He was not only forty-one years old, elderly by military standards, but he had never fully recovered from severe wounds he had suffered in World War I.

George, on the other hand, asked himself if it would be fair to leave his wife when, by returning to duty, he would have to give up his monthly disability check, which was vitally needed to supplement the family's income. And he knew the casualty rate among chaplains was high, especially since they did not carry arms. Who would care for his family if something happened to him? Besides, he loved the town and people of Gilman, his latest clerical post. Did it really make sense to leave home, even for a patriot? Finally, he decided he had no choice; he applied for enlistment in the army.

While George would go to war again, he worried that his teenage son might also enlist. He had always lavished on Wyatt a special, even consuming love, the kind he had been deprived of in his own childhood. And he was proud that Wyatt was so impatient to fight for his country, demanding to join the marines even before he graduated from high school. Hadn't his father run off to join the army before *he* had received *his* diploma? Wyatt argued.

But George would not let his son neglect his education. He agonized over the thought that Wyatt might take unnecessary risks on the battlefield, like those he himself had taken in the earlier war.

"There will be plenty of war to fight after you have graduated," George said.

And graduation was only months away.

2

With both father and son hoping to be accepted soon into the armed forces, a large crowd filed into the Methodist church in Gilman on Easter Sunday to make sure they would not be too late for farewells.

A RARE KIND OF LOVE

This meeting with George's congregation would be a far cry from the minister's reception when he had conducted services here for the first time. The people cherished their hillside church, which overlooked the main street of this small mill village, known mainly as the home of the Gilman Paper Company. And they had eyed this stranger suspiciously, feeling he was not the right man to represent them.

"We were so angry when we had to lose our other minister," one churchgoer explained, "that we talked it over and decided to be as mean as we could to our new one."

People hardly listened to the "new one" when he told them that he was like Abraham of old, who went out "not knowing where he was sent. . . . I am happy to be sent to serve you, but I will have to leave it to you to decide whether you have been given a black, a silver, or a fox of the more common red variety."

Most people did not seem amused by this play on his name. Whatever the color, they had been given a Fox they didn't want. As Isadore would say, "The inside of the church was cool, as most churches are the first Sunday in June when the windows have been closed all week. There was a chill of another kind in the air, however. . . . As I glanced at George, the look he gave me in return indicated that he felt the strange chill, too."

George decided he had to break the tension immediately or they might never accept him. Gambling on a quick solution, he deliberately pushed a small potted plant sitting precariously on the edge of the pulpit, and it crashed to the floor. Acting as if this mishap was accidental, he laughed, and the people laughed with him. They suddenly seemed mesmerized by the rest of his sermon. Afterward, one of them said, "Now we have made up our minds to love you just as we did the other minister and his wife."

And they loved him all the more when he helped farmers load their hay on a wagon, inspired them with moving sermons, thrilled them with his beautiful singing voice, tickled them with humorous stories, and had them roaring when he acted in church-sponsored skits, once disguising himself as a French girl, complete with curly wig and grapefruit breasts.

He became so popular in the town that the mill offered him a well-paid executive job, but he rejected it even though he was earning a pittance as a small-town minister. He explained to his wife, "How little people seem to understand that I am trying to live in the will of God, whatever the cost!"

George did, however, accept one connection with the company. He agreed to serve as a secret agent for the Federal Bureau of Investigation, which asked him to investigate a German chemist working for the firm who was suspected of engaging in espionage. If he was willing to die for his country abroad, George felt, how could he refuse to protect it at home? Would not the people praying for him agree if they knew?

Now, on Easter Sunday, they had gathered to thank him for his love and loyalty, for the joy he gave them as both minister and next-door friend.

That evening, Isadore was preparing a holiday dinner when, she remembers, she "heard someone sobbing in one of the chambers. I went upstairs and found Wyatt weeping and teardrops all over his bedroom floor. I was much surprised, as I had not seen him cry since he was a small boy. When I asked him what was troubling him so, he said, 'That may be the last Easter sermon I may ever hear Dad preach.'" Even as Isadore tried to console him, she herself struggled to hold back tears.

A few months later, Wyatt received his high school diploma and reported to the marine enlistment office. As he was about to leave by train for a training camp, Isadore related, he "began to shake hands with his father as a young man would do. Just then the conductor called out, 'All aboard!' Wyatt jumped into George's arms and kissed him"—as if it were indeed for the last time.

Isadore was worried enough about her only son, though he would have been called to war even if he had not volunteered. But no one was demanding that George risk his life again—no one except George himself, though she knew his decision to leave her home alone with their young daughter, Mary, was tormenting him. And yet she knew he must go, that he must heed God's will.

But like her son, Isadore had a premonition. One day the couple visited her sister, and as she was wiping the dishes after dinner, she "saw George laughing and talking with the people in the front yard." She told her sister, "Somehow, I can't see George growing old."

Trying to raise her spirits, her sister replied, "I think that is just because he is so young and full of life and is always so happy."

George never seemed younger or more full of life than on the day in August 1942 when he passed his physical examination despite his war wounds and received his commission in the Chaplains Corps. He would not fight in this war or even carry a gun, but he would try to ease the pain of men who *were* fighting—and dying—and reach into their hearts with prayers of peace.

3

Resplendent in his military uniform, the commandant of the Harvard Chaplain School, a priest from the Brooklyn Diocese, welcomed his fellow men of the cloth with the passion he might have reserved for members of his parish. But even before the new recruits took their seats in the campus stadium, they had felt sparks of inspiration as they roamed hallowed grounds and reflected on how religion had played a crucial role in the country's glorious past.

They had passed the spot where, during the Revolutionary War, a chaplain, the president of Harvard, had led soldiers in prayer on their way to fortify Bunker Hill. They had walked past buildings where some of these men had been quartered, and past a church where General George Washington had worshiped. Now the commandant's words seemed to fit the historical images evoked.

The speaker, a colonel, stressed to the priests, rabbis, and ministers seated before him that it was more important to meet the spiritual needs of the young soldiers than it was to meet those of their parishioners. And to give more of themselves to the soldiers, he said, they must strengthen their religious commitments to whatever faith they observed. They were, he added, religious ministers first and officers second. He quoted a Latin adage: *"Nemo potest dare quid non habel,"* or "No one can give that which he does not have."

After this statement one rabbi in the audience said, "It made me think of how many of us are purveyors of a religion we neither practice nor believe in."

George Fox was not one of them. He practiced his religion without cease, not simply in church but in every moral decision he made. And he unreservedly believed in his religion, especially since it had played so vital a role in the healing process after an agonizing childhood and the horrors of World War I.

The colonel's talk awakened in George some painful memories, since after that war he had abandoned Catholicism, seeking to shed every sign of his past in embracing a completely new identity. But now, at Harvard, it didn't seem to matter much which house of prayer one attended. George found himself suddenly assimilated into a strange world of clergymen where no particular faith predominated, a world in which a common God became the spiritual focus not only of separate religious concepts but of the individuals embracing them. Before this assimilation, most of these clerics had lived in their own religious cocoon and seldom, if ever, mingled with their counterparts of other faiths.

Now the practitioners of many religions were thrust together, six to a room furnished with two-tier bunks, in a dormitory called Perkins Hall. They ate together, studied together, marched together, drilled together, and even prayed together. As one chaplain, Rabbi Isaac Klein, later said:

"The arrangement proved to be a great source of a liberal education, and it started on the very first morning. As each one of us began to recite his morning devotion, I suggested that, instead of each of us eyeing the other with curiosity, we should, rather, explain to each other what we were doing. This suggestion was readily accepted by all in the room, and our dormitory room became a classroom."

After all, since each chaplain was responsible for the religious needs of all the people in his outfit, it only made sense to learn something about religions other than his own.

Alexander Goode was another rabbi in this "classroom." He shared the pleasure of this unique experiment in ecumenism with an Episcopalian, a Presbyterian, a Christian Disciple, and a Baptist. When "our neighbors found out that the only two rabbis in the class were housed in the same room," Rabbi Klein recalled, "they sent delegations to make offers of exchange. One offered two Catholic priests for one rabbi; the others, a Lutheran and a Congregationalist, of which we had none."

Who wanted a clergyman of his own religion or denomination?

Both George Fox and Alex Goode found this remarkable experience stimulating, even exciting. And the pair, a Methodist and a Jew, soon became close friends, though Alex, at thirty-one, was ten years younger than his battle-seasoned comrade. Aside from their ecumenical links, they had much in common. Both had been emotionally scarred by past personal conflicts. Both had charismatic personalities and were especially popular with young people and the less privileged and powerful. Both had lived on shoestring budgets in order to devote themselves to serving God, though they could have greatly fattened their bank accounts in other jobs, George as a businessman, Alex as an engineer.

Finally, both had an overwhelming faith in the future of their country. George had more than earned his patriotic credentials in World War I, while Alex had served many years in the National Guard.

Their friendship grew as they studied and trained together and learned each other's extraordinary abilities and character traits. They took courses in military law, hygiene, first aid, army organization, pastoral counseling, and map reading. And they drilled and marched with the other clerics for two hours every day except on weekends. Though many of these men were ten or twenty years older than the soldiers they would shepherd and puffed along on tender, blistered feet, Alex's breathing remained quite regular. For intense training in the National Guard and on the athletic field had toughened him physically and mentally. And his feet, it seemed, could have tramped over fire.

Nor was he motivated only by simple patriotism.

4

Like George Fox, Alex Goode was sitting in his living room after dinner on December 7, 1941, when he heard the radio blare the news of the Japanese attack at Pearl Harbor. And as most of the U.S. Navy's ships with their crews were sunk, so, it seemed, was Alex's dream. He had hoped to usher in a "century of humanity" imbued with a spirit of brotherhood and democracy that would bind together people of all religions, races, and classes. Would Pearl Harbor spell the end of the dream—or the prelude to its realization?

The question arose at a crucial moment in Alex Goode's life. The rabbi had only shortly before resigned as leader of the congregation of a temple in York, Pennsylvania, because his dream had come into conflict with the narrow, provincial views of the temple's administrators, though the congregation regarded Alex as a hero. Pearl Harbor then determined his next move.

How, he wondered, could he and his wife, Theresa, live the ideal life they had so eagerly anticipated amid the turmoil of a world gone mad? He would enlist in the chaplaincy and ask for overseas duty. He couldn't stay home while others did the fighting.

Theresa was distraught. "The night of Pearl Harbor," she recounted, "I nearly fell apart. Alex, the great patriot that he was, wanted to enlist immediately. I just looked at him and didn't say a word."

Her immediate reaction was similar to that of Isadore Fox when George expressed this desire. Since Alex was a thirty-one-year-old married clergyman and the father of a baby, three-year-old Rosalie, he didn't have to enlist. Why shouldn't he stay home to raise the spirits of the families whose sons and husbands were sent to the battlefields? The couple had been separated by circumstance much of their married life. Now they would be separated once more—perhaps this time forever.

Theresa was sure her husband would take any risk to save others. And the nine years he had spent in the national guard had only fed his feeling that with his training he was well prepared to do so. Yet for all her anxiety, she understood that she could not challenge a compulsion so deeply rooted in his psyche. She was silent even as she remembered what Alex had once written:

"Family tradition has it that there was a Colonel Goodkowitz [Alex's original surname] on the staff of Napoleon. This concession to the military by a peace-loving people is no doubt largely responsible for the fact that I spent the entire summers of the past few years in Army camps. The life of the soldier has encouraged my obedience to superiors, and my sense of duty."

This sense of duty was, in fact, apparent from his earliest years. At the age of ten, on Armistice Day, Alex trekked miles from his home in Washington, D.C., to Arlington National Cemetery in Virginia to attend a ceremony at the grave of the Unknown Soldier. Who was the man being honored? What religion? What race? No one knew. All anybody knew was that he was an American hero. And that was, it seemed, how it should be. This was true brotherhood.

Theresa realized that not even Alex's sense of duty to his family could compete with his devotion to his almost obsessive campaign to spiritually reform the world. And she was more than willing to be at his side in this crusade. But now a war to free much of mankind from tyranny had intervened, and however much she dreaded his departure, she knew he must enlist in the chaplaincy and request overseas duty.

To Alex's apparent surprise, it was his mother who vehemently dissented. Although she was normally disinclined to smother him with affection or display much interest in his future, she suddenly seemed to care about him. If he did enlist, he must not volunteer for overseas service, she insisted. Her two younger sons, Joseph and Moses, had enlisted and were going overseas, but they would be drafted anyway. Why should another son risk his life unnecessarily? How many sons might she lose?

Alex reacted to his mother's almost hysterical plea in an equally surprising manner: He raised his voice to her for the first time. How, he asked, could he stay home when everyone he knew was ready to fight in this war of survival? Didn't she know what was happening to the Jews of Europe? His mother obviously didn't understand what he was all about.

Theresa understood, even though she and Rosalie would be left alone with little means of support. She quietly hoped, however, that the services would reject him and was not unhappy when the navy did indeed turn him down, claiming there was no opening for another rabbi. But Alex was enraged.

Finally, after a long and frustrating wait, the Army Air Forces accepted him, and he immediately applied for duty overseas. His joy was tempered only by the despair reflected in Theresa's eyes. With a heavy heart, she packed his bags for the trip to the Harvard Chaplain School.

5

After training at Harvard for a month, it was time for the student chaplains to be sent to camps around the country to preach what they had practiced. In parting, Alex and George promised to meet again after the war—or, who knew, perhaps before then, on some front in Europe or the Far East. Anyway, it seemed that both would be sent overseas without delay. Wasn't the job of a chaplain to raise the morale of men fighting and dying at the front? That was why they had voluntarily torn themselves away from their families without being required to. They could hardly wait to be at the side of those who desperately needed them.

But to their chagrin, they kept waiting . . . and waiting. In August 1942, George Fox shipped out to the 411th Coast Artillery Battalion at Camp Davis, North Carolina, and Alex Goode to the Army Air Forces base at Seymour Johnson Field in Goldsboro, North Carolina.

Hoping his assignment would be temporary, Alex decided not to be particular about the housing he would find for his wife and child, who would be joining him. The problem was, he couldn't find *any* housing at all, and a hotel was too expensive. He knocked on door after door, without success. Finally, he saw a man walk out of a house with a suitcase. Perhaps there was a vacancy there. He knocked once again, and a woman with a little girl by her side answered. Yes, she would be glad to rent a room, the woman said.

"I have a child," the rabbi stated as he handed her a five-dollar deposit. "A wife and a child."

"That's fine."

Then the little girl noted a strange insignia on the collar of his uniform and asked him what those tablets were.

"I'm a chaplain," Alex replied.

"I've never seen that before," the child said in wonderment. "I've always seen a cross."

"Well, I'm a Jewish chaplain."

Alex felt a certain uneasiness—he could, after all, lose the apartment if the child's ignorance reflected a racial bias on the part of her mother. But he must also have felt the pride that had motivated a navy chaplain in World War I, Rabbi David Goldberg—who was often addressed as "Father Goldberg"—to persuade the armed forces to permit Jewish chaplains to wear a Jewish rather than a Christian insignia.

After a nervous pause, the woman said she was returning the five dollars. She didn't want to rent the room to Jews.

Alex was crestfallen. He was trying to serve at the front, and she didn't want to rent the room to him! Didn't she understand that they were on the same side?

Perhaps not, but the woman suddenly changed her mind. The stranger looked like a nice man, even if he was a Jew, and she should have mercy on his wife and child, who probably wouldn't do her any harm. The rabbi got the room, where he sat and pondered just how difficult his mission would be. But when Theresa and the baby arrived, a surprising conversion took place.

"It was a cold night," Theresa said, "and [the landlady] had a hot water bottle in the bed so our feet would be warm. And we became the best of friends."

Alex grew more hopeful. Incredibly, it took only cold feet! Maybe his job would be a little less difficult than he had thought.

He was especially heartened when all the men at Seymour Johnson Field gave him a warm reception. Once, a non-Jewish soldier stepped into his office and asked for counsel on a personal problem.

He would like to help, Alex said, but he was a Jewish chaplain, and a Protestant chaplain was available.

Yes, the visitor replied, but he knew how Chaplain Goode always stood by his men and went to bat for them.

This soldier's problem was soon solved.

Alex's problem, however, was not. He had applied for overseas duty, but as the weeks and months rolled by without a reply, he launched a relentless lobbying campaign. He wrote to an influential rabbi in New York, saying, "All I want is a better opportunity to serve at the earliest possible moment." And he pleaded for help from friends of his wife and father in Washington, in vain. He bitterly mused to Theresa:

"It is harder work getting into the foreign service than it was to get my Ph.D. If they don't say something soon, I'll go to Washington and blow my top. If they'd at least send me some kind of answer, the waiting wouldn't be so hard."

Finally, success. He was to report to Camp Miles Standish at Taunton to await a ship bound for overseas. Alex rejoiced, but the men at his base didn't. In a move troops almost never made on behalf of a superior, they drew up a petition to Alex's superiors asking that the rabbi remain with them.

Alex was deeply moved, but he pointed out that orders were or-

ders. He didn't have to say that this was one order he was only too eager
to obey.

6

Rabbi Goode's popularity with the troops followed him to Taunton,
where, during bitter-cold weeks, Theresa recounted, he "would get the
boys together around the small stove in their barracks, boil water for
tea, and tell them stories and jokes to keep them happy."

Soon Alex, to his joy, was preparing tea for a newcomer as well—
George Fox. George, who, like his friend, had feared that he might sit
out the war in the United States, had been sent to this staging area from
Camp Davis, where he, too, had won the affection of his men.

The two chaplains resumed their discussions of the Old and New
Testaments and subjects like the possible role of religion and democ-
racy in the postwar world. Shortly, more men were drawn into these
conversations, including two other chaplains of different faiths: Clark
Poling of the Dutch Reformed Church and John Washington, a Roman
Catholic.

The four immediately bonded, feeling linked not only by biblical
history and spirit but also by an extraordinary interaction of personalities. They shared a sense of humor that permeated their counsel and
conversation, and even extended to practical joking.

Yet all were driven men, spurred on by an irrepressible need, nour-
ished by compassion and a covenant with God to fulfill at any risk a
mission that would test their souls. They symbolized in microcosm the
concept of brotherhood they hoped would help to promote friendly
postwar relations among both individuals and nations.

7

Chaplain Clark Poling, thirty-two, representing the seventh generation
of his family to produce a Protestant minister, had argued, even as a
youth, for a world infused with brotherly love. Once when his father,
Daniel A. Poling, the well-known Baptist minister, radio evangelist, and
editor of *Christian Endeavor,* stopped a shouting match between Clark

and his less idealistic elder brother, Daniel Jr., the sibling complained about Clark: "Aw, he's talking all the time about peace and brotherhood, and I'm sick of it. I told him it was soft stuff."

This "soft stuff" was a matter of conscience and common humanity to Clark Poling. He even loved his enemies, arguing that hate corrodes the soul and makes a bad soldier.

"If our cause wins," he once said, "they will be free, too. We do not fight to win for ourselves and for our children any good that cannot be shared."

Clark, like many idealists in the 1930s, was almost pacifistic in his arguments. He saw man as inherently good and believed that education, not war, was the way to achieve a peaceful world in which people settled disputes as brothers would.

Even after the black clouds over Europe had exploded into war with the Nazi invasion of Poland, he so passionately clung to his vision of peace that he couldn't see that conflict as a reason for the United States to man the barricades. He would write in a magazine:

"The most effective way that men have of achieving happiness is by creating personal sanctuaries which cannot be stormed by the forces of adversity. . . . We can build such a sanctuary by returning to the fundamental pleasures of home and family, of good books, and most important, to the joy of worshiping God. If our happiness is dependent upon these, the outside world can tumble about us and we can still have peace."

But the Japanese attack and the German atrocities soon burst this bubble of hope and obliterated any trace of pacifism still lingering in Clark's psyche. Pearl Harbor made it clear: Not even the soul could find peace until the enemy was crushed in war. Waging war had become less sinful than permitting carnage.

Even before Pearl Harbor, Clark had thought of going overseas as a fighting soldier if the United States entered the war against the murderers.

"Dad," he had told his father, "if I go in, I'm not going as a chaplain!"

Dr. Poling merely smiled, joking, "I think you're scared."

He understood his son and knew the opposite was true. "I knew," he later wrote, "that he was thinking of the more difficult and, as he regarded them, the more dangerous duties of armed conflict. He couldn't think of himself in a softer or more protected place than some other man, or of accepting a special consideration or exemption granted the ministry."

But the chaplaincy, the father argued, had had one of the highest casualty rates among the services in World War I. The enemy could kill him, but he couldn't kill the enemy since he was forbidden to carry arms.

And Dr. Poling knew something about war. During World War I, he had been en route to Europe on a morale-building mission for the War Department when his ship was attacked four times by submarines and was barely able to reach safety.

God, Dr. Poling prayed, would protect his son, too, if he faced such danger. And the thought brought to mind a letter he had received at the front from Clark, who was then only four years old.

"Dear Daddy," the child had scrawled in large block letters, apparently with his mother's help. "Gee, I wish I was where you are. Love, Clark."

Dr. Poling, who would shortly be gassed at the front, later reminisced: "Thinking of his childish desire as I stood in that scene of desolation, I was glad that my boy could be with me only in spirit and that he, when grown, would never find himself in such a war—for surely, I told myself, the civilized world would never countenance another such conflict."

Now, twenty-seven years later, Clark was finally persuaded by his father to serve as an unarmed chaplain, though the son still found it unfortunate that chaplains could not bear arms like any other soldier—as in medieval times, when they had fought alongside their parishioners. They had no guns then, of course, and they did not wield bladed weapons, since it was felt that men of God should not shed blood, or very much of it. But they did use the mace to break armor and bones. And some chaplains fought in the Revolutionary and Civil wars.

But Clark resigned himself to the fact that he could, as a modern-day chaplain, at least comfort and perhaps save men who *were* able to fight.

The moment for Clark to act came when he heard the radio report on the Pearl Harbor attack while visiting a member of his congregation after services on Sunday, December 7. He rushed home to listen to new reports with his wife, Betty. She knew before he said a word to her that he had made up his mind but didn't know how to tell her. He didn't really have to. Like Isadore Fox and Theresa Goode, who understood their husbands' dilemma, Betty realized it was agony for her spouse to leave her and their baby, three-year-old Clark Jr., or Corky as he was called, to enlist. And the pain was all the greater since she was pregnant with another baby they had already nicknamed Thumper, after the little rabbit in *Bambi*.

So she spoke first. He must go; he could not defy his conscience.

Betty was prepared for this moment, as she had long suspected that Clark would immediately enlist if the country went to war. In fact, he had made this clear to one friend, who recalled him saying, "The decision had been made before [the attack] and December 7th just iced it and put it into definite terms."

Why was he in such a rush to sign up? his father asked.

"It is," Clark replied, "love of America, love of freedom, love of home, love of justice, that will win for us. Lincoln proved that for Americans, proved and demonstrated it. Read what he said!"

Almost immediately, Clark conferred with members of his Dutch Reformed Church in Schenectady, New York, to let them know he would resign as pastor so he could serve. But they needed him now more than ever, they argued, and they rejected his resignation. Finally, when they realized his mind was made up, they said that, regardless, they would keep the job open until he returned. A charismatic and beloved leader, he had through the sheer power of his personality rejuvenated a dying church, and they wanted him back.

Clark then went down to the army recruiting center to apply for enlistment in the Chaplains Corps, impatient to kneel by the fallen in bloody fields to comfort them with prayer and a willingness to listen to wistful memories of home.

Finally, after a long wait Clark was accepted. He was immediately swamped with invitations to farewell dinners, and none was more memorable than the one his church held for him. In one of the most moving speeches he had ever delivered, he expressed his deep love for his flock and his anticipation of an early return to them. Members of the audience, many with tears in their eyes, replied with their own words of endearment for him. One participant later said, half seriously, of the address, "You had to see him at the dinner rise to such speaking heights as to outdo completely the guest of honor, his illustrious father" (who was famed for his oratorical skills).

Shortly before he departed, at a family dinner after Sunday services, Clark brought up the question of his possible destiny. A family member recalled Clark saying that if he didn't come back, "there was no reason for any of us to weep." He was doing what he had to do. In a private conversation with Dr. Poling as they sat together in his father's study, Clark forcefully stated, "Dad, I don't want you to pray for my return— that wouldn't be fair. Many will not return, and to ask God for special family favors just wouldn't be fair!"

Then, standing up, Clark placed his hand on his father's shoulder and went on with a smile: "Don't misunderstand me, I'm coming back all right—in spite of your high casualty rate for the chaplaincy." He added with a more serious demeanor, "Pray, Dad, that I shall never be a coward. Pray that I shall have strength and courage and understanding of men, and especially that I shall be patient. Oh, Dad, just pray that I shall be adequate! That is the prayer, Dad, I want you to pray; and when I do come back, everything will be wonderful."

Finally, Clark, escorted to the train station by his family, released Corky from his arms, kissed the child and Betty, and stepped aboard the train that would take him to Camp Shelby in Mississippi. Here he would learn the duties of a chaplain.

On arriving, Clark was temporarily assigned to the 501st Engineer Company of the Third Army and immediately volunteered for overseas duty, writing to his commander, "I would appreciate very much a permanent assignment with a combat unit in which a chaplain could accompany the men."

While anxiously waiting for a response, Clark was overjoyed to learn that he would be permitted to see his wife and baby again. Shortly they were living together in a small hotel in Gulfport, Mississippi, near the camp where Clark would spend his days in training.

Clark found himself in an earthly heaven as he waited to be sent overseas into what he was sure would be a combat zone. How lucky he was to spend his last days in the camp with his wife and child! He was a bit embarrassed, however, when Corky took a doll into the hotel dining room. The son of a soldier playing with dolls? But Clark finally convinced the child that the doll should at least wear pants rather than a dress. Apparently to prove he was a red-blooded boy, Corky began returning salutes whenever his father did. What wonderful days!

Clark enjoyed his training and camp duties as well, for he became very attached to the men of the 131st QM, whom he counseled and addressed on everything from the need for education to "sex morality." And they grew just as attached to him. But to the dismay of both Clark and the men, in late September 1942, after little more than a month together, the unit was to be sent into combat overseas—without him. He would remain at the camp but would be transferred to another unit. Had he not asked to accompany a combat unit abroad? Why were they leaving him behind? Clark made another plea for overseas duty: "Again may I express the hope that I will soon be permitted to serve with fighting troops. I am young, I am healthy, and I do not want a soft job."

At last, in November 1942, the long-awaited orders arrived. There were a few more days at home in Schenectady, where his joy over these orders was tempered by thoughts of his brother, Daniel, who was also a minister and had wanted to serve as a chaplain, too, but had to remain home to care for his invalid son.

"You must be very considerate of Daniel," Clark told his father. "It is harder for him to stay than it is for me to go. It takes greater courage for him to do what he is doing than it does for me to do what I am doing."

After another wrenching farewell, Clark was off to Camp Miles Standish in Taunton, Massachusetts, from where he would embark for the front, wherever it might be. God had finally come through—for Clark if not for Betty.

As He had for the three other chaplains, who were fated to meet at the camp en route to glory: George Fox, Alexander Goode—and John Washington.

8

On December 7, 1941, Father Washington stepped down from his pulpit in Kearny, New Jersey, got into his car, and eagerly drove down the roads leading to North Arlington, where he would spend Sunday afternoon with his favorite girl. John, who often called his mother, Mary, "my girl," had been trying to bring a little sunshine into her life ever since his father, Frank, died three years earlier.

He had worshiped his father, and his grief had deepened when he noted his mother's anguish. He showered her with flowers and gifts, and on this Sunday afternoon he picked her up at her home and escorted her to a movie and a restaurant. What an enjoyable day they spent—until John turned on the car radio while driving his mother home.

America, the speaker announced, was at war. Mother and son were stunned into silence as the prospect of a deadly future suddenly wiped out any trace of their lazy contentment. Mary knew what John was thinking, and what his two brothers were thinking, too. Would they all soon be sent off to fight?

On arriving at his mother's home, John accompanied her to the door, kissed her, then said, "Sorry, I've got to run. Of course, you know I must try to enlist. Everyone will be needed."

At his lodging, John, an associate pastor of St. Stephen's Church in Kearny, called the pastor, Reverend George Murphy, to request permission to serve as a chaplain. He was sure that Father Murphy would agree. The man was a tough boss, constantly pushing him to expand the church's activities, especially in conjunction with an affiliated school run by the Sisters of Charity, which sponsored athletic events, theatrical productions, and clubs.

Yet Father Murphy was also loved by everyone for his determination to improve the lives of the poor and underprivileged. Since John was just as determined to achieve this goal, he got along extremely well with his superior, whom he regarded as a kind of second father, in the parental sense.

And just as John anticipated, the pastor, who had served in the army in World War I, supported his enlistment. The young assistant was relieved, but the road to the battlefield was still not clear. Would the armed forces accept him with his sight so seriously impaired? If only he hadn't gone hunting in "Africa" . . .

Actually, he had gone hunting in Newark, New Jersey, where John was born in 1908. As a child he had, in his imagination, turned the rutted streets of the neighborhood into an African jungle full of wild animals. Playing with a young "hunting" companion, John was warily creeping along when suddenly his BB gun, which he was using to shoot "elephants," went off with a pop and he lay writhing in pain on the street. A bullet had grazed his right eye, permanently weakening it.

This accident would seriously affect John psychologically. A leader of his gang, he suddenly became an object of merciless taunts when he was forced to wear glasses. To prove that he wasn't a "sissy," he sometimes struck back with his fists—after removing his glasses. He soon felt compelled to avoid appearing "different," and even refused to take piano lessons for fear of adding to an "effeminate" image, though he loved music. (He would eventually submit to his mother's pleas.) And when he played baseball, he made sure he was the catcher so he could hide his glasses behind a mask.

But despite his fear of rejection, John applied for enlistment in the navy, choosing this service even though he had never learned to swim well because of his partial blindness. He had almost drowned when some of his tormentors in school pushed him into a pond. Still, as a messenger of God, he felt, he should not shrink from taking risks.

After a physical examination and a long wait, the answer came. John's fear proved well-founded; his application had been rejected. Shattered though not surprised by the news, the young priest lamented to Father Murphy that he was losing hope of doing what he felt God wanted him to do. The old soldier gently encouraged him.

Why not apply to his old service branch—the army? he asked. John was skeptical; the outcome would be the same. But he said he would think about it. He then conferred with another priest, who offered a solution: "When they test you, just cover your bad eye twice and read the chart with your good eye twice. They won't notice the difference."

A great idea, John felt, but he was a man of God. Should he stoop to such deception? Yes, he decided. How could he serve God without a little chicanery?

So John applied to the army and fudged the eye test, then spent many hours praying that God would forgive him for his trickery and arrange a positive response. Finally, to his great joy, he learned that the Almighty, in His sliest wisdom, had come through. John's application had been accepted.

The joy, however, slowly drained away when John visited his mother and saw her tears. He knew they flowed from more than pride, especially with his brothers, Francis and Leo, signing up as well, Leo also with the army and Francis with the Army Air Forces.

In May 1942 John was sent to Fort Benjamin Harrison for training, then a month later to Fort George G. Meade in Maryland, where he was given several furloughs while waiting for the army to approve his request for overseas duty. While he enjoyed the training, he was uncomfortable wearing his officer's uniform, which distinguished him from the enlisted men, with whom he closely identified; many of them reminded him of the boys in his old gang. He was, he felt, not cut out to be an authoritative figure. Ironically adding to his image of authority were his glasses, which had elicited those painful taunts in his childhood. He wondered why a chaplain had to be an officer.

"The only pain in the neck is that saluting business," he wrote to his brother Francis. "When I go to town I always turn my back and look in the store windows whenever I see a gang of soldiers coming by."

Despite the lingering sting of the taunts, John missed the gang at home, especially the "Washington gang"—his two brothers. Once when these siblings, who were enlisted men, came home on leave when he was also there, they saluted him, mockingly. He told them in an equally mocking manner, "I'm still boss here!"

And the three were soon wrestling with each other in the backyard. They were Irish, weren't they?

How great to be happy again.

Still, John was as impatient to be sent overseas as the three other chaplains, whom he had not yet met. On September 23, 1942, he wrote for a second time to an official in the chaplains' office in Washington: "Once more may I ask you to consider my application for overseas duty. If I am too fresh in requesting it, then slap me down."

But, to his joy, he wasn't slapped down. In November 1942, John joined his three fellow chaplains at Camp Miles Standish, where, while experiencing a rare kind of mutual love, they marked time until God would deliver them from this miserable, muddy, half-built camp and send them on a sacred mission.

CHAPTER III

COLD CHILLS
AND A CAKE OF ICE

I

Colonel Frederick Gillespie Sr. sat at his desk at the New York Port of
Embarkation in Brooklyn with his eyes glued to the list of chaplains
waiting to be sent overseas. He ruminated over his choices. As head of
personnel at the command center for all army transports heading to
Europe from that port, it was up to him to pluck out names. Who
would go on what ship? It was like a lottery. Would his choices end up
on an ill-fated voyage? Only God knew.

Gillespie worked dizzyingly to meet his deadlines. But it wasn't easy.
Almost every time he drew up a passenger list for a ship, a snafu would
require sudden changes, which he would have to make quickly so the
ship could raise anchor on time. And as the war spread, more and more
ships joined the fleet of transports needed by the military. The elegant
Queen Mary and the run-down *Dorchester* would no longer take passengers on heavenly vacations but would instead be transporting troops to
far-flung fronts.

The *Dorchester* was ready to sail, but at the last minute two chaplains
were scratched from the roster. This crisis prompted an urgent call from
Gillespie's superior. One Protestant and a Jew were still on the list, the
man said, but a second Protestant and a Catholic were needed—fast!

Gillespie, who had accumulated a pool of chaplains waiting to be dispatched overseas, quickly scanned the roster. He noted that one man came from Newark, his own hometown: John Washington. He didn't know the man personally, but why not give a possible neighbor a chance for glory? Next, a Protestant. His eyes focused on the name Clark Poling. From his record, it seemed clear he was the son of the famous evangelist. He would surely be happy to make his father proud of him. Gillespie gave the two names to the appropriate official at Miles Standish headquarters; the *Dorchester* would soon be able to depart. He was relieved. But the ship's destination was so secret that even he did not know where it was going.

2

Isadore Fox awoke on the morning of January 15, 1943, with a heavy heart. It was the nineteenth anniversary of her wedding to George, but he was in Camp Miles Standish and his name was listed on his unit's bulletin board among those about to go overseas. Had he already left?

"I could not seem to accept the news as a fact," Isadore later wrote. "I kept praying that he would not have to go."

And her mood did not brighten when there was a knock on the door and she was handed a bouquet of nineteen roses. Had George sent flowers because he couldn't get a leave? Though depressed, she went to work; she had taken a job at a defense plant to help support her daughter and herself while George was away. As she left the plant at eleven P.M., she saw in the shadows a barely visible figure standing outside the door. Could it be . . . ? No, the figure was too large. But suddenly she cried in excitement, "You may come out now, George. I see you."

Still the prankster, her husband had been hiding behind a stranger. He ran into her embrace—an hour before midnight. He had made it home in time for their anniversary.

"I was so happy," Isadore said, "that I forgot that I had stood on my feet for eight hours that day."

But deep in her mind, she could not forget that this would be the last time she would see him—until he returned.

At home with their daughter and Isadore's sister, George told jokes and stories until the laughter was interrupted by his sister-in-law, who took him aside and asked apprehensively, "Aren't you worried about going overseas?"

"I have all the faith in the world," he replied. "I am going over safely and coming back safely."

But Isadore would say: "Cold chills ran up and down my spine as I lay beside him in bed those last three nights he was with us."

On Sunday the couple went to church and George conducted services. Afterward, a young man walked over to him and said, "I sing in the choir and I would give anything if I had a voice as good as yours."

Yes, a beautiful voice, Isadore thought. When would she hear it again?

The next morning, George was to return to Camp Miles Standish, but he told his wife, "You do not need to take that long walk to the bus station on this cold morning. I would rather leave you here in the home that I am coming back to."

"So I kissed him," Isadore would reminisce, "and saw him walk a short way across the street into a heavy fog and disappear."

3

Greenland! That was where he was going, Rabbi Goode told his wife, Theresa. He had learned of his destination through the grapevine, and was dismayed. The couple were meeting in New York on Alex's last leave a few days before he was to be shipped out, but as thrilled as the rabbi was to see his wife, he couldn't hide his distress. He had asked to be sent overseas so he could bring comfort to the fighters. But who was fighting in Greenland—the polar bears and the walruses? He would apparently be stuck at some snowy air base with nothing to do but make coffee to warm up the boys—just like in the United States.

"I don't want to go to Greenland," he wailed to Theresa. "I'm not going to sit on a cake of ice. I want to go where there's action."

But Alex appeared to sense that ultimately he would see action—and that the cost might be great. According to Rabbi David Max Eichhorn, who was with him at Camp Miles Standish, the two of them and Father James M. Liston had been playing a game of pinochle when both Alex and the priest said they "had a premonition that the ships carrying them to their respective overseas destinations were not going to make it."

But no premonition could keep Alex from appealing directly to General William R. Arnold, the chief of chaplains, for assignment to a more active post. The answer, however, was no. With deep chagrin, the rabbi was now resigned to sitting on a "cake of ice." But why think of ice, he decided, with Theresa in his arms?

Alex did think of his daughter, Rosalie. Why, he asked his wife, hadn't she brought the child along as he requested? The child had been vaccinated and was running a fever, Theresa explained, and so she had left her with Alex's sister.

"I should have taken her anyway," Theresa later lamented. "I don't know whether it would have harmed her or not. But he was so disappointed that he didn't get to see her."

Not, however, disappointed enough to spoil paradise.

"I spent three days with him," Theresa would reminisce, "and then we said good-bye. It was a very difficult good-bye, and I looked at him through the window of the train. I was crying and he was crying. I knew I would never see him again—I just felt it in my heart."

Shortly, Theresa would receive a farewell note from Alex before he left Camp Miles Standish:

Darling: Just a hurried line as I rush my packing. I'll be on my way in an hour or two. I got back yesterday just before the warning. Hard as it was for us to say goodbye in New York, at least we could see each other before I left. Don't worry—I'll be coming back much sooner than you think. Take care of yourself and the baby—a kiss for each of you. I'll keep thinking of you. Remember, I love you very much. Alex.

4

Hardly had Clark Poling arrived at Camp Miles Standish when he telephoned his wife, Betty. Good news! His departure for overseas would be delayed. So would she and their son, Corky, please come to stay with him?

"Would I?!" Betty replied. "I fairly dragged Corky out of bed, but I did wait until I bought him a warm outfit. . . . So off we went to Taunton, Massachusetts, and there in two rooms we spent the next two months. We had Thanksgiving and Christmas together and it was the happiest Christmas of our lives. . . . We lived always with the anticipation of what the next moment would bring."

Finally, Clark took his family home to Schenectady, and during a four-day visit he called on the sick and elderly and held his last communion with his church officers. He then went back to the camp expecting to return home on another leave the following week. But a few days later, a telegram arrived:

CAN'T PHONE AGAIN. WITH MY DEAREST LOVE. CLARK.

His last letter from American soil then arrived:

Dearest: I can't write a "noble, brave" letter. I would be a little self-conscious writing that sort of letter to you. All I can say is that always I will love you and hold our happy memories in the most sacred part of my thoughts until that time when we shall be together again. . . .

Betty knew it would be pointless to count the moments until that time.

5

When John Washington arrived home on his last leave, his mother saw that he had developed a case of hives and tried to keep him in the house. But in vain. Would a tough Irishman like his father have let himself be babied because of a few red spots? He visited all his friends and asked for their prayers, then, after conducting Mass for them and his family, left for his camp.

"Good-bye, Ma," John said as he embraced his mother before boarding the bus. "No crying. You'll be hearing from me."

But this prophecy did not ease the anxiety that had gripped his mother since she had learned about Pearl Harbor on that sunny Sunday afternoon she had spent with her son.

CHAPTER IV

An Odd Foursome

I

When Sergeant Michael Warish boarded the *Dorchester,* he gave the deck officer his name and serial number and was assigned to a stateroom on the main deck, though these private rooms were reserved mainly for officers. Michael, however, wanted no such honor. There were double doors to the room, and this could prove fatal if a torpedo hit the ship, for one door could easily jam, trapping him inside.

But before he could leave to seek other quarters, there was a knock on the door, and an officer with a cross on his lapel entered and introduced himself: "I am Father John Washington. The deck officer told me you were here. We are well represented in chaplains."

Michael, who was a nonobservant Catholic but was well aware of the dangers ahead and the desolation of Greenland, replied, "We sure need 'em."

Actually, he wasn't sure they were needed. Where had prayers ever gotten him? But in case of crisis, he felt, the chaplains could help calm the men and prevent panic. John and Michael exchanged talk about their hometowns and other mundane matters, and the priest invited Michael to come to him anytime he might need help or support.

"I'll see more of you," John said with a smile as he departed. After all, Michael was the chaplain's next-door neighbor.

But Michael was not eager to remain a neighbor for long. He soon left not only to find another place to sleep but to "look the ship over, . . . every stairway, every hallway, every doorway—I wanted to know where it went. . . . You got to know the ship." All he knew about it was that the navy operated communications, including radio and signals; the coast guard, the two forward guns and two aft guns; and the merchant marine, the entire ship.

As Michael descended a stairway leading to a lower deck, he noticed the four chaplains standing at the bottom in heated discussion.

"They were in a huddle," Michael said. "Just like a football huddle."

It seemed a strange sight. They were all of different faiths or denominations, yet they were conferring together as intimately as brothers. It was as if they were all of the same religion. Not, Michael thought, like the clergymen at home, who never mingled with their counterparts in other churches or synagogues. The "huddle" coagulated into a lasting image of spiritual unity that suddenly, and strangely, seemed so natural. An image that would also crystallize in the minds of the other men. Pfc James McAtamney thus observed:

"There was camaraderie among them that was hard to describe, because it was so unexpected. I was raised Catholic in an Irish neighborhood, and there the Catholics didn't talk to any Protestants, and none of us Protestants and Catholics spoke to the few Jews who were there, and there were no Baptists around. I don't know if there was a law against them or what. But to see these men in the same uniform but of different faiths getting together and actually talking and laughing and smiling and joking with each other was unheard of. I don't think I'd be very far from the truth if I said that the pastor of our church wouldn't be caught dead talking to a Protestant minister."

Now, aboard the ship, Father Washington introduced Michael to his three colleagues, Chaplains Fox, Goode, and Poling, as if this were a family gathering. Perhaps, one of them said, the sergeant could help them with some of their plans. They would like to hold services, but how could they inform the men when and where the services would take place?

"Just post the information on a bulletin board by the door of the mess hall," Michael suggested. "Everybody goes there to eat, and they'll see it."

The chaplains agreed, then told Michael of their plans to hold an amateur night to cheer the boys up. They had heard it could be a rough trip. The chaplains would personally seek talent as they visited the various quarters. In fact, all four of them were pretty good singers, and Chaplain Washington was a fine pianist, though he might have a hard time with the dusty old piano left over from the days of pleasure cruising.

Chaplain Fox seemed especially eager to arrange such a night. He loved a party. What better way to counter the boredom and tensions of daily life on the ship, to pacify anger and even hatred? George Fox had learned how to filter moments of joy from adversity, to ease the pain lingering in memory since childhood. . . .

CHAPTER V

POOR OLD GEORGE

I

Altoona, Pennsylvania, in the early 1900s, was a smoky, grimy railroad town surrounded by hills that echoed with the shrill whistle of incoming trains, the clickety-clack of wheels grinding over steel, and the gravelly shouts of brawny freight handlers. Here in the gloomy shadow of the Alleghenies, George Fox grew up in an old duplex house crowded with five children, to whom home meant submitting to the iron will and rigid disciplinary rules of a violent-tempered, crippled father.

He was especially cruel to George, who was born in Lewistown, Pennsylvania, in 1900 and was taken to Altoona where he would serve as a kind of male Cinderella. It is unclear whether the man was his biological father.

While their classmates played ball in the street after school, George and his brothers had to work in the garden planting vegetables. They dreaded the sound of their father's uneven gait as he returned home on his artificial leg after a day's work on the railroad. If he wasn't satisfied with their efforts, there would be hell to pay. George in particular would be beaten and humiliated in odious ways. And not even his serene-natured mother could save him from the man's terrible wrath.

George spent some of his few happy moments in the classroom and received high grades. But perhaps because he never played with his schoolmates—many from more prosperous families—they relentlessly made fun of him, whether for his patchwork clothing or for the sparse contents of his lunch box.

He felt entirely at ease only when he stole off to a local library and pored over books on everything from history to the classics. Biographies of Abraham Lincoln were among his favorites, and he even memorized the Gettysburg Address. He seemed to identify with Lincoln, who, like him, had suffered through a difficult childhood.

George was also intrigued by adventure stories, which offered an escape into a whole new, free-spirited world, a world that took on a devotional hue with his study of the Bible. Every Sunday his mother, a devout Catholic, took him and the other children to church, where, as he leafed through the holy pages, he felt a tranquillity that helped relieve the tensions that seized him at home.

But the older he became, the greater were the tensions. And they grew unbearable when his father wanted to buy a farm and apparently threatened—if perhaps only for effect—to kill George if he did not agree to spend his life planting, harvesting, and cleaning up the manure. He would be trapped forever in a prison even more oppressive than the garden that yielded not only tomatoes and onions but the bitter fruit of his hatred.

Not even the sacred caress of God could now assuage the pain. George had turned seventeen, the same age an older brother, John, had been when he had fled home to find his own way. George had similar thoughts. And the idea crystallized when, in April 1917, the United States entered the Great War against the Central Powers, led by the kaiser's Germany. The kaiser was an international bully who was strangling Britain and threatening to overrun France.

On a family scale, there seemed to be a certain symmetry with his own victimization at home. He couldn't fight his crippled father, but he could fight the kaiser—while breaking loose from his father's stifling grasp.

The problem was that anyone under eighteen would need his parents' approval to enlist in the armed services. George knew *his* parents would never give it, and indeed he dreaded the thought of how his father would react if he learned of his intention to flee home. George therefore lied about his age, declaring himself eighteen when one day he sneaked out of the house and enlisted.

Unlike many other abused youngsters finally escaping from a nightmare existence, he was not infected with any inclination to commit crimes of his own or simply hobble through a life devoid of meaning or purpose. When he sailed off to France, he was determined to appease his anger by helping to destroy a dictator who was trying to impose his will on the world. He knew he might die, but he would die as a free man. And was not death the ultimate freedom—with God the eternal guarantor? Whatever his fate, he had escaped his father's clutches at last.

Attached to the 2nd Division, George was not, as he had expected, handed a rifle and sent to kill the enemy. He was instead given an ambulance and first-aid equipment and told to comb the killing fields for wounded men and bring them to hospitals, an assignment especially geared to his spiritual temperament. The danger he faced was as great as that faced by any rifleman, perhaps even greater since he was unarmed, but his job was to save people, not kill them. The anger he had felt at home was largely channeled into compassion on the battlefields of Verdun, Champagne-Marne, Aisne-Marne, Saint-Mihiel, and Meuse-Argonne.

While saving others, George was barely able to save himself. He earned several Purple Hearts for wounds sustained during mustard-gas and shelling attacks even as he suffered from the near-frozen condition of his feet, which were planted for days at a time in the cold, watery trenches of World War I. He won the Silver Star for action he took in a night attack at Champagne, removing his gas mask, placing it on a wounded American officer, and carrying him on his back to safety. And French field marshal Ferdinand Foch then pinned on him the Croix de Guerre with Palm, France's highest honor, for saving a French officer in the same way.

A day before the armistice, he himself was wounded when the stone building he was in collapsed from a bombing, burying him in the debris. As he later described the event:

"I was fixing up a room for operating and dressing in this stone farm house. I had just secured some sheeting to cover the windows and all other openings so the candlelight wouldn't penetrate the darkness. I was reaching up to hammer another tack when there was a roar and a crash. When I came to, I was in the hospital with spinal injuries."

No, doctors told him, he could not go back to the battlefield. There was none. The war had ended five days earlier.

And so now did his previous life.

2

In a sense, George was born again one day in 1918, shortly after he left the hospital in greatly improved but far from perfect condition. When he had emerged from a subway in Bay Ridge, Brooklyn, he asked a young boy standing nearby, "Do you know where the Foxes live?"

"Yes," the boy said, "I'm a Fox."

Oliver Fox had been sent to meet a particular soldier and bring him home. And soon George, a dashing figure in a bemedaled uniform with a pack on his back, was welcomed into the home of Percy and Florence Fox and their seven children, one of whom was Oliver. George had never met the family before, but he felt he knew every member well. For while he was overseas, Florence had corresponded with several servicemen whose names and addresses were listed in the newspapers so that people back home could write to them to help raise their morale. And George was one of them. So warm was their correspondence that George, having vowed never to return to his own home, decided to visit the Fox family after his discharge from the army.

The visit was prolonged; he stayed for weeks, then months. Months of pleasure for George—and his hosts.

"He was a happy-go-lucky fellow," Oliver said years later, "and he just fit in with everything. If he could help you in any way, he would. He used to make ice cream for the family, and he could do anything—climb up roofs and paint and help out with the housework. He would work in the garden and cut the grass. . . . And he really gave us a wonderful, wonderful time. He would often get us and the neighborhood kids together and tell ghost stories and scare the wits out of us. And he took us on all kinds of picnics and to Coney Island. We went on the scenic railways and saw the clowns. We loved that stuff."

And they loved George.

So at the age of nineteen he was adopted by the Fox family and became the eighth Fox sibling. To George, this was a dream come true. After having endured years of maltreatment as a boy, he now found himself a hero in a household of people who embraced him as one of their own.

But he also needed the love of God—especially now, after experiencing the horrors of war. He was haunted by the sound of men on the battlefield calling on a higher power for comfort and relief; by the memory of carrying a wounded man for miles through a trench so narrow that he had to walk over a carpet of corpses. He even thought he might join the clergy. At first, George would go by himself to a Catholic church on Sunday while his family attended services at their Methodist church. But as he sat among strangers, searing visions of the bitter past drifted through his mind. Wouldn't God like his family to be together? So he told his new father, Percy, "Dad, I'd like to go to your church and see what it's like."

The following Sunday he was praying to God surrounded by those he loved. And the more he prayed with them, the more he wanted to learn about their faith. After a while, he enrolled in the Moody Bible Institute in Chicago—where he met Isadore.

3

By chance, Isadore sat next to a neatly dressed, "almost handsome" fellow student when she started class at the institute.

"I was unimpressed," she later said of her first encounter with George, "until I heard his beautiful tenor voice as he joined in the group singing of a familiar old hymn."

When class was dismissed, George introduced himself, and "the ice was broken." Then he walked her back to her dormitory, but she made a mental note that she "did not care to make a habit of walking with him. My studies," she said, "not a boy friend, were on my mind." Besides, he told her he was planning to go to Africa as a missionary and "did not want to have anything complicate his lifework."

Nevertheless, they soon found themselves working in the kitchen together, and "when there was a nice bunch of grapes, or a pear, or a red apple left on a plate," he would give it to her as he passed her at the sink while she was washing dishes. Self-consciously, she wished he didn't show her such attention in public.

"One of my most embarrassing moments came one evening," she said, "when I attended a lecture in a large auditorium. George, too, was there and asked me to sit beside him. Thinking the room would be well filled, I went along with him. To my chagrin, we were the only ones to sit on that side of the room. . . . I sat through the lecture feeling my face getting redder by each passing minute. No wonder I had little knowledge of what the speaker said. When I remonstrated later, George said, 'that should teach you not to hide behind the post in the dining room so I cannot see you at mealtime!' "

Years later, Isadore would think back to this episode, reflecting on a revealing aspect of her husband's character. "I have come to believe," she said, "that George made me conspicuous because of his pride in me as much as he did it to tease me." He was a man of strong, serious feelings but also of whimsical, even lovably silly disposition.

"In a short time," Isadore remembered, "we were taking long walks on the shore of Lake Michigan, and I suddenly realized that I was happier than I had ever been in my life. He was witty and gay as we laughed and walked with the wind off the lake beating in our faces. Then we felt sad when we thought how the cold evenings of the Chicago winter would put an end to our walks. So it was when George suggested that I go downtown with him to pick out my diamond ring, I was in the right frame of mind to say yes."

But Isadore's sister discouraged her. Had she considered the burdens she would bear caring for a partly disabled man? Now she did.

"I was so upset, so uncertain about our future plans, that I decided to break our engagement. . . . [But then] it seemed as if the heavens had fallen all around me. There was no sun in my sky. Panic seized me and all joy went out of my life. I began to pray to God to send George back to me. All day long I prayed. . . . I now was certain of my feeling toward [him]. If God would only send him back to me, I would spend the rest of my life trying to help him forget the memories of eighteen months in the frontline trenches in World War I."

At about eight-thirty that night, God answered her prayer. As she sat in bed reading the Bible, she heard the click of pebbles striking the window.

"When I went to the window," she related, "my heart leaped with joy. There stood George. I flew downstairs and let him in the front door."

A new wedding date was set. But Isadore had been under such tension that she fainted hours before the ceremony. George, Isadore wrote, "had become well acquainted with fainting spells and blackouts from his experience in the ambulance company. He calmly picked me up from the floor where I had fallen, carried me upstairs, and laid me on my bed. Then he phoned the preacher, postponing the ceremony until seven o'clock in the evening."

The morning after the wedding, Isadore "awakened to find George in his dressing gown sitting at the foot of my bed. His first words were, 'I sat here and looked at you all night and asked myself over and over, "Did it really happen? Is she really mine? Or will I awaken to find it all a dream, like many other dreams of recent months?"'"

Isadore also found her groom to be a man of great patience: "To people who think that marriage must be consummated on the wedding night to start a marriage relationship successfully, this may appear as a sign of weakness on his part. I disagree. To those who knew him well during the following nineteen years of our marriage, this is but one more facet to add to the jewels of patience and self-control which he so fully possessed."

The couple would need patience and self-control to endure the hardships as the years passed. To earn money, George interrupted his studies at the Moody Bible Institute and went to work as an accountant for the Staten Island Edison Company. He was well on his way to success when he decided to resign and return to the institute. George could not take "himself out of God's will for him."

But he had to when Isadore became pregnant, forcing him to find various short-term jobs as a bookkeeper or accountant. Unable to afford a car to get to work in New Hampshire during a stormy winter, he had to walk two miles through deep snow, aggravating the lingering pain from his World War I bouts of trench foot.

Eventually forced to give up that job, he went from door to door trying to sell brushes and small household appliances to people reluctant to part with even a penny. He finally wrote to his new adoptive parents asking for financial help, but the Fox family had lost almost everything in bad investments and could offer little.

Giving up on the idea of returning to school after his son, Wyatt, was born, George persuaded the Methodist Church to appoint him, despite his limited training, the pastor of the West Berkshire circuit in Vermont, even if at minuscule pay. Isadore wrote:

"The change from the comparative luxury of an eleven-room house, the home of his once-prosperous parents on Staten Island (where they had moved from Brooklyn in the 1920s), to a parsonage in northern Vermont that was devoid of nearly all modern conveniences, did not discourage George. On the contrary, he was filled with exhilaration at the thought that at last we were on our own."

George didn't mind using an old-fashioned, hand-operated pump to fill a tank in the cellar with water for the kitchen and bathroom. And he could always borrow from someone an ancient copper clothes boiler to help out on wash day. Nor did he complain when the jingling of the improvised doorbell awakened him in the middle of many nights, a signal that a neighbor wanted him to comfort his ailing wife by sitting at her bedside and singing a hymn until she fell asleep. After all, what were ministers for?

But to be a better minister, George felt, he must have a better education. And so in the fall of 1928, he terminated his ministry and enrolled in Boston University's School of Religious Education and Social Studies. He and his family—recently expanded by the birth of a daughter—moved into a kitchenette-and-living-room arrangement created from two storerooms in a commercial structure. To pay for this living space, the couple scrubbed the floors and dusted the furniture in other rooms in the building every evening. To pay for food, George sold butter, cheese, and eggs at a local market, and for his books and tuition, he borrowed from the Methodist Student Loan Fund. When winter came, he bought a used overcoat for ninety-five cents. Isadore's sister, who had opposed the wedding to George in the first place, remarked to her sibling, "Poor old George. That must have hurt his pride."

Then another hurt. A minister told George, "You are twenty-eight years old now. It will take you seven years to earn your Bachelor of Sacred Theology. That will make you thirty-five years old. You know the churches are looking for younger men. You are foolish to try to continue your work at Boston University."

But Fox did not agree. Let people say what they wished; he listened only to God, and God, who would never engage in age discrimination, had given him the call.

During summer vacation, Fox temporarily served as a pastor in a little church in Bloomfield, Vermont, where he and his family lived in a parsonage more decrepit and unkempt than any housing they had previously experienced. In horror, Isadore cried when she entered one of the rooms, "George Fox, hurry and come up here! See what I have found!"

What she had found was a wall crawling with bedbugs. Desperately they tried to trick the bugs.

"After we went to bed at night," Isadore would explain, "George blew out the light and set it near at hand. In a few minutes he would re-light it. I would then turn down the covers on Wyatt's makeshift cot while George would hold the lamp at the edge and catch bedbugs in the lamp chimney. The heat caused them to drop off. We counted as many as eighty that we caught at one time around the edges of the cot. Soon we made up our minds that this method was too slow. Our little son was becoming poisoned from scores of bites from those filthy bugs—to say nothing of the nightly discomfort of it all."

Finally, they went to the women of the Ladies' Aid Society, who gave them money to buy a gallon of Flit. After spraying the infected rooms with it, they wondered how they could test its effectiveness without possibly continuing to submit the children and themselves to the hunger of the insects. Well, if someone had to be the guinea pig, it might as well be Isadore's father, who was about to visit them. When he arrived, he slept in one of the fumigated rooms. In the morning at breakfast, Father, who had not been informed of the test, was asked how he had slept.

"I slept fine all night," he replied.

Isadore smiled and said, "I guess it worked."

"So it seems," George muttered.

Dad didn't understand that these comments meant that his hosts had finally won the war against the bedbugs—or that it was *he* who deserved the Silver Star this time.

The bedbugs, dead or alive, could not dim George's joy on the job. Every two weeks he held a social affair on the church lawn, and people came from all over the region to participate in stunts, tricks, and group singing. His reputation as a fun-loving cleric swiftly spread. Once, after they could finally afford a rickety car, George and Isadore were driving at night when the headlights went out. George borrowed a lantern from a farmer and sat on the hood of the car, holding it, to light the way for his wife, who was at the wheel. When he returned the lantern to the farmer, the man said in awe, "Young man, I have seen you do all sorts of stunts to entertain your parishioners. This one is the best yet."

When summer was over, George decided to leave Boston University and take advantage of a scholarship at Illinois Wesleyan University, which had a Methodist heritage. The family once more packed their meager belongings and set out in their rattletrap car for Bloomington, Illinois. The scholarship paid so little, however, that George had to spend much of his time preaching in two small-town churches to meet his expenses. He and his family lived in a room without a kitchen, having been given the right to prepare meals in the basement of one of the churches.

The situation grew worse when his salary was paid less often, and the family had to depend on a church "pound party," to which parishioners brought a supply of fruits and vegetables. But when these contributions ran out, the Foxes could barely feed themselves.

"George would not ask for credit to buy groceries," Isadore lamented. "He too often heard about his predecessors' moving away leaving debts unpaid. Our children sometimes cried because they were hungry, and it wrung our hearts to hear them say, 'Why don't you give us something besides just bread to eat?'"

The following summer brought the worst news of all. A church official informed George, "Now that your school year is nearly over, we have decided that we can't pay what we owe you on your salary, and you might as well leave."

George, however, did not leave. He continued to preach on Sundays without pay, but on weekdays he spent much of his time out of school traveling around the region selling identification tags so he could put more than bread on the table. Finally, he was appointed to a church in the nearby town of Downs, where he regained a salary but had to live with his family in a parsonage right next to a pigsty with a stench that nearly suffocated them. But they ate slightly better here—at least one day when George returned home with poultry. He had visited one of his parishioners on a farm, who recalled that he said, " 'If you can catch that hen, you can have it,' and George did it!"

Soon the Foxes were breathing the fresher air in Boston, where George resumed his studies at Boston University while serving as a pastor in nearby Rye. Shortly, on June 3, 1934, he was consecrated as a minister in the Methodist Church. But poverty continued to plague his family when he was appointed a "circuit rider"; he would serve as a pastor at three Vermont churches, including one where still another congregation refused to pay his salary for six months, complaining that they liked their previous minister and had not been given a role in choosing his successor.

The Foxes were saved when a family from another church gave George permission to pick its garden vegetables. When George told his daughter to say grace that night, "she lowered her head, then in a slightly disgusted tone said, 'Lord, we thank you for these beans. Amen.' " Now at least they had beans *in addition* to bread.

Finally, at a meeting of church officials, one of them stood up and said, "I have been waiting for a chance to give Mr. Fox a promotion." He would now be sent to another Vermont town, Union Village.

The only problem was, this "promotion" would reduce his already skimpy pay of less than one thousand dollars a year by twenty-five dollars. When George met the leader and his wife later and greeted them with a smile, Isadore, who was furious at the man's "betrayal," said to her husband, "George, how can you be so nice to them?"

"Let's not let them know that we know the difference," he replied.

Was he not blessed just to be able to serve God?

Isadore would later reflect, "Although some may find this attitude hard to understand, that was the way George lived his too-short life. . . . I have long since come to believe that he was the winner every time."

To better serve God—and apparently to suppress an inner impulse to voice his disappointment—he pursued his spiritual work with extraordinary zeal, traveling many miles, often by foot, to visit five schools located from three to almost five miles from his parsonage. A fellow minister, amazed at his energy, asked him, "How do you make so many calls, George? Do you just ring the doorbell and run?"

Adding to George's tension was the bullying of his son and daughter by other children at school, who saw a minister's kids as appropriate targets of ridicule and attack. When the bullies pulled down Wyatt's pants zipper and yelled for the girls to "come and see a sight," George advised his son to "go back to school and lick those boys." And Wyatt did. But then the boys began picking on Mary and tore her new dress.

In frustration and anger, George delivered a sermon in church on the subject of malicious gossip. The church district superintendent was furious. "I don't have to tell you, George," he wrote him, "that no Christian minister would preach that kind of sermon."

George felt he had put his children through enough. It was time to move again. And in June 1938 the family went to live in Gilman, Vermont. Maybe here, with God's help, its luck would change. And here he stayed until the time came to fight new battles—in a new war.

CHAPTER VI

BLESSING THE BORED

I

Michael Warish continued to tour the *Dorchester*, still wondering where he could sleep in relative safety. As he moved along the twisting corridors, he opened doors and chatted with the men. Almost all of them were green, he found, and one passenger in civilian clothes lurking in a hallway seemed, to his dismay, to be only about fourteen years old.

What was he doing on the ship? Michael asked.

He had carried aboard the baggage of his uncle, a civilian, the boy explained. And he decided to stay so he could fight the enemy.

Michael stared at the youth, struck by how young he looked. He asked, "Why aren't you in school?"

"Everyone on the ship wants to know my age," the boy replied in frustration, "but it's nobody's business."

"I wasn't going to ask you your age," Michael retorted. "I want to help you."

And that seemed to place the boy more at ease.

The ship hadn't left the dock yet, and Michael could have had the youth thrown off the ship. But he thought of the drummer boy and the young fife player who symbolized the spirit of 1776, when a call to arms had meant grabbing a musket and joining the ranks of other patriots. He didn't have the heart to expel this young patriot. Yet he felt a twinge of guilt. What if the ship went down with this drummer boy of 1943? How could he ever forgive himself?

And the more Michael checked the vessel out, the more concerned he became about its vulnerability. For while some of the men, at first glance, confused the *Dorchester* with a luxury liner, the deceptive fog would soon lift: This ship was an old creaky tub that seemed to add credence to the prediction of the former undertaker that "this damn thing is never gonna make it."

Yet one could imagine what this ship had looked like in the past when the now steamy, sweat-smelling hold that housed most of the men was one of the grand ballrooms, as the walnut paneling still on the walls nostalgically affirmed. Pfc James McAtamney would colorfully describe his own disillusionment as he boarded the ship and entered one of the compartments, each crammed with eighteen or twenty men:

"We were taken aboard . . . and got a look at that thing and it wasn't your ideal dream cruise ship. It was a rust-covered thing, very cramped . . . , and it had been renovated to accommodate its passenger capacity for troop transport so that all of the bed space was down in the lower holds in C, D, and E, with bunks stacked [four high] and separated by two and a half to three feet on either side.

"Then I lucked out because I got E hold, which was way down in the bottom in about midship. I said, 'How the hell do you sleep here? Where do you hang things?' We had life preservers, we had duffel bags, our helmets, and all that other gear you clutter yourself with. And Charlie [a comrade] and I had extra baggage because we'd been on K.P. New Year's Eve at officers' mess at Miles Standish, and we stole everything that was not perishable, and had an extra bag full of that."

Making life even more unbearable were a couple of guitar players. They would probably have an appreciative audience at the party planned by the chaplains, but were "not at all good down in E hold when you're trying to sleep and they're up there twanging something from way back in Arkansas.

"Anyway," McAtamney concluded, "it was a dismal experience just to see this place."

It was for Michael, too. Now he knew what those stevedores had meant when they cried out, "You'll be sorry!" He should be hemmed into a sliver of sleeping space in a crowded room at the bottom of the ship?! A death trap as frightening as his stateroom, without its relative comfort. Michael thus chose to sleep on a fire hose that he found curled in a built-in container in a corridor. To think that if he had boarded this ship as a civilian a few years earlier, when it had accommodated little more than a third of the passengers now aboard, he would have been lying in the lap of luxury!

2

The *Dorchester* finally set sail at about seven o'clock on the cold but clear morning of January 23, 1943, ship number twenty-three in a sixty-four-ship convoy that included many tankers and freighters and was heavily escorted by destroyers and corvettes. The armada sailed in a single file through swollen waters, past ferry boats and smaller tooting craft, as the skyscrapers of New York receded in the mist. It headed due east on a zigzag course that, hopefully, would enable the ships to dodge torpedoes. With so many gun-bristling protectors moving so cautiously, few men on the *Dorchester* feared that a U-boat would dare attack.

Whatever the danger, the four chaplains lost no time in trying to ease whatever anxieties the men had. And they hadn't had to memorize the *Chaplain's Training Manual* to know that "the chaplain is the servant of God for all, and no narrow sectarian spirit should color his utterances, nor should his personal work assist only a special group." From their first day aboard the ship the chaplains visited the men in their quarters, usually together, stressing the gratitude that America felt toward them. And they pointed out that this ship made five earlier trips overseas and always returned safely.

James McAtamney would succinctly explain why the chaplains were loved: "They were always there. In any formation or any gathering of any kind, one or more of them was passing by, talking and joking and participating. You could see them at all hours, not just meal hours. They had tremendous empathy with what most of us were going through—

the uncertainty, the fear, and all the other sentiments. That's probably the standout thing about them—their togetherness. . . . It was almost like a symposium when they were sitting together and talking and fielding questions. Then they would split off and go either as a group or as individuals to speak to us one-on-one."

Nor did most of the men discriminate in their feelings toward the chaplains. In fact, they found that the four all exhibited similar personality traits. They were tolerant, selfless, and, most important, humorous even in moments of stress and crisis. One had only to ask Pfc Charles Macli, a former professional boxer.

"We used to talk," Macli would say, "and they used to tease me about boxing, making friendly jokes because word got around that I fought with [boxing great] Jake LaMotta." (Macli lost the fight.)

And Michael Warish reminisced: "Guys would line up to talk to them. We had a lot of young guys, and a lot of them had never been away from home before. The chaplains were like mother and father to them."

At the same time, it was noted, each chaplain had his own distinct persona. George Fox, the medal-winning hero of World War I, exuded a senior authority without trying to impose his will on anyone. Alexander Goode, the idealistic intellectual, carefully filtered his vast knowledge to others without patronizing them. John Washington, the sharp-witted street fighter, never tired of displaying his Irish talent for finding an intriguing story in virtually every event in his life. And Clark Poling, the sensitive poet and the only one of the four from a prosperous, well-known family, withdrew into anonymity as he sought with his fathomless curiosity to search the soul of anyone who came to him, to better understand the man's problems.

Some of their calming words were spoken at well-attended services held in the mess hall, as they took turns ministering to men of their respective faiths. Many, regardless of their faith, attended the services conducted by all four chaplains.

"Life on the ship was boring," James McAtamney explained. "We could play cards, tell lies, joke a lot with each other, learn a little bit about each other's background. . . . [But] for most of the army personnel, it was a totally new experience. We came from different parts of the country—first exposure to the ocean, first exposure to a ship. We couldn't identify with these coast guard men or navy crewmen, merchant mariners, and the few civilians on board. . . .

"Of course, officers were out of the realm of possibility. You just didn't associate. You saw them at the briefing, you saluted them if you thought about it, and that was it. But the chaplains were different. It was a pleasure to listen to each one, pray with them, and listen to their ideas. We left feeling better. After all, they all believed in the same God."

The chaplains also helped one another out when they could. One Friday night, Rabbi Goode wanted to hold Sabbath services in a room near the kitchen, but he was competing with a cook, who wished to use that room for a crap game.

While Alex was arguing with him, Clark Poling appeared and was as outraged as Alex by the cook's intransigence. Clark helped the rabbi persuade the cook to hold off on the game, and Alex was soon handing out small Bibles. The argument that prayer was more important than shooting dice had finally triumphed. And the men who attended the service were especially glad. As William Kramer, who was Jewish but nonobservant, recalled:

"I went to the service because I was going to war, and maybe the good Lord would watch over me. Rabbi Goode really helped to raise my spirits and understand the importance of what we were fighting for."

William needed his spirits lifted. His sister's husband had been killed in an accident when he was on maneuvers with the tank corps, shortly before William embarked on this trip—the same day his sister gave birth to a baby. And his own son had suffered brain damage from rheumatic fever when he was five years old. William cherished the Bible the rabbi gave him after the service. It was a good time to read about God.

Father Washington, who deplored gambling, also appreciated Alex's triumph over the craps shooters. When he found a dice game in progress, he protested to the man running it, a merchant marine, and the man scoffed: "Who are you? You're not my boss. I don't take orders from you!"

A military policeman standing nearby threw the man in the brig.

But if John sometimes revealed a temper, he was almost always good-natured, and could tell one hilarious story after another. As one survivor described him:

"He was your typical bluff, hearty Irish priest. And he had the ability to get you to confide in him without your knowing it. He had a tremendously wonderful sense of humor. He wasn't always preaching the traditional line—hell, damnation, and fire, and all that."

John, in fact, usually checked his temper with levity—sometimes even when gamblers irked him. Once, he saw several men playing a high-stakes card game and said, "Well, I see you're playing cards. Someday I'll tell you a story about cards."

One of the players asked, "Father, would you please bless my hand?"

The priest glanced at the hand and replied, "I should waste my blessing on a lousy pair of deuces?"

John was a conservative Catholic in the tradition of Diego Lainez, a general of the Jesuits, who had written to the Spanish officer leading an expedition against the Moors in North Africa:

"By prayer and good example, by preaching and hearing confessions, by nursing the sick and helping the dying, these men will do a tremendous amount of good. They will teach the soldiers and will call them to task for blasphemies and *gambling*. Finally . . . soldiers will profit from this, for by their peace of mind and confidence in God they will better fulfill their duties in war."

But John and the other chaplains were only too eager to bless the men and give them aid and comfort, whatever their vices. Daniel O'Keeffe, a merchant marine wheelman, went to the chaplains' quarters to have the priest take his confession and found him sitting with Alex Goode. John introduced O'Keeffe to the rabbi, and the three conversed about their past experiences and about their families. Alex then departed so that John could take Daniel's confession.

"Rabbi Goode knew or surmised that I was there because I wanted to talk to a priest," O'Keeffe said. "Like Father Washington, he made me feel he cared about me."

It was not surprising that Alex received so warm a compliment from someone of a different faith. He had been struggling throughout his life to bring people of all faiths together, inviting Christian leaders to speak in his temple, praising the moral principles of other religions, writing essays on the beauty of interfaith brotherhood. And now he was literally living with, and perhaps might die with, the brothers he had long been wooing. . . .

CHAPTER VII

THE PROPHET AND THE PRIZE

I

Alex Goode was well equipped to encourage the spread of the inter-faith spirit that today is still a grand if elusive ideal, for he relentlessly sought triumph in any effort he undertook. With his slim but wiry build he had excelled in tennis, basketball, track, and swimming. With his brilliant mind he had won prizes in debating and oratory, and could read over five hundred pages at a sitting with photographic retention.

While still in high school, he had so mastered mathematics that he devised his own formula for solving a complicated problem alge-braically. He was equally erudite in history and liberal arts; while in college he wrote thought-provoking, scholarly treatises on Middle Eastern and American Jewish history with impressive, sometimes esoteric titles like "A History of Jewish Philanthropy in America Until the Civil War," "The Jewish Exilarchate in Baghdad During the Arabic Period," and "A Critical Analysis of the Book of Yosippon as Compared to Josephus and Other Sources with a Discussion of the Literary Problem of Its Composition and Style."

His favorite subject, however, was covered in a book-length manu-script called "Cavalcade of Democracy," explaining his view of how a democratic world would evolve after the war as the result of the Judeo-Christian link being welded by war.

"Christianity and Judaism," he wrote, "have common enemies, [and] joining forces against [them] in defense of their common spiritual heritage and ideals, both will achieve mutual understanding and good-will." This will lead the way to a new world, "one of community ruled in the spirit of democracy. What has seemed like civilization up to this point is but a crude effort compared to the era that lies just before us."

Alex traced every detour, every twist and turn along the road to what he called the coming "century of humanity," starting with biblical times. Such a climax was possible, Alex wrote, because Christianity and Judaism "have influenced the progress of democracy through their common Bible. The moral standards of religion have become the standards of democracy. . . . The democratic element in religion lies in the fact that it regards God as the father of all men; consequently all men are brothers and as brothers are responsible to one another by ties of brotherly love."

Alex was especially driven by the horrors Hitler was perpetrating on the Jews of Europe, though when he was writing his book, persecution had not yet turned into the Holocaust. The future world must never again be dominated by racial or religious hatred, he stated, and only universal ties of brotherly love could prevent such a recurrence.

Alex himself had smelled the foul breath of anti-Semitism as a student, when gangs of rednecks had attacked him and his brother Joseph several times. He and Joseph had beaten up some of the bullies, but while brute force, Alex felt, might temporarily numb the virus of hate, only education based on spiritual values could finally kill it. In college, he wrote of the Bible to his fiancée: "It really is heartrending that more people do not seek out its treasures. Perhaps if Hitler read some of its valuable sayings he would be a wiser ruler than he is destined to become."

The passion behind his views is what influenced Alex to give up thoughts of a prosperous engineering career, or perhaps West Point and a military life, and to choose what he knew would be a struggling existence in the rabbinate, which would give him the opportunity to fight for his "new world" from the pulpit, from any pulpit in any community that would listen to him.

This decision did not entirely surprise his family. Alex, after all, was the product of three generations of rabbis, though he wanted to serve in the more modern Reform branch of Judaism rather than in the Orthodox branch of several previous generations. It would be easier in this branch to start a new tradition of aggressively fostering ties with other religious groups and pursuing his "new world."

But even Alex's father had hoped his son would choose an engineering career, which would virtually assure him a prosperous future. It was more profitable building a bridge between riverbanks than between different races and religions. And his father was speaking from bitter experience; he could barely provide for his wife and four children.

2

Born in Brooklyn on May 10, 1911, in a traditional Jewish home, young Alex showed early signs of a simmering impatience, a mulelike stubbornness, and an almost elastic resilience. He would write that "as the outcome of much pugilistic practice [against anti-Semitic bullies], I now find myself pugnacious enough to keep fighting life's problems long after defeat seems certain. Often, this apparent loss of the battle turns into victory."

Sometimes the battle was to protect his younger siblings, especially Agatha (nicknamed Berdie). One time their mother was away and Alex, an expert chef, was cooking in the kitchen when a lighted match set the curtains on fire. As the flames spread, Alex shouted to his siblings to run out of the house and smothered the fire with a wet blanket, saving his home. When the firemen arrived, they were stunned to see a boy with a black-smudged face and singed hair greeting them triumphantly. How could he think of his own safety when his brothers and sister were in danger?

The battles would erupt in many places, for Alex moved from city to city as his father sought rabbinical appointments wherever he could find them. Nor was his life in the sometimes dysfunctional atmosphere at home—wherever that might be—conducive to a stable, happy youth.

Alex was close to his good-natured if rather aloof father, Hyman, who favored him over his younger children, two sons and a daughter, apparently because, as an intellectual himself, he prized his elder son's scholarly achievements. But all the children except the youngest son, Moses, had only a flimsy bond with their mother, Fanny, an attractive, spirited woman whose taste for social life seemed oddly in conflict with her husband's austere, academic bent. She often preferred to spend a night out with friends than in the kitchen, though she could cook some tasty eastern European dishes. (Sometimes Alex took over the cooking.) Fanny left home several times, and years later the couple would divorce.

Alex was the first of four children Fanny would have in the initial four years of marriage. A rigidly independent woman, she refused to live only on the meager earnings of her husband (supplemented by income from Alex's paper route). After one separation, she opened her own beauty parlor in Brooklyn, and with the help of her shy young daughter, Agatha, and son Moses, transformed dowdy women into glamorous images of herself. Whatever siblings happened to be living with their mother at the time were housed in a back room of the shop, a situation that embarrassed Alex, who would not bring friends home with him when he was in town.

Surely life, he felt, would improve when he went off to college. But would he be able to go? Neither parent had the necessary funds. Besides, Fanny did not see education as a top priority in the struggle to achieve financial security. She herself, like many women who had emigrated from Russia in the early twentieth century, wasn't educated, though she was adept enough in business to open a beauty parlor that would eventually do quite well. In her later years, however, she would enroll in night school and perhaps regret that she hadn't been able to finance Alex's education.

In any case, Alex would not give up on the struggle to pursue his dream. In 1929, he appealed to the National Student League for the necessary funds, stressing his family's financial difficulties. He supported himself, he wrote, by working as a cape-draped theater usher. His father had moved to High Point, North Carolina, "and can offer me no help, nor would I ask it of him. Neither he nor my mother are able to maintain me during my summers so that the past several years I have spent the summers at . . . National Guard camps."

The league rejected Alex's application, but the sisterhood in his father's former temple in Washington, D.C., agreed to grant him a college scholarship. And he used the money to study for the rabbinate, even after having lived through the ordeal of his parents' poverty and watching them agonize over their inability to meet the needs of their children. Was not the struggle for the "new world" he envisaged worth the pain of deprivation that might lie ahead?

3

But if Alex foresaw the pain, he also found a way to relieve it. While still in high school, he fell in love—at first sight. Theresa Flax was a pretty brunette with soulful eyes and a beaming smile that helped make her the favorite niece of famed singer Al Jolson. But, extremely shy, she did not smile when her classmate—Alex—stared at her on the way to and from school each day, though she admired him for receiving top marks without ever needing to carry a book home. (With his phenomenal memory, he didn't have to.)

Neither his good mind nor his good looks, however, would count when he drummed up the nerve to telephone her, hoping she'd accompany him to a fraternity dance. Unfortunately, she wasn't home.

"If he calls back," Theresa told her mother on returning, "please tell him I'm not coming home until tomorrow."

She was only sixteen and had never dated a boy before. And his brilliance intimidated her. What could she talk about with him?

Alex, however, finally was able to attract her attention. He entered a French class one day without his book, and when he told the teacher that he didn't have one, she said he should look on with another student. Someone then tapped Theresa on the shoulder.

"And who was it but Alex," Theresa later reminisced. "And I must have turned beet-red because I was very shy. And he was, too, but not enough so he couldn't ask me to look on with him. So we shared the same book."

To win Theresa's affection, he sensed, would be to finally fill the void he felt in his heart, in part because of his feeling that his mother, occupied with her own affairs, did not love him.

Alex had tried to fill this void before. He had once thought of himself as "undemonstrative and unemotional," though girls were drawn to him by his charm, athletic glamour, and attractive features, with his searching blue eyes, slightly arched eyebrows, a cleft chin, and sensual lips often curled in a barely perceptible smile. But then he met Cynthia. Writing of his first love, he would say:

"I was violently in love with Cynthia, the much to be desired daughter of a house painter, and my work in class languished as I drew visions of learning the painting business from my future father-in-law. . . . Since my first amorous experience I have been stung by Cupid many times, until I learned to deal warily with women."

But now it was Theresa who dealt warily with *him,* and the road to the altar was pitted with uncertainty as she felt rushed by his almost obsessive desire for her attention. He was especially hurt when she turned down another dance invitation, telling him she was going with her brother. Alex went with someone else and, Theresa would later admit, "We kept eyeing each other the whole evening, and both of us were very unhappy."

Since she had noted that Alex, for all his athleticism, was a poor dancer, she later offered to give him dancing lessons. He was delighted and offered in return to give her tennis lessons. By the time they graduated together, Theresa no longer minded his attention. In fact, not at all after a memorable episode during the graduation ceremony. Alex was in such a hurry to collect his diploma that he tripped on the top step leading to the platform and fell flat on his face.

"That struck me so funny," Theresa said, "that I had all I could do to contain myself."

This humorous incident somehow lent a new spark to their relationship. But not for long; Alex went off alone to Cincinnati to study at both the Hebrew Union College and the University of Cincinnati after pleading with her in vain to go with him as his wife.

Despite the Depression with its massive unemployment, Theresa had gotten a well-paying job in the White House as a secretary to two of President Roosevelt's brain trusters, Benjamin Cohen and Thomas Corcoran. Alex, meanwhile, was earning hardly enough to support himself. It wasn't the time to marry, Theresa argued.

But how important was money, Alex countered, compared with the rich, rewarding life they would lead amid the scholars and curious-minded students who were drawn to Hebrew Union with its lovely landscaped campus? Alex was relentless. He wrote a letter to Theresa almost every day, each filled with passion and hope. Typically, he would write in mid-1933:

> *Dearest: Another day begins with me thinking of you, as always. When I fall to sleep at night and when I wake in the morning, at any moment in the day it is you, always you, darling. My depth of feeling is dangerous for if you were denied to me I really do not know what disastrous effects would result.*

After Theresa finally responded with her own declaration of love, he ecstatically replied, "I long to thrill again at your touch, to once more feel the impress of your delicious lips—but again I must be patient and wait. . . . Now I am reassured and inspired to greater heights than I could have reached without your sweet words. I feel I shall accomplish much from now on for an incentive has been given me—and that driving power is you."

Alex's feelings became almost surreal in their intensity with every exchange of letters: "I love you so completely I want to feel your spirit, your presence, in every fibre of my being, in every recess of my mind, in every spring of my emotion. . . . With you there is life, without you only mere existence. . . . I breathe you, eat you, dream, sleep you—my every effort is clothed by your vision."

Alex occasionally interrupted his declarations of love with statements of determination to win every contest he entered, whether intellectual or athletic. Thus, he wrote Theresa:

"My year would be complete if I won a couple of the essay prizes, the oratorical contest and the tennis tournament. Really small things but they inspire one to do bigger things."

To Alex, any contest was a metaphorical test of his ability to achieve "bigger things" as a spiritual teacher. Thus the stakes were high every time he competed, so high that he felt he couldn't afford to lose.

Before the oratorical contest, Alex sought feverishly to perfect his performance, especially the nuances of his voice, and stood for hours before a mirror pontificating to himself. He used his voice for another purpose, too. It was good enough to make the Hebrew Union choir.

He was just as meticulous training for a sporting event. When he lost in the finals of the tennis tournament, he vowed that next time he would reverse the results. To lose, and by so little! Yes, winning a contest was a "small thing"—but not really for someone who dreamed of helping transform civilization. He tried to make his dream clear to Theresa.

"Darling," he wrote in one letter, "I love you and I want to know that we have not lived worthless lives but have left some impress on the world. Together we will go far—storm the heights of achievement—not of money or fame—but accomplishment to our own satisfaction."

But when would their climb to the heights start? When would Theresa marry him? Alex's impassioned letters had finally captured her heart, but she was still reluctant to give up her prestigious, well-paying job. How could they live on his temple scholarship, even if he did augment his income by tutoring, typing term papers, writing magazine articles and prize-winning essays, and speaking in small, poor synagogues? And with the Depression, it would be difficult for her to find a job in Cincinnati.

So desperate did Alex become that he began, it seemed, to lose faith in his ability to do "bigger things" without the eternal bond symbolized by a wedding.

"I feel almost like leaving school and getting work in Washington near you," he wrote. "What use is it to work for a whole people when you yourself are unhappy?"

This suggestion, however, quickly evaporated, though the very idea reflected his agony.

Finally, in February 1935, Theresa surrendered. Yes, she would leave her job and marry him. He replied ecstatically: "I may be a little delirious with joy now, sweet, but I know how much I love you—surely more than man loved maid before and all I can say is a thousand times—I love you, I love you, my sweet. . . . I'm walking on air."

Alex soon realized, however, that they might be *living* on air as well. But they married regardless, at Theresa's home in Washington, with her grandfather, a rabbi, performing the ceremony before about fifty relatives and friends. When she walked down the stairs toward the altar, Theresa followed her mother's instruction: "Now start on your right foot so everything will always be right."

Yes, everything would be right.

But not always. Hardly had the couple set off for a short honeymoon in Virginia Beach, with tin cans tied to the car crackling in rhythm with thoughts of the future, when the decision was made. They would have to separate once again; the struggle was simply too difficult. Theresa kept her White House job, and her husband went back to Cincinnati to complete his studies. Five days after their wedding, Alex wrote his bride: "Keep well, sweet, and remember that our taste of heaven is only the beginning of more wonderful things to come."

And as the months rolled by, they met on passion-filled vacations made possible when Alex bought a rickety old Oldsmobile they called "Betsy." It was truly indulgence on a luxury. After one meeting, he wrote his bride that after paying his bills, he had only enough money left "for carfare and incidentals—about three dollars. In fact, I'm in training to be a miser. Pretty soon I hope to get along on a dime a month—then I can get rich and retire."

Actually, Alex, who was obviously joking, had little reason to believe he would ever get rich, nor did he appear confident he would live to retire. Thus, presciently, it seemed, he said in another letter: "Life is so fleeting we should be happy for the moment, live for the now—who knows what lies in the future?"

4

Adding to this uncertainty was a tinge of fear that his application to serve after graduation as a rabbi in a prestigious temple in Philadelphia might be rejected. He didn't give up hope, however, asking Theresa to "keep your fingers crossed and our dreams may come true."

But crossed fingers didn't work. When Alex graduated from both his schools in May 1937 and, resplendent in tailcoat and striped trousers, was ordained a rabbi, the couple finally moved into a common abode. It wasn't, however, in Philadelphia; he had been beaten out for the job there with another crushing second-place finish. It was in York, Pennsylvania.

Alex had also applied to serve as rabbi in Temple Beth Israel there and was asked to deliver a trial sermon. So, on a steamy day in July 1937,

Alex visited the little temple, and with the light streaming through a stained-glass window showing David playing a harp, sweatily delivered his sermon, topped off with inspirational words reflecting his dream of an ideal world:

"God in His love for us is our friend and comrade Who will aid us in the titanic task of bringing the universe to perfection. Our love of Him and His creatures smoothes the path upward. For love is not the victory, but the effort; not the goal, but the struggle; not the result, but the mighty research of the soul and heart of man."

Alex, who was competing with several other aspirants for the job, was silent for a moment. He knew he had done well, but would he come in second again? He soon found out. His listeners, at least the rank and file, were thrilled. He had touched them deeply with his visionary rhetoric, unfurled with a dramatic flourish.

Most members of the board, however, were skeptical. They were German Jews, some with roots in America reaching back to about 1860, who considered themselves the elite members of this seventy-five-year-old temple and of the Jewish community as a whole. They wanted an experienced rabbi who would deal strictly with the Bible and temple affairs, ignore politics and other controversial subjects, and, most important, make no decisions without their approval. He must show them the utmost respect.

Would this young man fit into their traditional mold? They weren't sure. He seemed rather aggressive and might be too ambitious. But they bowed to the wishes of the congregation, which clearly wanted him. And so Alex, with his first rabbinical post, would now finally embark on his perceived sacred mission.

Yes, he had preferred Philadelphia, but perhaps, after all, it would be better to preach in a relatively small town that he could more easily shape into a role model for the nation, even the world, than to serve in a large city where his efforts might have limited effect. Also, in his free time he could study at Johns Hopkins University in nearby Baltimore, earning a Ph.D. in Middle Eastern languages so he could better understand the history of his people in the Holy Land.

But Alex first gained a better understanding of the obstacles he would face as soon as he telephoned the president of the temple.

"Hello, Mr. President," he said. "How are you? This is Alex."

"Alex!" the president exclaimed.

After a tense, silent moment, he continued patronizingly in a heavy Germanic accent: "Let me talk to you like a father to his son. You know, people in this town are very funny. They like to treat their rabbi with proper respect, you know. I myself don't mind being called by my first name, but you should remember that you are a rabbi all the time. All of us will call you by your title, Rabbi, so we'll know what we are paying for."

And then there was Daisy.

Daisy Grumbacher, a widow who owned the largest department store in York and was the perennial president of the temple sisterhood, was reputed to be someone who, years later, could be described as a small-town "Evita." Her docile, indulgent husband had plucked her from a Baltimore boardinghouse owned by her mother and sent her to a finishing school. Shortly, with her husband catering to her every whim, she was running his department store and intimidating her way to the social summit of her community. Daisy's family, after all, was the town's largest financial contributor to the temple.

Soon after Alex's arrival, Daisy invited him and Theresa to dinner—the first and only time—and in unequivocal tones told the rabbi what she expected of him by relating the story of a fallen predecessor:

"He called me a dictator. Can you imagine that? I had never attempted to dictate to him. All I was trying to do was to give him the benefit of my experience and make it easier for him to achieve the common objectives that we all have in trying to improve the unity of Jewish life. Well, you can be sure that after that unpleasant conversation that young rabbi was not with us very long. I saw to that. But imagine his nerve!"

Alex could well imagine it, especially after one particular incident. A representative of a national fund-raising campaign visited York and asked who had written "the letter that was so effective in winning the support of the community?" Daisy responded, "It would be false modesty for me to deny it. I did."

Alex was furious. *He* had handled all the publicity and had written the letter. He looked at her "with mouth agape," he later said, "but she did not meet my eye. I did not correct her; to do so would have been fatal." Still, it seemed, their relationship was already collapsing, and Daisy surely knew, Alex felt, that he could hardly harbor any respect for her after what he regarded as a false claim.

The rabbi quietly went about improving conditions and expanding activities at the temple, and his success was reflected in soaring congregational attendance. He reorganized the religious school, modernized the long-neglected appearance of the temple, prepared talks for the pulpit, made pastoral calls on the sick and bereaved, attended meetings of the many Jewish communal organizations almost every night, and published a new temple *Bulletin* that, if not delivered on time, would draw angry protests. One of its notable articles revealed a moment of supreme joy for the rabbi:

"The congregation is happy to welcome into its fellowship its latest member, Miss Rosalie Goode, daughter of Rabbi and Mrs. A. D. Goode . . . . Miss Goode is a slender brunette of moderate proportions weighing about seven and a half pounds. . . . When interviewed, Miss Goode was enjoying a real Pennsylvania Dutch breakfast. So we say: 'Welcome to you, Miss Rosalie Goode.'"

At the same time, Alex played a leading role in a program to revolutionize York's social pattern, a triumph that Daisy and her supporters saw as beyond the ken of the job he was paid to do. What did it matter that the *York Dispatch,* the influential local newspaper, would quote him as saying:

"Where there is intolerance and bigotry in our midst let us take steps to enlighten the uninformed. The best cure against religious hatred is information. Let us know one another better and thus learn to appreciate the good inherent in every man."

Alex's partner in finding ways for people to learn about one another was Victoria Lyles, the superintendent of primary education for the schools of York, who was intrigued by the rabbi's ideas and his optimism that they would work. They soon developed a plan of education in human relations. Gradually, bias and segregation vanished from the night schools and some school boards as they set up a special library on the subject and published school bulletins offering information on all races, religions, and creeds.

The rabbi also made other efforts to spread interfaith understanding. He hosted a weekly radio program on religion (with Theresa providing background piano music). When the Jewish community formed a scout movement, he refused to cooperate until it agreed to accept youths of all religions and races. He invited teachers of all faiths and races to celebrate the Sukkoth harvest festival at the temple, and when St. Paul's Evangelical Lutheran Church burned down, he offered to let its congregation conduct services in his temple (though the minister had to refuse because the temple was too small to accommodate everyone).

On one occasion, Alex and the pastor of another Lutheran church held a joint service of the two congregations. Speaking from the pulpit of that church, Alex stressed the importance of cultural pluralism to the United States, showing the great contributions of each group to American civilization.

The rabbi's sermon to the Judeo-Christian audience became the talk of the town, and the local newspapers quoted it at length, with one editorial warmly endorsing his views. In the face of this overwhelming positive reaction, even some of his foes in the temple expressed approval publicly.

Daisy and a few others, however, carped in private that the speech would probably cause more harm than good. And they grew increasingly disdainful of Alex's outside activities. Was he running for mayor of the town or working for the temple? Finally, they decided to meet in secret to decide what to do. They couldn't fire him—he was too popular with the congregation, especially with the adoring younger people who crowded his classes on Judaism. In fact, he had become a highly admired teacher throughout town.

Alex learned of the meeting and angrily joined it. Insults soon flew and, according to the rabbi, one board member sprang toward him. Alex lashed out in self-defense, striking "Mr. G." in the left eye, as the attacker, his blows missing, was restrained by the others.

Alex hurried home and, virtually in tears, described what happened to Theresa. "I shouldn't have done it! I shouldn't have done it!" he moaned. Hadn't he always preached that people should settle their differences peacefully?

Theresa tried to console him. He had only tried to defend himself. How shameful and shortsighted of those elitists, wielding the power derived largely from their financial contributions, to drive her husband to this. Instead, he deserved praise for trying to move people out of a stagnant, parochial social past and into a new world in which democracy would have real meaning and everyone would be everyone else's brotherly neighbor. Didn't they know what Victoria Lyles thought of him?

During World War II, Ms. Lyles would make clear what she thought of him. She would write: "Rabbi Goode educated the whole town of York in social relations, and the plan he and I started has now gone through the whole state of Pennsylvania. Rabbi Goode's influence directly or indirectly touches every primary school and high school in the state. In this regard at least his life goes on in a wider sense among the young men and women of our nation, and it is only a question of time until his name will be remembered everywhere."

In any case, Alex could no longer work with people of such narrow vision. Besides, he had already done a lot for the temple and the town, and he now had a doctorate from Johns Hopkins University. It was time to accomplish "bigger things."

In December 1941, destiny dictated the circumstances that would make this possible. The United States, which was to be the engine of Alex Goode's democratic world revolution, was under attack.

CHAPTER VIII

En Route to a
Safe Place

I

Not only fear tainted the dreams of men going to war as the *Dorchester* rocked with a sickening rhythm in the roaring winter North Atlantic. Ben Epstein, for one, was more concerned about his curdled stomach than his pounding heart. For he soon learned that he didn't need the strawberry jam jokingly prescribed by an officer as an antidote to keep him from rushing to the sink.

"The trip was terrible," Ben related. "The ship lurched forward vertically, then horizontally. We weren't controlling the water; the water was controlling us. And everybody on board—most people—were sick as dogs. We just laid in bed and moaned."

Not even Ben's closest buddy, Vincent Frucelli, whom he had met a few months earlier at the Army Air Forces Administrators School, could take his mind off his misery.

The two young men had become so close that they had attended each other's place of worship together; Ben, who was Jewish, had gone with Vince to his Catholic church, and Vince had accompanied Ben to his synagogue.

"Ben," Vince now said, "the trouble with us is that we're allowing ourselves to get ill. I'm going to the galley. I hear the food is great on board, and I'm going down to eat."

"Vince," Ben replied, "don't you even talk to me about food. You go and do whatever you like."

Vince left and shortly returned.

"He looked fabulous," Ben remembered. "He must've eaten for six people. He stood at the door and said, 'Ben, it's great. You've got to get up and go to eat.' . . . And he kept on reciting the menu. . . . Suddenly, as he was talking, he began to turn color."

Vince ran to the sink, then crawled back to his bunk and demanded, "Ben, don't even talk to me until we reach land."

They didn't know where this land would be, but they prayed they would get there soon. Meanwhile, how could they survive their ordeal? Not even the four chaplains together, it seemed, could save them.

Nor would their stomachs be spared still another shock. Though Ben and Vince, as the ship's record keepers, would later have their own stateroom on the main deck, they were at first assigned to the hold. From there, during an "abandon ship" drill, they and the other men sharing their quarters had to run all the way up to the top of the three-deck ship and inflate "doughnut" rafts, which, in an emergency, they were to throw into the water, then jump in themselves and swim over to these rafts. (The commander of an escort cutter would later write in his report that these drills "had been poorly conducted and improperly supervised.")

Ben, however, wasn't thinking about abandoning ship, at least as he peered from this height into an infinity of dancing white-tipped waves. He had experienced the same feeling in the pit of his already roiling stomach when he had once gazed down from the top of the Empire State Building. And the shock was not eased when he heard a fellow soldier cry, "It would be suicide to jump!"

Still, that was one way, it seemed, to settle his stomach.

How long would the torture last? Until they reached North Africa, many guessed, since Allied troops had landed there. Others correctly surmised they were heading toward the Arctic because they had been issued parkas, heavily padded boots, and other clothes that would be needed in extremely cold weather. But few were sure of their final destination as the ship continued to sail eastward.

On January 27, after five days at sea, fear replaced nausea as the primary concern of Ben and many of his fellows. For they awakened to find that virtually the whole convoy had disappeared, having broken off to head for Russian waters to unload arms and equipment for the embattled Red Army.

The *Dorchester,* though showing its age with its faulty steering gear and gyrocompass, was now the commodore ship leading two other vessels, the Norwegian S.S. *Biscaya* and the Panamanian freighter S.S. *Lutz,* on an unswerving eastward course behind a British corvette.

The following night, at about eleven P.M., the ships, with official permission, glided across lowered protective steel nets into the harbor of St. John's, a fishing town in the Canadian province of Newfoundland. They edged their way to a dock area and berthed, facing a town that stretched across a hill dominated by a twin-towered church with a British Admiralty flag fluttering from one tower over a large eyelike clock. Land at last! At least for refueling.

Many ships, some with large holes that had been blown in their sides, crowded the port, while other craft, mainly British warships, patrolled the outer harbor. As the men saw the ice partially blanketing the vessels and traces of ice floating in the water, a frightening thought entered their minds: If the ship continued into more dangerous U-boat territory, they could, if torpedoed, find themselves freezing alive in a frigid sea.

The ship's loudspeaker suddenly blared: "All troops, repeating, all troops, get ready to disembark, fully clothed with packs."

They were to march to an American base situated high up on the hill. Were they to remain here? Those who wanted to fight wondered why they weren't heading toward the front. Those who wanted an easy war were hopeful they would stay. Only the four chaplains and people like Michael Warish, who were returning to their outfits, knew they would not remain here for long.

Before debarking at five A.M. the next day, the men went to the mess hall for a breakfast of pancakes and coffee. Speaking of the chaplains, whom he had joined, Michael recounted: "They were joking around, having a good time among themselves. I got my plate and I got pancakes, and the food was super, super on that ship. We sat down and had breakfast and I told them about St. John's. And they said they have to get a master of ceremonies and they have to get ready because on the first of February they're gonna hold amateur night. Nine acts, and very good acts."

What a great time the boys would have!

When the sergeant told the chaplains that he had made several trips to Greenland in the past few years, they were eager to hear all he could tell them about this colony, which the Danish government in exile placed under American protection after Denmark fell to the Nazis in early 1940. There was a lot to learn, though they had apparently studied the basic facts.

Nearly as big as the combined twenty-six states east of the Mississippi River, Greenland was the world's largest island, with more than 80 percent of it covered by a massive glacier known as the ice cap. In winter, the arctic nights were long, dark, and freezing cold, growing all the colder when a biting wind, sometimes near hurricane force, howled across the land.

So forceful was the wind that one officer based there, on stepping out of his hut, had suffered two broken arms when a gale had thrust him twenty feet against another hut. Sand driven by the wind could act like emery paper on everything it hit, and the men had to wear huge goggles to protect their eyes. Occasionally, it was even necessary to wear gas masks.

After a dark stormy night, one observer wrote, would come the "season of perpetual day, when no shadow crept over the landscape at evening, no hour of darkness called the weary to rest. The weeks went round unmarked by dawn and sunset, till the eye was dim with the continued brightness and yearned to close itself in the pleasant shade of night."

But while the chaplains would have been glad to serve under any conditions, they would find that southwest Greenland, where two American airports were located, was far more livable than other areas. It had a relatively temperate climate, with the beautiful fjords that deeply indented the coastline sheltering the area from both the ocean storms and the fierce winds off the ice cap. Tall arctic willows, white birches, and other vegetation sprouted there.

Still, the island in general was not hospitable to visitors, and not only because of the climate. Denmark had banned foreign trade and tourism so as to shield the unsophisticated Eskimo natives from corruptive outside influences. Indeed, the American soldiers based there, with their cigarettes and urge toward fraternization, were forbidden to mingle with them.

This urge to isolate the natives from foreigners apparently had not characterized the attitude of Erik the Red, the great Norwegian explorer who discovered the ice-blanketed island in 982. Hoping to colonize it, he misleadingly called it Green Land in order to draw settlers there.

Michael told the chaplains "about the midnight sun and the northern lights, but they didn't want to hear that anymore. They wanted to know what it was like up there." So he went on:

"Greenland is not green. Mother Nature offers no welcome mat. You don't have the area to play ball. You can't bat a ball there. If you want to pitch horseshoes, you're gonna have a problem putting the pegs in. If you want to go anywhere, there are no streets, no roads, no paths. We had no power, either. I never seen so many candles in all my life. And the fleas and the gnats—they were so thick they got in your nostrils, in your mouth, in everything. You could hardly work. And after work? All you can do in Greenland is play poker."

Poker? The chaplains, especially Father Washington, were not going to Greenland to play poker! The chaplains had been aware of some of the hardships in that forbidding land, though not of the fleas. And now they were reminded that there was no fighting there. They could only entertain the boys and comfort them in the cold.

Where were they likely to be based in Greenland? the chaplains asked.

They shouldn't count on hanging up their hats at the same base, Michael said. Troops were spread around. There were two air bases in southwest Greenland, the largest at Narsarssuak, code-named Bluie West One, meaning Base One on the West Coast. These bases permitted planes to fly from Newfoundland to Greenland for refueling and zoom on directly to Britain; to attack U-boats and reconnoiter the North Atlantic; and to facilitate the rescue of downed airmen.

The chaplains could also be sent to a huge open-pit cryolite mine in

Ivigtut, where many of the Danish workers aboard were headed, to comfort men who, in a black and claustrophobic world, burrowed into the earth for a mineral that contained aluminum, vitally needed for the manufacture of aircraft. They might be based in one of the several weather stations, where meteorologists scanned the skies to discover storms that could alter flight plans over battle areas in Europe. Or they might find themselves at a radio and aerological station that was sprouting on Akia Island.

Michael could sense the chaplains' disappointment; it wasn't just that they might be separated but that none of the possible assignments offered the hardships they thought they should undergo. They still felt cheated of the opportunity to serve on the battlefield.

2

While only a few of the passengers knew their destination was Greenland, it seemed that everyone ashore knew. As the soldiers debarked and started marching up the slippery, snow-covered hill, crowds gathered along the road. Ben Epstein later commented, "Would you believe it that . . . the kids on the street were telling us where we were going!"

"Greenland! Greenland!" they cried.

One paper boy shouted, "Where were you guys? You were supposed to be here yesterday."

In fact, almost nothing was secret in this town, which was infested by German agents arriving on merchant ships and operating water taxis, or "bum boats," that kept the U-boats informed about the comings and goings of every ship in the harbor. One spectator warned that there were "enough submarines out there to walk on the water without getting your feet wet." Such suggestions of impending doom did nothing to make the soldiers feel more secure. Now they knew not only that they were heading to a desolate, glacier-bound island but that they would be lucky to get there!

The chaplains marched with the troops. They felt that in the brisk air the walk to the American army camp about an hour away would reinvigorate them, especially after having spent so much time listlessly moving from room to room in the stifling holds.

On arriving at the camp, the men were delighted to step into a hot shower and find a hot meal waiting for them. They also had a chance to wire or mail home messages, some of which the chaplains had helped them write. Alex, in his wire, assured Theresa that he was as safe as he would be at home. And John wired similar assurances to his mother.

John was especially happy, for in the camp he met another Catholic chaplain, Father William S. Bowdern, a close friend whom he knew from Camp Miles Standish and who was now based here.

"It was a real treat to be together again," Father Bowdern later reminisced. "We talked about the danger of the trip ahead, and the great blessing it would be to the soldiers—if anything happened—to have a priest on board to give them all absolution. Just before leaving me to go back on his ship, John and I made a visit to the Blessed Sacrament and he went to confession to me. He was happy, and wanted to get back to the 'boys' on the ship. We shook hands, and bade farewell."

Clark Poling wrote a letter to his wife, Betty, expressing his regret that he was being sent to a country he could not name, but which she understood to be Greenland from their conversations at home. He wrote:

> There is a part of my mind that is quite satisfied with the turn of events that send me to the safe but lonely post we have talked about. However, you know there is another part of me that is disappointed. Perhaps all of us are drawn to the heroic and hazardous. I have done all and more than is legitimate to get into the thick of it. . . . Dearest, I love you, and wherever I go and for all time I am yours, and you are mine. Read to Corky for me and spank him, love him, keep him away from the river, and feed him the oil! You must let me know how things are with 'Thumper' and send me a wire. . . . God bless you, my darling wife. . . .

Yes, it was somehow selfishly comforting to know that he was going to a "safe" place and so would be likely to return to his loved ones, but was it right? His job was to help people in dangerous places. He would do his best to ease the hardships of the men in Greenland, but he yearned for a greater challenge.

To Clark Poling, challenge was the fuel that drove him to success in whatever endeavor he undertook. . . .

CHAPTER IX

THE POET
AND THE CARPET SWEEPER

I

As a teenager, Clark Poling weighed only about 135 pounds and, with his dreamy eyes and gentle manner, resembled more the poet he in fact was than the athlete he aspired to be. But he turned out for football at Oakwood, a Quaker prep school in Poughkeepsie, New York, even though he wondered how long it would take for some human tank to flatten him.

"Dad," he lamented to his father, "I'm punk. I can't run and I'm too light and too brittle. Yes, I'm punk."

Clark had good reason to worry about his brittleness. He still had nightmares about the day when the family car struck a telephone pole and turned over. Eleven-year-old Clark and several other family members suffered serious injuries, and it seemed a miracle that any of them survived. Clark was hospitalized for a long period with a wounded hip that had to be broken and reset. Would a sharp blow now in the injured area cause new damage? It wasn't clear, but Clark, though concerned, was determined to overcome his self-doubt.

He succeeded. In his freshman year he led his team to victory in every game, causing his coach to comment that he was the best freshman defense back in the Michigan Small College Conference. A teammate would observe:

"Clark overcame handicaps by utilizing his indomitable courage and stamina. Also, a certain effervescence suffused Clark's personality. This spirit he carried with him constantly and was conveyed to his associates. It was this quality that seemed to glow in his eyes and give him the determination to conquer."

Clark's father, while proud of his son's performance, watched him play with apprehension. How could so slender a boy take all that punishment? But he would not intervene. It was better that his son risk wounds to the body than wounds to the spirit. And Clark did suffer a broken wrist that ended his short but glorious football career. The important thing, however, was that he had overcome a formidable obstacle.

His dramatic success against all odds in a sport normally requiring much physical strength was apparently due not only to his spirit and technical skill but also to a gift for analysis. As he analyzed the foe's playbook in seeking counteraction, so he mulled over the meaning and implications of almost every serious book he read and argued vociferously in support of his view whenever any controversial question was raised in conversation, sometimes playing the devil's advocate. His aim was to piece together the truth independently of conventional wisdom, even the wisdom of his parents.

Usually, his search for truth would yield passionate but flexible conclusions, reached as circumstances tipped the scales either toward mysticism or reality. Thus, influenced by teachings at his Quaker prep school, he embraced pacifism for a time, a philosophy consistent with his deeply held antiwar sentiment, but he later modified this conviction to approve fighting in self-defense.

Clark questioned everything. Once, after shoving a chair under the doorknob of his father's office to make sure they would have privacy, Clark sat down across the desk from his father, stared quizzically into the elder man's eyes, and cautiously asked, "Dad, what do you know about God?"

His father was numbed with astonishment. "Mighty little do I know about God," he finally replied. "[But] what I do know about God changes my life."

And so Clark departed, still frustrated by unanswered questions.

The subject of God's role in the universe led to constant verbal combat between Clark and his elder brother, Daniel Jr., who believed in God with a fundamentalist passion and had known from childhood that he would follow his father into the ministry. Once, as the two youths and their father lay on a sandy beach, the brothers engaged in a heated argument over Clark's seeming doubts, with Daniel denouncing his sibling as a "son of heresy" and a "flaming liberal."

Their father, perhaps surprisingly in view of his own unquestioning devotion to God, supported Clark, admiring him for seeking answers that might confirm his faith.

Many years later, Daniel Jr. would affirm that Clark "was very different from me. He was born an inquirer, a questioner; I was born an accepter—I accepted and believed. My brother inquired. . . . The things that [Clark] heard, he . . . searched to know their meaning and their purposes."

Clark even tried to make contact with God Himself in order to question Him. While vacationing with his family, Clark hiked up a mountain one day and failed to return that night. After about thirty-six hours, Clark's frantic father went looking for him and finally found him.

Why had he not come home? Clark's father demanded.

"I had some things to settle," Clark replied, "and I thought that . . . I might hear The Voice. I did not hear it. . . . But, Dad, I am glad I went. . . . Some things are clearer now and other things will be, I know."

The elder Poling hoped his son would follow the sacred path that he himself and his father had chosen, but he felt that Clark must follow his own instincts, and it appeared that his son preferred the legal profession. So Dr. Poling was overjoyed when he finally heard Clark say, "Daddy, I'm going to preach; I've got to do it!"

"Clark," Dr. Poling said, "you come from a long line of ministers— none have given up the fight. I do not wish for you a life of ease, nor do I desire to see you free from suffering and heartache. Rather do I desire for you a life of real conflict against the forces of evil. Be true to your calling."

Clark would be, but he had to be honest. Thus, during the ordination, he stunned most members of his family and guests with his reply to a question involving basic Christian dogma: Did he believe in the virgin birth? After a brief, uncomfortable pause, he stated, "I do not disbelieve, but I am not convinced."

Clark then quoted from the Second Epistle of Saint Paul: "For he hath made us able ministers of the New Testament, not of the letter, but of the spirit, for the letter killeth but the spirit giveth life."

Dr. Poling, who already knew of his son's lingering doubt, would later write of this dramatic moment:

"He had an answer that was direct and courageous. It was hard for him to give his answer . . . with his fundamentalist grandfather, whom he loved and greatly admired, right in front of him; hard for him to speak with his mother and father listening in."

In young Poling's view, it was the spirit, not the letter, of biblical lore that was important, as taught by Saint Paul. A spirit that could harmonize with that of every faith.

2

Clark's independent attitude, so often expressed with exasperating frankness—and incisive truth—had frequently landed him in trouble even as a child. He and his brother, Daniel, were constantly arguing or even fighting, not just over God but over everything, despite the most vigorous efforts of his parents to intervene. (Occasionally Clark would join his more mischievous brother in rousing the ire of the community, one time dragging a dead but still highly scented skunk across town, nearly creating a panic.)

Nor could his parents get Clark to concede that he might be wrong about anything. After one endless argument with his mother late into the night, he finally gave in. But the next morning, he took his concession back.

"Mother," he said, "I've got to be honest with you. You didn't get anywhere with that proposition last night. But I just got so sorry for you I had to let you go to bed."

Clark's father received equal treatment. The boy, unimpressed by the way his father argued in one debate, told him "in a burst of deep confidence," "Daddy, when I become a father, I'll show you how it should be done."

Clark's noisy tussles with his brother and his blunt but well-meaning counsel to his elders reflected the atmosphere of slightly chaotic freedom and barely restricted independence enjoyed by the Poling children—the two sons and two younger daughters, Mary and Jane.

However happy life was in the Poling household when Clark was a child, many painful events diluted his joy. In fact, the boy was in distress even on the days following his birth in Columbus, Ohio, in 1910, for he had contracted whooping cough from his pregnant mother. His parents wrapped cotton bandages around his body, and when coughing spasms turned his face purple, they held him up by his feet until his throat was cleared of phlegm. They feared he would die. But even as a small child, he somehow found the strength to survive and live an enjoyable life, though his father at that time earned little money as a student pastor in a small Columbus church.

Still, it was not easy adjusting to new environments as the Polings, like Rabbi Goode's family, frequently moved from city to city. Clark had to make new friends in new schools in unfamiliar neighborhoods in New York, Boston, Philadelphia, and elsewhere, depending on where his father preached. But with the family bond so tight, the joie de vivre weathered not only these difficult physical and psychological dislocations but even the tragedy of death.

Clark's mother, Susan, was the angel in Clark's life, a delicate, beautiful woman with gray eyes, dimpled cheeks, and a diminutive five-foot-one figure. When her husband returned from the war in 1918 after recovering from the effects of gas, she was waiting at the open door of her mother's home in Auburndale, Massachusetts, "looking . . . radiant—more lovely, if possible, than I had remembered her," Dr. Poling later reminisced. Clark and the other children "came rushing over . . . to fling themselves" on their father.

The family's joy, however, would not last long. Before Clark was born, eight years earlier, Susan had contracted the whooping cough that would affect him, but she kept this a secret until the disease finally developed into tuberculosis.

"It was as if she had willed herself to stay alive until I could return to be again the father to our children," her husband mused.

Some days after his return, Susan died.

Clark would never forget his mother and his last moments with her. Years later, when he was in college, he would write a poem reflecting the depth of his wound, a work praised by teachers as one of the best student productions of the year. In part, it read:

> *Gentle Mother,*
> *May I ask*
> *Why your face*
> *Is like a mask,*
> *Still and white?*
>
> *Dearest Mother,*
> *Can't you hear,*
> *Don't you see*
> *That I am near?*
> *You're so white.*
> *Oh! My mother,*
> *You are dead;*
> *Lying there*
> *Upon your bed,*
> *Cold and white!*
>
> *Mother! Mother!*
> *Lift your head;*
> *Rise again*
> *From your bed,*
> *White, all white*

The Poling family moved in with Clark's paternal grandparents, and about a year later, when the boy's tears had crystallized into memory, his father married a woman who had been close to Susan, a widow with two little girls, Rachel and Ann. If Clark was shocked at first, he soon realized that his second mother, Lillian Diebold Heingartner, also had a heart filled with love. She had helped to set up a home for underprivileged children in Canton, Ohio, and, after World War I, had organized special community hospital service during the influenza epidemic.

Probably more important in Clark's eyes, she reacted only mildly to his penchant for disorganization. His clothes were scattered all over his room, and when he had an appointment, he would usually arrive late, if he hadn't forgotten it altogether. Anyway, he thought it was fun playing with two new sisters, who would eventually be joined by two newborns. Merriment once again permeated the Poling household.

"The gracious 'second mother' came into our lives," Clark's father exulted, "and for the next twenty-two years Clark had her constant care and love."

With Dr. Poling's growing celebrity as a religious leader, the family would gradually own many homes, especially in the New York area, but also a twenty-room summer home in New Hampshire purchased when Clark was fifteen. The appropriately named Long House, which had been built in 1767 in the territory of the old Massachusetts Bay Colony, offered Clark a tantalizing journey into early American history. It became, in his father's words, "the beloved place toward which our wandering feet had pointed through all our traveling days."

"With Clark," he would say, "it was love at first sight and a sort of mystical union. . . . No, he was not the best farm hand I have known. He was too often the dreamer and too much the poet to be that, but he loved every rock on her mountainside and every blade of grass."

With sweaty exuberance, Clark planted elm trees, built a road, traced weedy Indian trails, and tramped through a rugged wilderness of brush to a dirt-floored "lodge" he built with clumps of granite at the top of the mountain, known as Wolf Hill. Here, in a rustic environment of almost sacred beauty and peace, he would, like Moses, wait hopefully for a word from God, when he wasn't making the trek with friends, including youngsters he had organized into a Boy Scout troop.

But Clark didn't have to leave the house to explore a wondrous world. Within its musty rooms lay the relics and artifacts of unknown heroes—original furniture, old family Bibles and records, inky-noted ballads from the Revolutionary War, and a yellowed book proclaiming on the first page the watchword, "Let only Patriots be on guard tonight."

An even more thrilling reminder of the glorious past was the ancient burial ground that graced the pine-sprinkled slope of a granite hill. Here, beneath crumbling, moss-covered stones, rested men who had fought under Washington's command. And here Clark would linger and silently ponder what these sleeping patriots had wrought in the service of their country and all freedom-loving people.

The lesson of Long House reached deeply into Clark Poling's psyche. It steeled his resolve to help make sure that their sacrifice would have meaning for the future.

3

The next lessons would be taught in the classroom. At the Oakwood prep school, Clark deeply absorbed the essence of its Quaker teachings. The teachers' emphasis on pacifism reinforced his natural antiwar instinct, though his experience at Long House, with its mementos of Revolutionary glory, helped convince him that war was permissible for self-defense and preservation of freedom.

Clark earned a reputation for more than crashing through a line of scrimmage. Headmaster William Reagan said, "He was one of the outstanding boys in my forty years of teaching experience.... As president of the student body and a member of the Council, he would at times find himself in opposition to most members of the faculty. At other times he would oppose the great majority of students. He was kindly and open-minded."

But not always serious. He was also known for his horseplay. To the shock—and laughter—of the whole school, he once hid in a laundry basket in the girls' dormitory until he was discovered by several screaming residents, who dragged it down the hall. But he had seen nothing, Clark claimed. The cover had been on all the way!

Upon graduating from Oakwood, Poling entered Hope College in Holland, Michigan, a religious school with Dutch Reformed traditions that stressed prayer and discipline. Unable to play football after he broke his wrist, Clark, in his non-study hours, devoted himself mainly to literary pursuits. He stayed up late reading the classics and modern literature and writing poetry, some apparently inspired by a senior-class girl who had taught him how to dance. The quality of his prose and poetry grew with almost every effort as he extended his literary repertoire to short stories and plays for children.

Clark also starred on the debating team and spent much time writing for the college newspaper—too much time, in the view of some school officials. For though he personally enjoyed studying the Scriptures, and, in fact, decided while at Hope to become a minister, he stated in his writings and speeches that less religious students should not be compelled to attend chapel services. With his cool view of excessive discipline, he even wondered why testing was necessary. For Clark, studying people's problems took priority over studying math problems.

From Hope, Clark transferred to Rutgers University in New Jersey. Here he made close friends with a blind Jewish boy and read to him for at least two hours every day to help meet his expenses. After two years, Clark was off to Yale Divinity School, where he took time off from his studies to be ordained.

That summer, Clark gave a sermon from the pulpit for the first time. The church in the neighboring village of Clinton Grove had suddenly found itself without a minister and asked him to take over temporarily. People from all around swarmed in to hear the son of the famous Dr. Poling. Clark stared at the crowd as if he were facing a jury about to convict him. What if he failed? What if the congregation rejected him? How could he explain this to his father, who expected so much of him? A church adviser later critiqued his performance:

"How they loved him; how quickly he became a vital part of their community life! He was their pastor as well as their preacher."

When summer was over and Clark returned to Yale Divinity, he was given a student pastorate at South Meriden, Connecticut, where his ministry really began. He immediately won over the congregation, as he had at Clinton Grove.

In his last year of college, Clark served as associate pastor in the First Church of New London, Connecticut (Congregational). Here he joyously wrote children's plays and conducted religious pageants while teaching the Bible at Connecticut College. He still found time to look after his elderly, motherly landlady, whom he "adopted" and took care of. And—whenever he could get home to Philadelphia, where his father now preached—he courted a particular young lady.

The courtship took some time to slip into gear, and was largely engineered by Clark's youngest sister, Billie. In the fall of 1936, Billie spotted the girl in Dr. Poling's church and whispered to her father, "Oh Daddy, I wish that Clark could meet her!"

Daddy glanced at the guest, Elizabeth, or Betty, Jung, an attractive, dark-haired young woman with warmly luminous eyes. Noting that Betty, a teacher and youth-movement activist, was "lovely, gracious, and with an infectious quality of charm," Dr. Poling immediately agreed with his daughter. "It was for us love at first sight," he would later say. And he was especially happy that she was the daughter of a minister.

But how could it be arranged for Clark to get *his* first sight of her? Billie decided to throw a party for him on one of his visits home and invite Betty. At the party, Clark, who was shy in the presence of young women, seemed to ignore the girl. He excused himself, claiming he had a severe headache, and ran upstairs to his room.

Billie was furious. He had ruined her party—and her scheme. The next morning at breakfast, she cried, "You never had a headache in your life. . . . And she was the nicest . . . girl you ever had a chance to meet."

Clark silently agreed and sheepishly asked his father for her phone number. He called her, and from then on he phoned Betty almost every day from school. On one of his visits, Clark returned from a night out like a man possessed. Shouting with glee, he grabbed Billie and swung her around, then dashed into his parents' bedroom, shocking them awake. Had their son gone mad? He had—with joy. He was engaged to Betty Jung!

4

Distracted by wedding plans and his extracurricular activities at Yale, Clark once more neglected his studies and after submitting his thesis late, failed to graduate with his class. He was shattered. What shame he had brought on his family! His father, however, said of his son's sorrow,

"His innate fairness would not allow him to indict the decision, though he was wracked and broken by it."

Clark quickly corrected the deficiencies and received a diploma shortly afterward, but the pain remained. The setback, however, drove him harder to achieve his goal of ministering to the people. Yes, good grades *were* important; he needed them to shorten the path to this goal. Though he was only in his early twenties, he feared that his youth was too quickly slipping away. When would he have his own parish? Who would hire a young minister just out of college with only part-time experience? How much time would he lose?

Actually, not much. On returning to his room one day, he found a special-delivery letter awaiting him. He glanced at the postmark: Schenectady. He tore open the envelope and pulled out an invitation: Would he be free to "supply the pulpit" of the Dutch Reformed Church on the following Sunday? Would he!

Clark, proud of his birth mother's Dutch ancestry, had always felt close to the Reformed Church, with its Dutch origin. He had visited the church—the original building on this site had been built in 1682— and treasured its traditions and its simple Gothic beauty, especially the tower room under the spire, whose stained-glass windows portrayed the death of Dominie Peiter Tasse Macher, America's first Protestant pastor and the church's first as well. Ironically, though this was one of the first mission churches devoted to the Indians, Macher was killed and scalped by Indians in the French and Indian massacre of February 8, 1690, during the destruction of the Schenectady settlement.

Since then, four Reformed churches had been built at the same site, two of them having been burned to the ground. The church that now requested Clark's services for a day was built in 1867. It was a magnificent structure with arched trusses and an elegant sanctuary. To serve there, Clark felt, would be like living on the fringe of heaven.

Yes, he replied to the offer, he would be free. Even, he felt, if it was only a one-Sunday deal. He learned as much as he could about conditions at the church, finding that it was in deep economic trouble, its congregation shrinking almost weekly. Just the kind of challenge that energized him. In his test sermon, he must inspire members to look optimistically toward the future, and he had just the theme. On March 20, 1938, he stepped to the altar and delivered a sermon with a theme taken from Exodus 14:15: "And the Lord said unto Moses, Wherefore criest thou unto me? Speak unto the children of Israel, that they go forward."

Clark's audience understood. The church must go forward despite all its problems. The sermon so thrilled the congregation that it met within days and voted unanimously to appoint him its pastor, offering a salary of three thousand dollars a year with free housing. Less than two months later, on May 6, Clark was donning his ministerial robe in the church he loved, with his father proudly giving the sermon.

5

Shortly, wedding bells would harmonize with church bells, as Clark and Betty were married by the bride's father in his church—but the groom almost missed his own wedding. Magnificently dressed, with his ascot neatly tied, his gloves on, and one hand cradling the ring, Clark was leaving home when his siblings, despite all his splendor, shuddered at the sight of him. Still the disorganized poet, he had forgotten to shave!

As he raced upstairs to wield a razor, his family was thankful that a perfectly organized wife would soon be asking him, however gently, if he realized how important methodology was to her. Miraculously, a smooth-faced groom made it to the church altar just in time to say, rather breathlessly, "I do."

After a short honeymoon, the young couple moved into a small apartment, where, Dr. Poling reminisced, "began the five golden years of their life and ministry together. It is good to remember how truly it was their ministry together; no person of that congregation ever thinks of one without remembering the other. Theirs was a beautiful and complete human partnership."

Everyone who knew Clark, including Betty, loved him all the more for some of his quaint gaffes and eccentricities. He would sometimes forget to tell Betty that guests were coming to dinner, and would then have to rush out to buy food when they showed up. He spent much time roaming the streets searching for his car, having forgotten where he had left it. And his boundless generosity would sometimes aggravate even his mild-tempered wife. She would try to prevent him from giving away a second pair of shoes or trousers, but he would reply, "Why should any man have two when another has none?"

And Betty found herself feeding almost any poor person who knocked on the door until Clark agreed to arrange for hungry callers to go to a restaurant, which would bill him for the food.

6

The new minister wasted no time before trying to fill every seat in his church, especially with young people, who were so few that the shrunken congregation had come to resemble an old folks' home, with gray the predominant color, and the tap of the cane rhythmically vying with the clang of the bell calling people to prayer. He appealed to women by revolutionizing their role in the church, encouraging them to become more active in its affairs.

He made a promising start, indeed, as curiosity about the new preacher drew to his church more and more people who had heard about his warmth and charm and his simple but powerful way of telling biblical stories in his sermons. He wasn't a great speaker like his father, but each listener felt the young minister was speaking directly to him or her. Even when the congregation wasn't particularly interested in the subject, it didn't make any difference. They simply loved to hear him talk.

But it wasn't enough, Clark felt, to have the people come to him. And so he went to the people. When someone was sick, the person would not *feel* sick, at least by the time Clark cheerily left the room.

"The moment you were ill," one church member recalled, "he would casually drop in on you. He didn't overwhelm you with bounding vitality, and he didn't come in to depress you with long, lugubrious prayers. . . . The first thing you knew he sort of picked you up and you felt better inside, just because he was there. I wasn't much of a church-going man before Mr. Poling came to Schenectady, but he changed all that."

Some children even came to think he was Jesus. Gradually, the youth began taking an interest in religion for its own sake. Under a program called the Character Research Project, parents gave children religious training at home and the whole family was expected to come to church regularly and worship together.

But religion was mixed with fun, and all young people in the community were invited to share in it. The Polings thus led members of a boys' club and others on camping trips, sometimes to the top of Wolf Hill, where they, like Clark years earlier, could listen for the voice of God while the minister and his wife cooked them a meal over a campfire.

Dr. Ernest Ligon, an associate professor of psychology at neighboring Union College, who worked closely with the Polings on the Character Research Project, recalled, "Clark came to Schenectady and in five years transformed a church that was virtually dead into one that was fast becoming the most influential in the community."

At the same time, the minister viewed his mission as extending beyond his own place of worship, much as Alex Goode did. He planned to build a chapel for people of all religions in the tower room, under the magnificent spire that depicted Dominie Peiter Tasse Macher being killed by Indians.

Meanwhile, he moved to improve interfaith understanding, especially with the Jewish community, in response to the persecution of the Jews of Germany in the late 1930s and early 1940s. He invited the well-known rabbi Aaron Wise to address the church several times.

But while Clark tried to spread the message of brotherly love across the community, he reserved in his heart a special nook of love for a new little citizen: Clark Vandersall Poling Jr., who would always be known as Corky.

How wonderful to imagine watching his son grow up as the boy pursued a righteous, happy path to manhood. Clark could hardly wait to hike with the child along the winding trails in the land of his beloved Long House, and to climb Wolf Hill to contemplate the realm of God.

Clark spent almost every spare moment with Corky, even when he was helping Betty with the housework. The boy's earliest memory of his father reaches back to his third year of life; his father was giving him a ride on a carpet sweeper.

"To me," Clark Jr. reminisced, "that always meant that he was playful, that he was loving, and that he was inventive."

What a beautiful life lay ahead.

CHAPTER X

RUNNING THE GAUNTLET

I

Late on the afternoon of January 29, 1943, the troops from the *Dorchester,* after feasting in St. John's, sloshed back to the ship, past new crowds lining the path. Once more shouts of their destination hung eerily in the chilled air, punctuated with the warning, "Watch out!"

At about four P.M., the *Dorchester* creaked northward out of the dock, together with five other craft in a new, bare-bones convoy called SG 19. It comprised the two freighters, *Biscaya* and *Lutz,* that had arrived in St. John's with the *Dorchester,* and three U.S. Coast Guard escorts— the *Tampa,* a 240-foot heavy cutter, and the *Escanaba* and *Comanche,* 165-foot cutters that had served as Great Lakes icebreakers in the early 1930s.

The cutters were part of the Greenland Patrol, established in June 1941 to protect ships and bases in the North Atlantic. The *Tampa* was the convoy's senior ship and carried not only its own commander but the convoy commander, Captain Joseph Greenspun, who would issue all orders pertaining to speed, course, and formation. Since radios were silent to avoid enemy interception, signal lamps would transmit all intership communications.

The *Biscaya* sailed on the starboard side of the *Dorchester,* the *Lutz* on the port side; the *Comanche* and *Escanaba* patrolled farther out, about two thousand yards from the *Dorchester*, slightly astern of it on the port and starboard sides, respectively; and the *Tampa*, with a speed matching the *Dorchester*'s, churned the waters about five thousand yards in front of the former luxury liner, plowing a winding, evasive course intended to thwart a U-boat attack. This formation would later be criticized by the commander of the task force the cutters belonged to:

"The disposition of the escorts appears logical. However, it is believed that the wisdom of forming the convoy in three columns with subsequent broadening of the convoy front to be covered is open to question. It would appear that greater protection would have resulted by having only two columns, one containing two ships."

John Pearse, chief boatswain's mate on the *Tampa*, later said, "It would have been nice to have had a fourth cutter to ride shotgun, but escort ships were in short supply and one played with the cards dealt."

Pearse and many of his shipmates were puzzled. How could three coast guard cutters, which largely lacked modern equipment, protect the *Dorchester*, the two freighters, and themselves from a pack of U-boats? It was like a few Chihuahuas trying to fend off a pack of wolves!

The large luxury liners that carried fifteen to twenty thousand troops on each trip to Europe moved swiftly, at more than fourteen knots, and seldom sailed in convoys with smaller, slower ships; they usually arrived safely. But the *Dorchester*, while able to reach fourteen knots, could not carry enough troops to make voyages to Europe worthwhile. So it sailed to Greenland at great risk.

The risk was especially great because the *Dorchester* was forced to pace its speed to match that of the slowest ships—the *Escanaba* and *Comanche*, which had a maximum speed of eleven and a half knots but averaged about eight. This creeping movement made the *Dorchester* extremely vulnerable to a submarine attack, particularly if the U-boat chose to glide on the surface and thereby expose itself to a possible counterattack. A U-boat could make ten or eleven knots on its diesel engines but, if submerged, only five or six knots on its batteries.

In any case, Allied ships seldom escaped attack en route to Greenland early in the war, though, in a cat-and-mouse game, a submarine was sometimes sunk or frightened off when an escort ship made sound contact with it and dropped depth charges.

As the vessels reached the lowered steel nets, the gateway to Torpedo Junction, the men on the *Dorchester* saw with a sudden surge of fear how vulnerable the ship might be. John Pearse later wrote, speaking of himself in the third person:

"Drawing past the . . . *Dorchester,* he noted the soldiers lining the rail and waving a 'V for Victory' to them, jabbed at his life jacket and pointed at them—indicating that they should have theirs on. Some nodded—others laughed and turned away. All gazed in awe at the listing remains of the torpedoed freighter grounded just inside the nets—the gaping hole in her hull a grim reminder that there was a war on out here."

Once the ships had filed through the nets, the fear seemed to subside, perhaps because the weather was fairly calm, a good omen. The four chaplains were among the hopeful as the little fleet advanced, zigzagging in unison to make it hard for a submarine to focus in on the ships. Perhaps God, they may have thought, heard the warning of the crowd and recalled that He had paved the way across the Red Sea to save other foes of tyranny.

But hardly had the *Dorchester* and its companion ships churned into the open sea when, it seemed, God chose to challenge their faith with a storm that might have disheartened even Noah as his ark rode the waves.

2

At about this time, officials at U-boat Control keeping track of Allied ships sunk in the North Atlantic were chagrined. The main purpose of the 1943 U-boat campaign was to strangle enemy supply lines in the Atlantic and Mediterranean and thereby prevent the Allies from invading continental Europe. But during January, there were no easy pickings—only four vessels, the least productive month in two years. Yet thirteen convoys, comprising about 520 ships, had sailed the North Atlantic run in both directions that month. At the same time, many of the two hundred U-boats patrolling the waters in all theaters had been cruising in the North Atlantic. Could the Allies have broken the German naval code? the officials wondered. No, they decided, the code was too complicated; the Allied knowledge of U-boat operations was due instead to spies, agents, and happenstance. But in fact, the British *had* deciphered the code, though the procedure was still very crude.

The battle in this zone had erupted in September 1939 when Britain, then fighting alone, had begun its struggle to receive vital military supplies from overseas. With America's entry into the war, the struggle had intensified, though neither side had gained an advantage until the fall of 1942. At that time, many U-boats that had been sent to American coastal waters after Pearl Harbor were transferred to the North Atlantic because they could not penetrate the improved United States coastal defenses.

They did a much better job in Torpedo Junction. By November 1942, a record 509,000 tons, or more than one hundred Allied ships, had been sent to the bottom of the sea. And Germany was now building U-boats faster than they were losing them. But in January 1943, fortunes changed when the Allies, having broken the German code, largely managed to evade the submarines.

(The tide would turn again in February, when U-boats in the North Atlantic would sink a record thirty-six merchant ships, and in March, a record forty-nine. But in May, there would be a final reversal: The U-boats would virtually abandon the battle in the North Atlantic.)

In any case, with January 1943 a barren month, there was joy aboard *U-223* on February 1 when twenty-six-year-old Lieutenant Commander Karl-Jürgen Wächter and his crew learned that a convoy was heading east toward Greenland, apparently from the United States. A most timely opportunity!

A few weeks earlier, on January 12, Wächter had boarded this U-boat in Kiel, Germany, for its maiden mission after training on it for hardly more than a month. His orders were to stop Allied supply and troopships from reaching Greenland, at any cost.

U-223 was part of a five-submarine "wolf pack" patrolling Torpedo Junction, and Wächter had good reason to worry. He was a young officer with little experience, and many members of his crew had even less. Moreover, the Americans were technically superior. As Sergeant Kurt Röser, who served in the submarine's control room, would later say:

"[The Americans] had plenty of information about our radio systems and knew from our captured U-boats how we were equipped.

And in their Secret Service, they had about one thousand people sitting just to detect us in the sea. It was a feeling of deep fear and uncertainty among us, especially when we listened for the sound of the AZTEC sonar."

If his U-boat struck a target, Röser asserted, the danger to the craft would, ironically, become even greater. For he and his comrades would then be the hunted, with depth charges raining on them. Little wonder, he felt, that the U-boat arm was knosn as a suicide force.

Still, Lieutenant Commander Wächter hoped to have the cherished honor of sinking a ship on *U-223*'s initial voyage. This goal seemed possible when he was informed, apparently by spies in St. John's, that the convoy consisted of only five (actually six) ships and was probably en route to Greenland.

Only five ships? U-boat Control decided to order four submarines, also new ones from Kiel, to reinforce *U-223*, fewer than would normally be sent on such a mission. German policy was to send U-boats in wolf packs to give each boat maximum security, a policy initiated by Admiral Karl Dönitz in 1935, when Adolf Hitler ordered him to build up and train a new U-boat arm.

But Wächter, it seems, was impatient. He would not miss this opportunity to impress his superiors, especially since only days earlier, on January 30, Hitler had promoted Dönitz to the rank of grand admiral and made him commander in chief of the navy. Dönitz would surely appreciate so auspicious a beginning to his new authority.

Without waiting for the reinforcements, Wächter decided to shadow the convoy until the raging storm had subsided. Once the smothering mist in its wake had lifted enough, he would move in, thwarting what seemed like a devilish cosmic plot to deprive him of well-earned glory.

CHAPTER XI

THE WIND
AND THE WARNING

I

Hardly had the *Dorchester* reached the open sea when gale-force north-west winds propelled it through towering waves that coated much of the ship with ice and stirred fears, which were fueled by loud creaking; the vessel, it seemed, might disintegrate or capsize. This fear was all the greater since the ship was zigzagging through the waves to avoid enemy torpedoes rather than plowing through them frontally, as naval practice normally prescribed.

Meanwhile, the two freighters riding on either side of the *Dorchester* at times almost smashed into the smaller outriding cutters, which tumbled ahead even more crazily than the other craft, looking from the *Dorchester* like toy boats in a bathtub of frothy water. A *Tampa* seaman, John Pearse, later wrote of the three cutters caught in the storm, "Their mastheads appeared occasionally—resembling fly rod tops being warmed up for casting."

The sailors aboard the troopship who had made the trip before were familiar with the winter storms in the North Atlantic, but even they were shaken by this one, the worst to hit the area in more than fifty years. Some men rushed below and, more nauseated than ever, threw themselves on their bunks, only to increase the risk of being crushed by collapsing bunks above them when the ship crashed through one of the leaping waves.

When three men were seriously injured, two of the chaplains carried them to bottom bunks and sat with them for hours, bandaging and feeding them, unable to heal broken bones but trying to heal broken spirits. The two others walked all over the ship, offering crackers and fruit to men almost too seasick even to talk. Yet the chaplains, while trying to cheer up the hapless men, were themselves turning gray with nausea.

"It was so rough that they had to walk with both hands holding on to the railing or something," Michael Warish said. "They lost their sea legs like everybody else. Yet they kept going."

Still, navy hands, more used to a fiercely rocking ship than most of the army passengers, were also busy, making sure the guns were in place, repairing damaged pumps needed to control the constant flooding, and, whenever the ocean fury subsided, chopping the tons of ice from frozen spray that coated the decks and superstructure so heavily that the ship began sinking under its own weight. The men also had to put back in place the anti-submarine-rocket launching pads that the fierce wind had ripped from the deck and two life rafts that had been torn from their lashings. And since there were only about five hours of daylight here this time of year—from about ten A.M. to three P.M.—the men had to work mainly in the dark.

"As the ship plowed through the [snowfield]," Seaman Roy Summers recalled, "it just parted, and you know the water is cold when snow won't melt on the water. [The snow] built up pretty fast and the winds blew and we just had some bad weather."

So bad that this ancient ship had to slow to about six knots to match the pace of the small coast guard cutters in the convoy. This mere crawl could accommodate the lust of a U-boat even more easily than the normal convoy speed—once its crew could see through the fog blanketing the area.

2

On the morning of February 1, Michael Warish felt sick. "Even I couldn't take it," he later commented.

He was not only seasick, however, but sick because the "amateur hour" he had helped the chaplains plan was scheduled for that night.

Now it would have to be canceled. Most of the men were too nauseated even to leave their bunks, much less entertain, and almost nobody could eat a bite. And those who did eat had to make do with K rations, for the cooks could not prepare hot meals with dishes and pots and pans crashing all around.

Indeed, almost everything on the ship not bolted down had broken or ricocheted around the rooms. The bathrooms, or "heads," reeked with the odor of vomit that stuffed the overflowing toilets and sinks.

Michael consulted with Chaplain Fox about the show scheduled for that evening, and the chaplain, with deep regret, agreed that the amateur hour should be cancelled. He would, he said, inform his three fellow chaplains. Like him, they were weaving their way around the ship, trying to comfort the men who had been injured in the storm and those, like Ben Epstein, who were experiencing an almost unbearable nausea.

Although the storm finally calmed, most of the men were still sick and could not focus on the threat of a torpedo attack. How could their suffering be greater than it already was? They would soon learn how. At 3:30 P.M. the next day, February 2, the *Tampa,* which, as the escort commander, had been in the vanguard seeking signs of danger, found some with its sonar equipment. It blinked a terse message to the *Dorchester:* "We are being followed. Submarines estimated in our vicinity. Inform all ships to close up tightly and stay closed for the night."

A signalman on the *Dorchester* urgently informed Captain Danielsen and then the other ships. Soon the *Dorchester* "was almost bottled up in the center of the convoy," in the words of Chester Szymczak, a fellow signalman.

Navy Lieutenant William Arpaia, the armed guard commander, immediately buzzed out the twenty-three men in his gun crew, who rushed to battle stations. The breech on the 3.5-inch gun forward was opened, the 20mm guns were cocked, and magazine tension was cranked at sixty-pound pressure. Arpaia consulted with Captain Danielsen, and they put all of their confidential papers in a perforated sheet-metal box, which would be thrown overboard if a torpedo hit.

The lieutenant then instructed the crew: If you see a wake, open fire in front of it with the 20mm guns. Don't wait for orders!

Together with the army group, he increased the number of lookouts throughout the ship. Report sightings not only of submarines, he ordered, but of icebergs.

Were all these measures enough? Arpaia wondered why Captain Joseph Greenspun, the convoy commander aboard the *Tampa,* did not order the *Dorchester* to zigzag in this U-boat-infested zone in order to make it a more elusive target.

Meanwhile, Captain Danielsen told his officers that if the *Dorchester* was not torpedoed by midnight, U-boats would find it more difficult to operate because of icebergs in the area, and by the next morning the ship would be in Greenland. The problem now was to let the men know that there might be danger ahead without alarming them, and he would do so at dinner.

3

Michael Warish, like the chaplains, continued to check the men's quarters, offering support and advice, even helping the less literate write letters home. But when he learned of the *Tampa* message before an announcement was made, he felt even sicker than before. He hadn't eaten since the storm started; instead, seeking relief, he had chain-smoked. Now he still couldn't take food, but he headed for the mess hall to get a cup of coffee.

On the way, Michael met Father Washington carrying a tray of food for the three men wounded in the storm. Referring to the *Tampa* warning, he said, "Father, I guess you heard the news."

The priest hesitated to answer since no official announcement had been made yet. But with an expression of pain, he nodded that he had. Then he said, "Sergeant, I'm going to hold a Mass at six o'clock."

Michael later remarked: "From the way he looked, I felt Father Washington wanted to tell me something."

Whatever the priest wanted to tell Michael, he was evidently preparing for the worst. And the pain he felt so intensely was surely not for himself, but for his men. In fact, he was, it seemed, almost immune to the fear of death. Not only because of his deep faith, but because he had already been so close to death in his youth that a priest had been called in to deliver the last rites. He was a man who had already peered into heaven and was living on borrowed time. And when his time expired, he would at least be going to a place where gambling was forbidden. . . .

CHAPTER XII

GOD AND THE
EIGHT BALL

I

John Washington had been placing his full trust in God since he was a child growing up in a middle-class, churchgoing Irish neighborhood in Newark, New Jersey, together with six younger siblings: Mary, Anna, Francis, Leo, Thomas, and Edmund. At times, it seemed, John was living more in the green fields and lush forests of Ireland than in the teeming urban jungle of his birth. For seldom was dinner served without the background music of his father's poetically cadenced brogue describing to his children the celestial beauty of his native country, which he felt symbolized a special relationship with God.

And didn't history confirm this spiritual connection? John and the other children were fascinated by legends of the heroic priests of the past century who had helped people hiding from the British oppressor. To young John, Ireland's history was the microcosmic story of man, supported by God, fighting for freedom and justice.

As the eldest child, John delivered newspapers door-to-door to help support the large family. He would stay up later than his siblings and have intimate heart-to-heart talks with his father, which helped cement their close relationship. His curiosity was often sparked by questions arising from his studies at St. Rose's, a Catholic school.

If there was darkness on earth, he asked his father, was there also darkness in heaven?

His father replied: Heaven was bright even at night because God and the saints were there.

At school, John learned a catechism that seemed to bring heaven closer to earth—and himself closer to God: "Man is a creature composed of body and soul and made in the image and likeness of God."

The thrill of first communion followed, and when John became an altar boy in his sixth year at school, he felt so close to God that he told his family he wanted to be a priest. Members of his family were as surprised as they were happy. His sister Anna later said, "I suppose I must have known all my life that my brother was the backbone of my family, sturdy and reliable. But I just can't help but remember him as a laughing boy."

John continued to delight people with his infectious laugh as he immersed himself in the study of a spiritual world with rigid moral and sacrificial demands. Finally, the day of confirmation arrived. As the bishop in the ceremony tapped him on the cheek, John was suddenly overwhelmed with the realization that he must endure any suffering for his faith, for humanity.

With his destiny now decided, he enrolled in Catholic Seton Hall in Orange, New Jersey, where he would work for his high school and college diplomas, then transfer to a seminary in Darlington, New Jersey. He was on the way to the priesthood—and successfully, it seemed, as he chalked up excellent marks and became one of the chief altar boys. Yet he didn't feel he had a more sacred mission than any of the other boys who felt chosen by God to preach His biblical teachings to the people. His mission was simply to be a good spiritual leader.

But suddenly his road to destiny was blocked. He returned home from school with a severe throat infection and a high fever, and his mother put him to bed and called a doctor. The doctor was alarmed when he couldn't get the fever down, even with ice packs and pills. Finally, John fell unconscious, and shortly the doctor went for a priest. The boy, it seemed, was dying.

The clergyman put on his purple stole and read a prayer: "Peace be unto this house and all who dwell therein." He then sprinkled a bottle of holy water over John while blessing the boy with the words "Sprinkle me, O Lord, with hyssop and I shall be made clean; wash me and I shall be made whiter than snow." Finally, the priest anointed John's eyes, ears, nostrils, lips, hands, and feet, and prayed again. The boy's parents were filled with dread—even after the priest said that the sacrament of anointing was also a sacrament of physical healing.

"Don't give up now," the priest told them. After all, miracles do happen.

And one now did. By morning, John's fever was going down. Shortly, the boy would tell his family with a grin, "I guess I nearly put on my wings. But God must have kept me here for something."

John's wonderment about God would grow when He didn't keep his fifteen-year-old sister, Mary, "here." Why, he asked, had God chosen to take this kind, saintly soul, and to leave him among the living? Had he spent too much time perfecting his expertise at the pool table? Had he erred in puffing occasionally on a cigarette in order to show members of the South Twelfth Street Boys, his boisterous, sometimes rowdy gang, that he was one of them? Yes, inexcusable vices, he felt, reproaching himself. About the only ones he couldn't tolerate, it seemed, were gambling and dirty jokes (though he loved nothing more than telling or hearing good, clean ones). Yet God had apparently reserved a special mission for him.

If John couldn't quite figure out God, he felt a new sense of holiness after his own near death and his sister's untimely one. How much closer to heaven could he be? He studied harder than ever at Seton Hall, trying to better understand the mysteries beyond.

Yet even here in this religious setting John never grew too solemn, apparently convinced that God, like his father, had a rollicking sense of humor. Thus John became a star in school plays, mostly comedies, and on weekends he was the life of the party, especially when he was tapping out a tune on a piano or cavorting playfully at the beach on short vacations.

He found it especially amusing to put down people who thought too much of themselves. One summer day when he was home working at a gas station as a "grease monkey," he boarded a bus in his dirty clothes and sat next to a well-dressed young woman with a haughty air. He winked at her, and every time she glanced at him with disdain he stared back with a big smile that reddened her face with fury. When the woman finally got off the bus, John burst into laughter. He had taken her down a notch or two.

Though John loved to hike, play baseball (as catcher), and talk about sports—he was an ardent Yankee fan—he was not a very good athlete, largely because of his poor eyesight. In the water, he could do little more than dog-paddle, and on the golf links he could hardly see the little ball. But when anyone laughed, he laughed with him, realizing this was the best way to endure a ribbing.

In his serious moments, John studied hard, while philosophizing that "it's not what's in your notes, but what's in your head." It was a philosophy that easily qualified him to enter the seminary in Darlington. Here, in a castlelike building nestled in the shadow of beautiful, tree-embroidered hills, John and his schoolmates attended Mass and meditated, then rushed back to their rooms to make their beds and sweep the floors with military efficiency before heading for class dressed in their brown cassock robes. He couldn't understand some of the lectures in Latin, but in the silent, sanctified atmosphere he didn't need words to bring him ever closer to God. And he was now more certain than ever that one day he would learn why He had spared him on his deathbed.

John earned top marks in the classroom, but sometimes he found the discipline stifling, and he occasionally dreamed of his carefree days with his friends in the pool hall, gleefully shooting the eight ball into the pocket. He had thought of becoming a missionary, but he felt he wasn't virtuous enough for the task, even though he was constantly trying to improve himself. What sort of example could he set in showing doubters the way to God?

Although John was dedicated to serving the Almighty, he was not eager to serve Him from a superior hierarchical niche that more ambitious, power-loving men coveted. Humility formed the core of his soul, his personal connection with God, and as a common priest he could more directly help the poor and the powerless, those who needed him most.

In his final year at the seminary, John was elected prefect of his class, but he felt enormous relief when appendicitis sent him to the hospital and another student had to replace him. His efforts to hide his talent for leadership, however, could not stop his superiors from advancing him a rung in the hierarchy. He was soon appointed a deacon.

Even so, the unpleasant thought of joining the "pompous" men at higher levels did not mellow the satisfaction he felt at completing his intellectual training and moving into the practical phase of priesthood: how to help common people and win over their hearts, his ultimate aim.

In June 1935, the time for his ordination came. Before a great crowd crammed into the campus cathedral, John, dressed in a simple cassock, moved down the aisle with his classmates, nodding proudly toward his teary-eyed parents and siblings sitting among the spectators.

The evening before, he had dined with them, once more filled with zest, laughing, joking, singing. When his father had questioned whether such merriment was appropriate on the eve of John's special relationship with God, John replied, ironically in view of what lay ahead, "After all, Dad, this is an ordination, not a funeral."

2

John thrilled at his first opportunity to serve people, as a priest at St. Genevieve's Church in Elizabeth, New Jersey. His deepest yearnings had been answered—he was soon visiting the sick, comforting the dying, baptizing the newborn. How he enjoyed taking children on scouting trips, coaching their baseball team, singing with them at church parties. Their parents loved him for loving their little ones, and were inspired by his usually short sermons, which he delivered without even glancing at notes. Never had life been so full of meaning. God had blessed him with this destiny. Was this why He had saved him from a premature death?

After a year, John was transferred to St. Venantius Church in Orange, New Jersey, where he continued to serve the common people, with whom he had quickly bonded. When friends marveled at his frequent midnight visits with his churchgoers, he would reply with humor that would bring a smile even to the dying, "The customer is never wrong. I can't ask people to die at hours to suit *my* convenience."

When John moved to St. Stephen's Church in Kearny, New Jersey, he treated his new "customers," dying or not, with similar deference and respect. But who deserved respect more than God? he asked in his sermons. And why wasn't He getting it? Why, for example, did many of the churchgoers simply rattle off their prayers to Him without thought or dedication? John demanded that they repeat the prayers until they were said clearly and distinctly, with the heart necessary to reach the Almighty.

But outside the church John found time to meet with his friends and play catchy tunes like "Girl of My Dreams" on the piano while leading a rousing songfest. He also organized dances, formed a choir, took kids to baseball games, and bought hit records for them after testing their popularity with his own nieces. He himself was mesmerized by Louis Armstrong.

Father (now Monsignor) Edwin Sullivan, who had been a student of John's at St. Stephen's, later said of his teacher, "He was a happy person and thought all priests were naturally happy. He never asked me to become a priest. He sold me on the idea without being a smart-ass. He sold me by example. I wanted to be happy, too."

Father Murphy, John's pastor, remarked, "He was my right-hand man. Funny thing is that I was never conscious just how much he was doing. He was chuckling so hard all the time that I never realized how truly powerful his work in the parish was."

But one Sunday in December 1941, after John had taken his mother to a movie, happiness suddenly dissolved in the horror of Pearl Harbor.

✧⁓✧⁓✧

CHAPTER XIII

TOO LATE FOR COFFEE

I

When Michael entered the mess hall after the storm, he found himself "ankle-deep" in broken dishware that glittered under a sign caustically warning, "If you don't see what you want, don't get caught asking for it!" The sergeant saw what he wanted—coffee. And he wouldn't have asked for anything else even if it would go down. He found an unbroken cup, poured some coffee, and stood amid overturned tables and chairs tied together, watching a crewman carefully shovel the broken crockery into a G.I. can. It seemed ironic. The ship was about to enter Torpedo Junction; what wasted work if the ship went down.

"I didn't finish my coffee," Michael recounted. "I got nervous and threw the cup into the can, lit a cigarette, and went on my rounds."

He wouldn't wait for the captain to announce the news, thinking that before he did "it would be better if the men actually knew that the possibility [of a torpedo attack] exists, not to be caught by surprise. It might stop them from panicking." He flitted from room to room, telling the men to stay in their life jackets and to wear shoes and not boots, which would drag them down in the water. He didn't reveal that a U-boat had been sighted, only that the ship was entering Torpedo Junction.

Some of the men objected to his advice, even calling him a "liar" for suggesting they were in danger. Besides, wasn't it hot enough down in the hold without wearing that life jacket?

Michael was shaken. The men were either angry or, it seemed, indifferent. Perhaps they hadn't recovered yet from their seasickness.

"After this real severe storm," Michael said, "nothing was right. Men couldn't get back to the normal way of walking or doing anything because many of the men were very sick. And take into account, too, that many of these men, about seventy percent of them, [had] never before sailed in the North Atlantic."

Would they panic when they heard the news from the brass, as he had feared? He wondered how they would act if the worst happened, how many of them would survive.

2

At about six-thirty P.M., as the men stood in line to be served dinner, home once again was a world away. For even before they could swallow a bite, the voice of Captain Danielsen blared over the loudspeaker:

"Now hear this: This concerns every soldier. . . . Repeating, this means every soldier. Now hear this: Every soldier is ordered to sleep with his clothes and life jacket. Repeating, this is an order! We have a submarine following us. . . . If we make it through the night, in the morning we will have air protection from Bluie West One, which is the code name for the air base in Greenland, and of course we will have protection until we reach port."

He repeated his order for the men to sleep wearing life jackets and dressed in all the clothes they had, including shoes, hats, gloves, and parkas. Then he wished the men luck.

A grim silence reigned as the men stopped eating, their appetites suddenly gone. But then Chaplain Fox stood up and said it was time for a party. The amateur night that the chaplains had planned for a day earlier was called off because of the storm, but the sea was calmer now and quite a few men who had been too nauseated to eat now showed up for dinner. Anyway, this would be the last evening meal on the ship, which was less than one hundred miles from Greenland.

In just a few hours, the convoy would have air protection, and a little later, at about ten A.M., it would arrive at its destination. With the sea now relatively calm, the chaplains decided to reverse their decision, reached during the storm, to cancel the party they had planned. A little impromptu fun would be especially appropriate now to relieve the stress resulting from the submarine threat and to celebrate the end of this rocky voyage. Assuming, of course, that they met a safe end.

Informed by the loudspeaker that there would be a party that night in the mess hall, many men came and remained until about eleven-thirty P.M. Father Washington sat at the old piano from the *Dorchester*'s pleasure-cruise days playing popular tunes, as he once had for his parishioners, while the other chaplains, with their melodious voices, helped him lead the audience in a songfest. Contributing to the harmony were two soldiers who sang while one of them strummed on a guitar.

For the first time, in a sense, the four chaplains were doing what they had wanted to do when they volunteered to serve in the war. To their great disappointment, they had not been sent to the battlefronts of Europe or Asia. But this peripheral war zone had become the front line for the men on the *Dorchester*. God willing, the ship would arrive safely in Greenland. But they might die at any moment, and the chaplains could now perform duties more meaningful than those they might perform in a peaceful environment.

They hoped to give the men at least a few hours of joy that would bring alive memories of home, of loved ones, of a life—perhaps short if God should call for them—that had been full and even beautiful. Memories of a life that had not been void of meaning could soothe wounds or make death less painful. But while the men dreamed of home, they did so largely in silence. Seaman Anthony Naydyhor recalled, "I didn't have much time before I had to go on duty again, but I did go in there and enjoyed it, but the place was not really festive, because most of the people had heard the news during the day about subs being in the area."

The chaplains themselves must surely have returned home in their imaginations as old, familiar songs sprang from their throats and echoed nostalgically, soulfully, through the hall.

Hardly had the fear-induced nostalgia ended, however, when the light harmony reminiscent of life back home dissipated into the harsh reality of Torpedo Junction as the chaplains urged the men to follow instructions, repeating what Michael Warish had already told them— go to bed fully dressed and wear a life jacket. Somehow, at least some of the men were a little less tense; they kept humming the happy tunes in their blacked-out rooms or on the decks, where lookout stations had multiplied.

Their hopes grew when depth charges fired by the escort cutters punctuated the rhythm of their imaginations. Perhaps the bombs would destroy, or at least chase away, any threatening U-boat. A few more hours and they would be safe.

But then Captain Krecker called a meeting of his men in the hold and, reviving the feeling of impending doom, added urgency to Captain Danielsen's instructions:

"This will be the most dangerous part of our mission. We're coming through the storm and now we're in calm waters. And they can really spot us out there. I want you to go back to your quarters, lay down on your back with your life jacket. Be sure to wear your life jacket and even your parka. We're not here for a beauty contest. It's going to be a dangerous thing."

The chaplains followed up with visits to the staterooms to raise the spirits of the men, and Father Washington held services in the mess hall, attended by men of different faiths.

3

Roy Summers, one of these men, recounted, "When I got off guard duty I went down to the chapel. I didn't know which chaplain would be there. But the Catholic Chaplain Washington was there and I enjoyed his service very much, although I'm a Protestant. I would have listened to any of them."

And Roy listened to a troubling, if heartfelt plea: "All of you know the Lord's Prayer," the priest said. "Go and sing it, say it, whatever. It'll help you."

A soldier later commented on the priest's advice: "That's the only time that I ever saw that he brought his religion in. The rest of the time he was just a man who wanted to take care of other men. I would imagine that would make him a very, very good priest, because people could get with him."

But if many of the men took the advice of Father Washington and looked to God to protect them, many also ignored the earthly orders of their military commanders and removed their heavy clothing and life jackets when they returned to their insufferably stuffy rooms in the hold. How could they sleep or enjoy a game of poker while sweating in bulky garb, strapped in by a straitjacket-like canvas life jacket stuffed with cork? After all, God would protect them.

Michael Warish had been too busy to go to the party, despite his initial efforts to organize one. At ten P.M., he went on deck in the thirty-six-degree weather to encourage the soldiers who were helping the naval crew look for a submarine or a more frightening sight: the wake of a torpedo streaking toward the ship. He wanted to see how God was doing, and it wasn't clothing that made him sweat. A gaze at the thirty-four-degree water was disconcerting. It appeared to be a vast mosaic of undulating, interlocked ice pans that, in the words of one observer, "suggested the marble-chip terrazzo floor of an uptown bank lobby." No wonder a man could live only twenty minutes in that water.

"I look at the lifeboat," Michael recalled, "and I see the canvas covered with ice, the block and tackle and ropes, too. And I noticed on the ship railing there was a coat of ice."

Adding to his apprehension was the weather. Not because the waves were leaping high, but because the sea had calmed with a slight chop. A submarine could now surface with just its conning tower awash and be almost invisible to the radar of those days.

4

One guard post Michael didn't check out was the crow's nest, about one hundred feet above deck level. James McAtamney, who had been so disappointed when he had boarded the ship and found himself crammed into the steaming, overcrowded hold, could hardly wait to leave that precarious post. A construction worker in civilian life, he commented:

"In construction work I was used to ladders; I was always crawling up the side of a tank or something of that nature. But that was a different breed of cat with having to climb up holding that narrow steel, ice-covered handrail wearing a parka and long underwear and sweaters and everything else you could think of, and to get up on this swaying thing and into that little compartment. And once up there, you're encircled with this thing that came maybe chest high. My job was to look out for U-boats, but cornered as I was with a face mask and all the other stuff, and with the wind howling and the ship doing what ships do in a storm, it was very uncomfortable and I'm sure I chickened out a couple of times and crouched below the level of the parapet."

And James added, "I don't know why I was up there to begin with. I wouldn't recognize a submarine if I saw it. There was an uncanny luminescence on the ocean at night and with the waves breaking and that sort of thing, I wouldn't be able to tell a torpedo coming toward us, or a sub for that matter, from a flying fish. It was an impossible task for a landlubber, but I put in my stint and I came down at the end of my tour at midnight. I beat it back to the mess hall for coffee, then went down to my E hold and got into more comfortable clothing. I then went back up"—at a few minutes to one.

5

At about the same time, Daniel O'Keeffe, who had pleasant memories of his talk with Chaplains Washington and Goode when he had gone to the priest for confession, was in an optimistic mood, especially since the danger seemed to be over. He had been on lookout duty on the bridge outside the wheelhouse for about an hour, the critical period, and he had seen no sign of a submarine. He could hardly wait to go down to the mess hall, where guards, on being relieved, could get some coffee. He would then climb back to the bridge, where he would take over the wheel and steer the ship to Greenland. It was a job he cherished.

Born in Syracuse in 1923, the son of a high-ranking official of the U.S. Department of Labor, Daniel had turned down a law school scholarship to join the merchant marine when World War II broke out. He had chosen that service when a romanticized movie about it helped convince him it was the "coolest" way to fight the war. After being trained by the coast guard, he would steer tankers and other vessels to Britain, South Africa, Egypt, India, Australia, South America, the Caribbean, and now Greenland—if his relief ever turned up.

As Daniel glanced at his watch, he wondered why his relief, who was scheduled to replace him at 12:50 A.M., was late. He couldn't leave his post until the man arrived, and as it was, he would have only ten minutes to go for coffee before returning to the wheelhouse at 1:00 A.M.

Though he was eager to take the wheel, Daniel knew from his stint there earlier this night that the usually relaxed atmosphere had become tense. The men had told jokes but, it seemed, only to conceal their fear. They had tautly watched the clock, drifting into a silence broken only by the roar of the dark, wind-swept sea. Finally, midnight. A feeling of relief pervaded the room. Only one more hour, and the danger would probably be past.

It was this hour that Daniel O'Keeffe was spending on guard outside the wheelhouse, and so far it had passed without incident. He had wanted to celebrate now with coffee, but it was probably too late. Bum luck! Still, he was looking forward to the companionship of his buddies. The danger was apparently over, and they could laugh at the jokes again.

6

Shortly before 1:00 A.M. on February 3, Lieutenant Commander Karl-Jürgen Wächter stood in the conning tower of *U-223* as it floated on the surface, cloaked in mist, and peered through his binoculars. In the heavy fog, the bearded, stern-faced commander had for some time been shadowing the silhouettes of what appeared to be at least two ships. Were they freighters? The haze was too thick for him to tell. He worried that the enemy might see his U-boat and target it before he could attack. The submarine had already picked up the sound of several depth charges roaring through the deep. The convoy obviously knew that a U-boat was on its tail, though sonar could not detect a submarine floating on the surface.

The depth charges he had heard, Wächter felt, were obviously intended to force his submarine to submerge so it couldn't catch up to the convoy. On the surface, he could make ten or eleven knots on his diesel engines. But if he was forced to submerge, he would be down to five or six knots on his batteries and would find it harder to overtake the ships.

Wächter didn't know that while he could discern the ghostly silhouettes of two vessels through the mist, four others were also slicing through the relatively tranquil waves. Nor did he know that one of the ships, the *Escanaba,* was the only one without radar, or that it happened to be screening the starboard side of the large ship, the side he luckily had a clear shot at. According to Lieutenant Commander Carl U. Peterson, the commanding officer of the *Escanaba,* "If the *Escanaba* had been equipped with radar, it is believed that the enemy could not have made his approach without being detected."

Wächter, fearing detection, decided not to wait any longer, even though the four other U-boats that were to join his own and provide a protective screen for him had not yet arrived. He hoped to return to his base after scoring a hit on his submarine's first mission.

Kurt Röser in the control room was thus ordered to have Erich Pässler, the torpedo man, prepare to fire a fan of three torpedoes when *U-223* advanced to about one thousand yards from the larger ship. Normally Pässler would fire only one torpedo, as Germany was short of munitions, but in this weather he couldn't take a chance on missing the target. If a single torpedo went astray, there would be no time to fire again before fleeing the scene to escape the depth charges that the screening ship would surely launch.

CHAPTER XIV

Countdown to Hypothermia

I

When midnight had passed without incident, Michael Warish recalled, it seemed "too good to be true that we were getting so close. I forgot all about [the danger] and started to make the rounds. I felt like talking to the men and sharing the good news that we were apparently safe."

As Michael sat down on a bed in one room, he happened to glance at the new wristwatch his mother had given him when he was home. The time indicated was 12:45 A.M. (though the actual time was 12:55 A.M.).

"Hey, Sarge," a soldier started to ask, "what if—"

At that moment there was a great crash, followed a second later by a muffled explosion.

"The lights went out, the steam pipes broke, and there was screaming," Michael related. "Then the bunks, three to five decks high, went down like a deck of cards. Shortly after, there was a very strong odor of gunpowder and of ammonia from the refrigerating system."

Michael had been right; his feeling that the ship had reached safety *was* too good to be true. At 12:55 A.M. on February 3, one of Erich Pässler's torpedoes smashed into the *Dorchester* amidships slightly aft on the starboard side near the engine room, ripping a hole from below the waterline to the top deck.

The explosion was muffled because the torpedo had struck underwater, but it opened the way for a virtual tidal wave that flooded the engine room, drowning the oilers and engineers who hadn't already been scalded to death by vapor escaping from the broken steam pipes and burst boiler.

At the same time, the flood roared into the lower compartments, trapping and killing between two and three hundred men, including many who were washed into the sea. Within a minute, the ship listed thirty degrees to starboard and lost way.

The water did not immediately ravage the compartment Michael was visiting, but a heavy piece of flying wood struck him on the head and back as he sat on the soldier's bunk. At the same time, the collapsing bunk above him fell on his right leg and caught him in a vise. He tried to lift the bunk, but it wouldn't budge. Other men in lower bunks were crushed to death in their sleep.

Meanwhile, the men in the room with Michael who were still alive and able to move stumbled out the partially jammed door, some trailing blood from their wounds, some wearing only their underclothes, having ignored instructions to "wear everything" they had. Michael, too, had disobeyed the orders he was supposed to enforce and wore only shoes, socks, dungarees, and an old T-shirt under his life jacket.

Now, in the dark, those who were mobile couldn't find anything and would have no protection in the thirty-four-degree water, which could kill them in a matter of minutes. Cries of "Where's my clothes? Where's my clothes?" echoed through the room. Some men could not find their life preservers.

Michael, who had tried so hard to prepare his men for such a moment, was, ironically, in the greatest jeopardy of all. He lay abandoned, trapped in the debris-strewn dark, breathing in the suffocating ammonia fumes escaping from the refrigeration unit lying in ruins just above the engine room.

2

After firing three torpedoes, Erich Pässler remembered, "It took quite a long time before [we] heard the detonation, and because of the hazy weather and heaving sea [we] didn't know what [we] were shooting at and what [we had] actually hit."

Only one of the torpedoes had struck home, though Commander Wächter, on the tower, "pretended," according to Pässler, "that [we had] hit several targets to make [us] feel like heroes."

But Pässler and his fellow crewmen did not feel like heroes. In fact, another member of the crew, Kurt Röser, put it bluntly: "In the end we were the hunted."

The captain immediately ordered his men to submerge the boat to more than 500 feet and to stay at that depth as long as the submarine's sonar continued to pick up the echo of screening ships in the area, since those vessels could move faster than his U-boat and had superior detection devices. Wächter realized that as soon as the enemy sonar detected a pinging sound like peas striking metal that indicated the location of the U-boat, depth charges would rain down upon it.

And so the captain and the crew of *U-223* waited with creeping alarm for their heroic end—or less likely, it seemed, commendation for having sunk a ship on the submarine's first mission.

3

After checking all the guns and lookouts, Lieutenant Arpaia, the armed guard commander aboard the *Dorchester,* had retired to his cabin at 12:15 A.M. to get some sleep. But forty minutes later he was abruptly awakened by the explosion. He jumped out of bed and rushed to the bridge to confer with Captain Danielsen, who seemed dazed by an attack that he had thought was no longer possible. A witness would report that the captain had run from his room to the pilothouse yelling, "That's it!"

Had Danielsen thrown the perforated metal box of confidential papers into the sea? Arpaia asked.

Not yet, Danielsen replied, but he would do so the moment he was convinced the ship would sink.

Persuaded by Arpaia that it would, the captain instructed the lieutenant to throw the papers overboard. But the skipper himself would not move from the bridge, apparently determined to go down with his ship if it did indeed sink.

After tossing the box with the papers overboard, Arpaia rushed to his gun stations to see if they were firing and discovered that one of the gunners on a 20mm gun had been "blown out" of the gun circle onto the gunwale and into the water. But another man, though having been thrown about fifteen feet by the explosion into a bulkhead, had returned to his 4.5-inch gun and was determined to use it.

The man, navy gunner Roy Summers, never lost his coolness. Before the torpedo hit, he had been sitting by his gun searching the cold, black sea for some sign of a submarine, though he knew that in the darkness without even a glimmer of moonlight, pinpointing a U-boat would be like finding an ant in the sand. Yet he would not give up the search. He longed to fire his gun even after he had limped back to it.

Roy had felt comfortable with guns since childhood. A gun was like a security blanket that would protect him from all the miseries of his young life. One of six sons of a coal miner in Murphysboro, Illinois, Roy learned what hunger meant at an early age when the roof of a mine fell on his father, crippling him and leaving the family without an income.

They moved to a small farm, where they could at least grow their food, and Roy worked on other farms while going to school. About the only meat his family could afford was from squirrels, each costing the price of one bullet. Roy thus made sure that when he went squirrel hunting his one bullet would strike his target. He became an expert shot and a lover of guns, which not only provided food but gave him status in the neighborhood. He was the envy of all the other hunters around.

Shortly before Pearl Harbor was attacked, Roy joined the navy and was soon off to the naval gunnery school in Chicago. He figured he might as well enjoy his job. He sailed to Greenland twice, and on one of these trips, in August 1942, he survived the sinking of the USAT *Chatham,* a sister ship of the *Dorchester.* A U-boat sank the *Chatham* at Torpedo Junction, but almost all of the 569 men aboard were saved by a cutter from the Greenland Patrol.

Now, once again a U-boat was lurking in the area, and Roy yearned to fire the shell that would avenge the attack on the *Chatham.* But try as he might, he could see nothing in the dark mist. In any case, Lieutenant Arpaia found that all the guns were inoperable anyway because of the ship's growing list to starboard.

At the same time, with the electricity cut off, no white rockets signaling the attack to rescue craft could be fired. The ship's whistle wailed six times into the moonless night, like a last lingering lament before fading into a throbbing silence when the steam ran out. Signalmen tried to contact the rescue cutters with one-way blinker-tube signal lights, but they failed. Aside from a few flashlights, the only other lights that worked were the little blinking battery-charged red ones, turned on by a twist of the lens, that were attached to the life jackets of the men. "After becoming certainly convinced that to open fire would be futile and that the ship was sinking and listing rapidly," Arpaia later reported, "I gave orders to the entire gun crew forward and aft to abandon ship." (The order was apparently directed to everyone aboard.)

Roy would have to give up his cherished weapon once again. How many comrades would die this time without being able to defend themselves? The question was especially pertinent since, with communications knocked out, the loudspeakers did not work and Lieutenant Arpaia's order never reached most of those aboard.

4

Meanwhile, the four chaplains leaped from their bunks determined to save as many men as possible, apparently realizing from the moment the torpedo struck that the ship would sink. Perhaps this was what God had primed them for. They were finally in the battlefield, and their souls would be severely tested.

It was a test that past experience had well prepared them for. George Fox had dashed into an area permeated with gas in World War I to save men who had fallen. Alex Goode, as a child, had rescued his siblings when his home nearly burned down. John Washington had become immune to a fear of death when he himself had barely survived an illness so serious that a priest had been brought in to perform the last rites. And Clark Poling felt he had a special relationship with God after experiencing a revelation on a mountaintop and would do anything he sensed God wanted him to do.

The four chaplains, driven by a powerful union of the spirit, ran from their stateroom on the main deck to hand out life jackets to men who might have left them behind. They would also urge those who couldn't make it into a boat or raft on deck to climb down a rope, if possible into a craft already afloat, or else directly into the water, where they could swim to one.

The chaplains would fulfill their destiny, whatever that might be.

5

At 12:55 A.M., seconds after the explosion, lookouts on the coast guard cutter *Tampa,* about five thousand yards in front of the *Dorchester,* observed what seemed like searchlights on her port side. Two minutes later, at 12:57, they saw the ship "veering hard to port and showing numerous small lights." The various lights, actually flashlights, convinced Captain Joseph Greenspun, the convoy's commander aboard the *Tampa,* that the *Dorchester* had been torpedoed, since otherwise there would not have been such a violation of blackout orders.

Yet the captain must have been puzzled, since a little earlier the *Tampa* had swept the waters around the convoy in response to a suspicious sonar sounding but had found no sign of a U-boat's presence. Now it was too late. The *Tampa* sounded general quarters.

6

In addition to the men killed instantly in the crowded hold of the *Dorchester,* many died trying to find an exit; one was blocked by crates of cola bottles that had cascaded into the corridor. Still others perished after inhaling air swirling with ammonia fumes; some made it out alive by breathing through handkerchiefs. Only a small number in the hold managed to survive.

In the confusion, most of the passengers ignored what little they had learned in lifeboat drills, even how to find their assigned boats, a system based on a person's initials. The panic, fed by clanging bells, screaming sirens, and frenzied cries, might have eased if all the craft aboard could have been put to use. The ship had sailed with thirteen motorless lifeboats, one motorboat, forty-five rubber, rope-floored "doughnut" rafts, and two square wooden rafts kept afloat by an oil drum installed at each end. These boats and rafts could accommodate 1,286 persons, more than enough space to save the 900 people aboard—if terror, temperature, and inadequate training had not dictated disaster.

Without waiting to board some life craft, many passengers jumped into the freezing water even before the hapless ship drew to a halt. These men not only would be in the lethal sea longer than those who waited until the vessel stopped to abandon it, but would be strung out so far in the wake of the ship, their little red lights flickering for at least a mile, that rescue before they froze to death seemed unlikely. Their countdown to hypothermia, a deadly loss of body heat, began too early.

Partly as a result of the panic that prevailed, many other men were injured or died fighting each other as they raced to crowd onto a few overwhelmed lifeboats and wooden rafts or to grab a doughnut raft and throw it into the water, hoping to swim to it. Some, half-blinded by smoke and dust as they scrambled across the decks, fell into the crater created by the torpedo. One maddened kitchen worker wildly swung a meat cleaver as he sought to clear a path through a desperate throng trying to climb onto a boat. He was shot dead by an officer before he could reach the craft, one survivor remembered, " 'cause otherwise he would've chopped everybody up."

Amid the frenzied cries were those of a cook who, trapped in the kitchen, had tried to escape through a porthole; his corpulent body had become stuck in it and his screams would be silenced only when the ship plunged to its demise.

Others trapped in the wreckage were luckier. Private Felix Poche had been knocked unconscious by the torpedo blast but was revived by Technical Sergeant Lloyd Phelps, who then helped Felix find and fasten his life jacket and led him from the wreckage of the hold onto the deck. From there they jumped into the water. Felix would manage to survive but his savior, Lloyd, wouldn't.

Some soldiers, sailors, and merchant marines competed to commandeer a life craft. Navy Lieutenant Arpaia had several of his men hurl a doughnut raft overboard for naval use, but "discovered," he would later report, "that some soldiers [took] our raft" when it hit the water. Two of his men, however, "volunteered to climb up to topside and get another one, and they threw it down. I then dove into the water, got into the raft and held it for them."

Several doughnut rafts were cut loose by members of the crew and left on the deck to float clear if the vessel sank, but not many of these rafts would survive the suction of the plunging ship. Adding to the tragedy, a few rafts that were dropped over the side fatally hit people in the boats or in the water. Survivor Charles Macli reported that a soldier had "jumped right off the ship on top of a lifeboat full of guys there. He must've broken a couple of heads."

No craft could be launched on the starboard side due to the torpedo damage, which caused the ship to gradually roll to that side and make the life craft impossible to reach. Thus, the port side was overcrowded with panicky people who piled on top of one another in craft that quickly capsized in the water. Some boats couldn't be lowered because their cables were encrusted with ice. Still others struck the hull of the ship on the way down and dumped their occupants into the sea.

As lifeboat number 9 started down, someone unexplainably cut a supporting rope, and everyone spilled out—except one soldier, Walter Boeckholt. His foot was caught between two planks of the boat, and he hung upside down by one leg with his head about a foot above the water.

All right, his time had come, he thought, but what a hell of a way to go!

CHAPTER XV

THE PEN
AND THE PENNILESS

I

Daniel O'Keeffe, who had been on guard near the bridge waiting for his relief so he could return to the wheelhouse and steer the ship, "happened to be looking aft when the sky seemed to light up in this orange-red light." Though Daniel had been searching the sea, he had not seen the torpedo speeding through the waves. It appeared to hit the engine room, near the place where he would have been drinking coffee if his relief had come in time. He thanked God that the man had been late.

As a crewman, Daniel, who had been trained to lower lifeboats in an emergency, now rushed to boat number 4, his assigned boat. He packed the craft with soldiers, then lowered it into the water, where they were to wait for him to shinny down a rope and join them. But when he had slid about halfway to the water, he looked down and saw in shock only rolling waves. The boat had cast off without him.

That was army gratitude—leaving a sailor to die!

2

Before the torpedo struck, Acting First Sergeant Edward J. Dionne, who worked with Michael Warish, had gone to the mess hall to get some food and coffee for men who were returning to their quarters after suffering through forty-five minutes of guard duty in the biting cold. He then joined some of his comrades in the head, which "was a nice place because it had more air in it." He met with his comrades there "so we could talk and we wouldn't be disturbing anybody." One man asked him for a pen so he could write in his diary. As Edward passed him a pen, a fellow soldier remarked, "No sense in doing that now. Wait about ten hours—then you'll either have something to write about or you won't be here anyway."

The would-be writer didn't have to wait ten hours. Or even one minute. For at that second, the torpedo tore through the ship. Edward and the others ran to the ladder leading them to the deck, but the hatch at the top wouldn't open. Finally, when all seemed lost, they managed to force it open and spilled out onto the deck. The diarist would never record that day's events. For as Edward would recall:

"He still had my pen in his pocket. And the last I saw of him he was standing next to me at the railing, and he decided it was time for him to jump. And he jumped. He went right straight through the bottom of a raft (already adrift), and it took care of him real quick."

3

Walter Miller had returned home from Greenland on emergency leave to visit his ill mother, who died while he was there. He attended her funeral before heading back to Greenland on the *Dorchester*. Now, as the ship churned through Torpedo Junction, Walter wondered if he wouldn't soon be joining his mother. But why worry about the future when he was one of the few lucky soldiers assigned to a stateroom on deck—and when he was about to clean up in a card game on his bunk with his three roommates? He had four deuces and three kings, and when he reached out for another card, he had a fourth king. Rummy!

"I raised my hand," he later related, "and instead of saying 'Gotchya,' was going to snap the cards on the bunk, when everything went black and we couldn't even see each other. I said, 'What the hell was that? We're hit!' "

After they had fumbled around in the dark looking for their parkas and life jackets—Walter couldn't find his—"one fellow felt for the door, and we finally found the latch; we opened the door and stepped outside."

Walter had been about to win a mint. Now, it seemed, he might die almost penniless.

4

Henry Geoguen was also playing cards that evening—cribbage. He and four comrades, divided into teams, felt that since they would be reaching shore in the morning, they might as well enjoy their last night together aboard ship. Besides, how could they sleep knowing that a submarine was lurking nearby? That afternoon they had seen the spray caused when the *Tampa,* the lead cutter, dropped depth charges, and the sight seemed to confirm that the order to wear all one's clothes and a life jacket throughout the night was based on more than suspicion.

The game relieved their tension; it was an alternative to the forbidden cigarette that might, in the darkness of night, make the ship the target of a torpedo. And Henry and his friends didn't much care who won—they were trying only to make one another forget the sight of that telltale spray.

Suddenly the lights went out, and they dashed out the door to the deck, where their assigned lifeboat was located—among the first to arrive there. Henry leaped into boat number 13 and cried, "Come on!" to his comrades behind him. But they didn't move. No, they would remain and "ride it out." Even a stricken ship seemed safer than a rowboat tumbling through the hungry waves into a dark, terrifying infinity. The ship was huge and solid and would probably not sink. No one dared doubt that they would meet again in Greenland and finish the game.

5

James McAtamney, who had returned to the hold after descending from the crow's nest, where he had been on guard duty, had hardly gone back to an upper deck to shower and "shoot the bull" with friends when—*bang!* He had come up from the hold just in time. "Basically, it was a question of 'What do I do now?' " he later said. He was a soldier, not a sailor! "We tried to remember which was port, which was starboard, what was aft, what was stern? Where was our lifeboat supposed to be?" He and three comrades "waded through these other bodies that were wondering what to do."

They finally found their lifeboat station but "where we thought our lifeboat was, there wasn't any lifeboat." With hearts pounding, they looked down at the black currents and saw their lifeboat, number 6, already bouncing in the waves. They took turns shinnying down a rope, but James missed the craft and landed in the bone-chilling water.

6

Roy Summers, the gunner who had agonized over the order to abandon his weapon, suddenly realized that he didn't have his life jacket on and went to look for it on the gun mount where he had placed it—but it was gone. Some soldier, he thought, had grabbed it. He was thankful that he was wearing a parka, felt-lined boots, and headgear. He knew the importance of being fully dressed if he had to jump into the freezing water.

With the ship listing forty-five degrees toward starboard, Roy rushed up to the top deck on the port side and with another sailor tried to release a lifeboat bulging with men, but it was frozen to its moorings and couldn't be broken loose. The two then tried to release a second lifeboat, but it, too, was immovable. Nor were any more rafts to be found. With the ship listing more by the minute, Roy would have to go over the side without a life jacket. He placed his faith in God, who had saved him when the *Chatham* had gone down and would probably want to be consistent.

7

Ben Epstein, still suffering from seasickness, had fallen asleep between ten and eleven P.M. on the night of the sinking. He slept soundly, as might be expected of an inveterate optimist. Why worry about the submarine danger—or about anything beyond his control? He had followed all the instructions announced by the captain and felt certain he would survive no matter what happened. Before falling asleep, he had tried to allay the fears of his friend, Vince Frucelli.

"Just put on all your clothes and your life jacket. Don't give up, whatever happens. Don't worry, I'll take care of you, but we must stick together."

"Okay," Vince replied, "anything you say."

And Ben dropped off to sleep—only to be awakened shortly by the blast of the torpedo.

Jumping out of his bunk, he told Vince, "We're gonna creep along the outside of the deck until we come to our assigned position of the lifeboat."

When they had climbed over heaps of debris to the deck, they entered a refrigerated world. Ben recalled, "I don't have to tell you how cold it was, you can imagine. And I don't have to tell you that the North Atlantic is not the most pleasant place to go sailing. It was vicious. There were icebergs around. And so we walked around the outside of the deck until we came to our assigned boat position, which was on the port side, the opposite side of where the boat was torpedoed. We felt our way along the side, and I sort of led Vince."

When they came to their position, they saw a rope hanging from the side of the ship to a boat.

"I want you to follow me," Ben said to Vince. "Do you understand? You will follow me. I'm jumping over the railing."

"Yes, I'll follow you," Vince replied.

But his voice was shaky, his eyes glazed with fear.

8

Meanwhile, Walter Boeckholt continued to dangle by one leg from the end of boat number 9, which had been partially cut loose as it was being lowered and was hanging by a davit, having dumped all the other occupants into the sea. He was praying for a craft to come by and for someone to pull him free. But he finally managed to release his foot and crawl up the side of the ship to the deck.

With most survivors lining the railing on the lower starboard side, Walter, on the port side, could see only dead bodies lying around. Hoping not to become one of them, he grabbed a rope and started climbing down once again toward the sea, this time feet first. He dipped a foot into the water to test the temperature; it nearly froze. He suddenly realized that it didn't make any difference. He couldn't swim a stroke, but there was nowhere to go but down. He dropped into the water and went down, deeper and deeper.

CHAPTER XVI

A DEADLY DECISION

1

At one A.M., Lieutenant Commander Peterson, skipper of the *Escanaba,* which was stationed about two thousand yards from the *Dorchester* on its right flank, signaled Captain Greenspun aboard the *Tampa* that the *Escanaba* was heading toward the sinking ship. Peterson reported to headquarters that he would "investigate the picture, which indicated that there was a man overboard and the *Dorchester* was attempting to make a pickup." But it soon "became apparent that the *Dorchester* had been torpedoed since the red lights attached to survivors dropping over the side and swimming in the water became visible."

Instead of permitting the *Escanaba* to sail amid the red lights and pick up survivors, however, Captain Greenspun "advised" its dismayed skipper to sound general quarters and return to the cutter's previous location. And so the *Escanaba* "went to full speed, swung out and around the stern and bow of the *Dorchester,* and back to station."

2

The *Comanche,* about the same distance from the *Dorchester* on its left flank, was first aware of the attack when Storekeeper First Class Richard Swanson, who operated the cutter's sonar, an acoustic location and ranging device, heard at 12:55 A.M. what sounded like an explosion. He was stunned. "The sound quality was not good that night," Richard later recalled, "but there was no doubt about what it was."

He immediately reported the sound to the *Comanche* skipper, Lieutenant Commander Ralph Curry, and Curry passed the report to Captain Greenspun, who was apparently already aware of the explosion.

The men on the three cutters, *Tampa, Escanaba,* and *Comanche,* were alarmed about the fate of their brothers aboard the *Dorchester.* If the ship sank, hundreds might die in the icy waters before they could be rescued. They hoped that Captain Greenspun would send at least one of the cutters to rescue survivors immediately. But they were disappointed; their humanitarian instincts clashed with Greenspun's view that the potential danger to a second ship deserved priority over saving the lives of those who were doomed to die if not reached immediately. They felt this view tainted the spirit of the Greenland Patrol, to which they belonged.

The Greenland Patrol, established in June 1941 to help counter the Nazi infiltration of Greenland, grew in strength and importance when the coast guard was transferred to the navy five months later. The job of the patrol, which worked out of ports in Newfoundland and Nova Scotia, was to keep open the convoy routes for vessels and the air routes for planes. It sought out and destroyed German submarines, rescued passengers of torpedoed ships, reported weather and ice conditions, broke ice obstacles, and transported men and supplies.

These functions helped counter increased enemy activities that were facilitating submarine attacks. German radio stations hidden amid the glaciers, for example, were transmitting data to Berlin several times a day and informing U-boats in Greenland waters of the weather and enemy ship movements in the area. The Allies feared that Hitler might even try to take over the island because of its strategic importance and to keep them from using it.

Knowing the stakes, the men aboard the more than thirty vessels in the Greenland Patrol were proud to serve in this special naval arm, a pride akin to that of firefighters. They were, in fact, the firefighters of the sea, undertaking some of the coast guard's most hazardous missions. They were constantly battling icebergs, blizzards, and towering waves as they rushed to help victims of torpedoed ships, often while in the crosshairs of a torpedo dispatcher.

It was hard for these oceanic firefighters to countenance failure and watch men die. But they knew they would have to, for vital minutes were ticking away and none of the three cutters had yet been given the order to save the survivors of the *Dorchester*—even though the *Escanaba* was already at the scene.

Greenspun was not a man to ignore official rules or even unwritten doctrine, whatever the circumstances. And one such doctrine held that when a ship in a convoy was torpedoed, other vessels in the group, before picking up survivors, should seek out and destroy the responsible submarine in order to prevent an attack on a second ship. This was the order he now gave.

A German crew member later said, however, that the Americans should have known that U-boats seldom wasted scarce torpedoes on a nearby smaller craft, particularly after a hit on a larger one, since staying around to prey on a secondary target would not be worth the risk of being knocked out by an Allied depth charge.

Men could survive for hours or even days in warmer waters, perhaps justifying application of the navy doctrine in this case, but critics question whether this rule logically or ethically should have applied when men were certain to die in icy waters if not rescued quickly.

"I can't understand this decision," one expert said. "The rescue of hundreds of men in deadly water should come before efforts to protect a small vessel with far fewer men from possible attack—especially since one of its purposes was to save survivors in the water."

In any case, while the sound of a patrolling cutter might keep a submarine at bay, the vessel would not have fired a depth charge even if the U-boat was located (though the Germans could not be sure of this), for the blast would kill the survivors speckling the area.

Captain Greenspun's decision is particularly puzzling in light of a document entitled "Screening Instructions for Escort of Convoy Operations" that the United States Atlantic Fleet issued on November 14, 1942, less than three months before the sinking. It read:

"It is obvious that detailed instructions for all eventualities are impracticable. In applying these instructions, commanding officers will be guided by common sense, good judgement, the seaman's eye, a sense of proportion, and good sound imagination."

Critics say that Captain Greenspun displayed none of these qualities in reaching a decision that navy rules didn't require him to make, a decision that would not simply risk but *cause* the death of hundreds of men in one of the greatest sea disasters of the war.

The irony is that after sinking the *Dorchester,* the *U-223* crewmen, in a standard U-boat maneuver, rushed into the deep, where they settled for hours, too fearful of an attack from another ship in the convoy to strike a second time.

Meanwhile, the *Escanaba* log indicates, "various courses and speeds" were ordered so the cutter could evade the U-boat. None of the courses would immediately lead to the men who were dying.

CHAPTER XVII

FULFILLING DESTINY

I

Roy Summers, the navy gunner who had lost his life jacket and was unable to loose a lifeboat on deck, decided to descend into the water without one. Like Ben Epstein, he was confident he would survive. Had he not survived when the *Chatham,* the *Dorchester*'s sister ship, was torpedoed a few months earlier? An escort cutter had come to the scene without delay and had saved him and almost everyone else on the ship. Similarly, at least one of the cutters escorting the *Dorchester* must already be on its way to the rescue.

But as he was about to abandon ship without a life jacket, he remembered that jackets were stored under an antiaircraft gun on the top deck. He rushed there and, reaching his hand into an opening, found the depository empty. The chaplains had already distributed the jackets to men still on the ship or had thrown them overboard to those already in the water. And the jackets kept in lockers elsewhere on the ship, he was sure, would be gone by now as well. As Roy withdrew his hand from the opening, he touched what felt like canvas and cork. The last life jacket!

With the ship listing ever more sharply, Roy put it on and ran to the aft part of the ship to jump off, but he changed his mind when he heard terrifying cries. Unable to see in the black night, some men had blindly leaped into the claws of the still whirling screw, or propeller, which had risen from the waves like some monstrous sea dragon and was grinding the men up.

As Roy started back, he saw two of the chaplains by the railing. They had already distributed all remaining life jackets to men without them, and were trying to persuade two soldiers to lower themselves on a rope into a lifeboat bobbing below.

"One chaplain," he recalled, "was shaking this one boy very hard and even slapped him a few times. This boy was hysterical. He was screaming, and this chaplain was trying to get him to quiet down to talk to him. He said, 'I want you to take this jacket, get on the lifeline, and drop off the ship. You can save yourself.' Another chaplain was there beside him lowering the men, putting them on that lifeline."

Finally, the hysterical young soldier grabbed the chaplain who was seeking to save him by the neck, as if to choke him. Roy, who couldn't identify the chaplains by name, rushed to the scene and pulled the pair apart. Unruffled by this unfortunate encounter, the chaplains moved on, encouraging other terrified men to abandon ship.

"Come with me," Roy urged the reluctant soldier. "We can go down the rope together."

But the man broke away and ran down the sloping deck, possibly to his death. Then Roy, who needed no urging, climbed over the railing and lowered himself into the water, hoping that a lifeboat or raft would float by and pick him up—if a coast guard cutter didn't arrive first. He remained calm, he later said. He didn't panic like that army guy. He was a navy man, and the navy never let a sailor down. He had learned that when the *Chatham* had sunk.

2

Meanwhile, the chaplains continued to move around the decks urging men to climb down a rope, if possible into a craft already afloat or, if necessary, into the water, where they could swim to one. When Chaplain Washington, who was administering absolution to men going "over the side," urged Charles Macli, the boxer, to join them, Charles cried, "Father, get off the ship yourself! It's going down!"

"No," John replied. "But *you* must get off."

Charles, realizing that the priest would not give in, slid into the water.

3

With the ship listing at an ever sharper angle, men still on deck tumbled to the lowering starboard side. Almost catatonic with fear, they stood two or three deep by the railing, which many gripped until their knuckles turned white. Staring at the beckoning sea as if into the heart of hell, they groaned in agony, wept, and pondered whether to submit to its terrible lure or to wait for some supernatural force to save them.

Walter Miller, who would never collect on the winning card hand he had held at the moment of the explosion, later reported on these miracle seekers:

"I walked down the railing, but they were man to man—there was no way to get between them. They were solid. I walked right down to the middle of the ship and I came back again. Then I put my hands on the shoulders of two guys standing side by side. And I said something like, 'C'mon, guys, we have to get the hell out of here. This thing's going down.' And they didn't move. . . . These guys were frozen in fear."

At that moment, with "amazement and disbelief," Walter witnessed a remarkable scene. He heard "a loud voice with terror and panic in it saying over and over, 'I can't find my life jacket.' I turned and looked in the direction of the voice and . . . I heard another voice say, 'Here's one, soldier.' " And this man took off his life jacket and helped the panicky youth into it. Walter recognized the voice of Chaplain Fox.

Grabbing a steel bar running under the floor of the deck above, Walter now vaulted over the barrier of flesh to get to the rail. He reached out for a rope hanging from an upper deck, but the greater the tilt of the ship, the farther out the rope dangled. He finally managed to pull it in and, with his legs wrapped around it, slid down toward the sea. It then suddenly occurred to him that he wasn't wearing a life jacket— and he couldn't swim. He seemed to be in a position as perilous as that of Chaplain Fox—except that the chaplain apparently wasn't trying to save himself.

4

Chaplain Washington still wasn't trying either, as a survivor, Hugh Moffett, can testify. Hugh, a former sergeant in the New York police force and a naval veteran of World War I, was helping to lower a jammed lifeboat when he saw the priest grab a jacketless soldier by the arm, unhook his own life preserver with his free hand, and slip it over the head of the man.

"God bless you, Father," the soldier mumbled and moved toward the railing.

Edward Dionne, who had lent his pen to the diarist who would not live to record the disaster, faced the same fate, for he, too, had left his life jacket behind. Suddenly, he saw Chaplain Washington, now also without a jacket, and asked the priest if he knew where he could find one.

"He said," Edward recalled, "that he believed that one could be found on the top deck in a container. . . . We went up on the top deck together . . . but none were there."

John was clearly dismayed. If only he had a second life jacket to give away!

As the *Dorchester* gradually rolled farther to starboard, Edward, realizing it was too late to jump straight down without being sucked into the water with the vessel, climbed to the "side of the ship and ran down from the aft end to the bow, and when I saw the water boiling up, that's when I made the world's record running broad jump and swam at the end of it." He managed to climb into a wooden raft, ignoring protests by some of the sixteen men already aboard that one more person might sink the craft.

5

Meanwhile, navy lieutenant John Mahoney, after running out onto the main deck, realized that he had left his gloves in his cabin. He later wrote:

"Chaplain Goode overheard me swearing at myself for my stupidity. When he saw me heading back to my cabin he called after me, 'Don't bother, Mahoney. I have another pair. You can have these.' He pulled off his gloves and gave them to me."

The lieutenant refused to take them. It would be hard for anyone to survive in the icy water without gloves, and it would be unconscionable to condemn the rabbi to some terrible end.

But Alex said he had another pair and that the lieutenant needn't worry. Mahoney then took the gloves and lowered himself into the water. Later, he would realize that a man preparing to abandon ship wouldn't burden himself with a second pair of gloves.

"I owe my life to those gloves," Mahoney said. "I landed in a lifeboat that was awash, and for eight hours had to hold on in [freezing] waters. My fingers would have been frozen stiff had it not been for the gloves. I would never have made it without them. As it was, only two of us survived out of the forty who were in the boat."

Lieutenant Mahoney found it difficult to understand how anyone could be *that* selfless. But the rabbi was, characteristically, thinking of far more than himself. He had a dream, a dream to bring all people everywhere into a world of peace, democracy, and brotherhood. The intensity of his idealistic drive suggests that he may have handed his gloves to someone he hardly knew and whose faith was irrelevant to him as a symbolic expression of his belief that young people like that navy lieutenant would ultimately help bring his dream to fruition.

Since this deed seems to indicate that Alex intended to go down with the ship, it also suggests that he was saying good-bye to his beloved wife, Theresa, and his baby, Rosalie. They would understand—his daughter, in the future—why he had to leave the world he wanted to change. Theresa had always understood that he had to pursue his destiny. How apt, it seemed, was the remark he had written in a letter to her after their wedding: "We can both take it, sweet, and we'll handle this separation like champions. Together now we can be brave in our love and laugh at time and distance because now we are one."

6

Second Engineer Grady Clark viewed another heroic act by a chaplain, though he couldn't identify him.

"I stood just five feet from [him]. I watched him. I saw him force his life jacket over the head of an unwilling service man, who was crying hysterically, and the boy said he knew what it meant. The boy said:

" 'Damn it! I don't want your jacket!'

"The chaplain showed his rank. He said:

" 'Get into it, soldier, and get into it fast!'

"And then he gave him a shove with his open hand down the careening deck, against the rail, and slid after him, and lifted him up and dumped him into the water.

"Then," Grady continued, "he turned and saw me, and he came slushing up the deck, and he said, 'Soldier, what are you doing here? Get over the rail.'

"He spun me around and followed me to the rail, and I got over the rail. He said:

" 'Swim out,' and he stood looking at me, and he had a funny laugh."

Grady then "swam out" and managed to scramble into a boat.

Who was the chaplain? Dr. Poling would later note that when his son, Clark, "was terribly afraid or very mad, he had a funny laugh, or a nervous laugh."

7

Merchant marine Daniel O'Keeffe felt betrayed as he clutched a rope and saw that it led directly into the water. He had helped all those army guys get into boat number 4 and had lowered it, expecting them to wait for him to shinny down a rope, but they hadn't waited for him, and now he was dangling over the sea.

Daniel was glad he had never joined the damned army—and, with the end near, grateful that he had received the blessing of Chaplain Washington. He let go of the line, dropped into the sea, and paddled around, his body numb, until he finally saw the chance for a second miracle. Lifeboat number 6 sailed into view. But it was jammed with people, mostly soldiers lying in a heap, and some of them wanted to ignore his pleas for help, fearing the boat would capsize.

"But I'm a seaman," Daniel cried. "I know how to run the boat. Let me on!"

Someone then pulled him into the boat—which was built for forty people, but was now crammed with more than fifty—apparently because of his expertise. And he probably saved the boat by telling the army oarsmen to crash it frontally into the waves to avoid being tipped into the sea. *Now* the army needed him!

Later, Daniel would learn that lifeboat number 4 had capsized and that he probably would have died with the rest of the occupants if they had waited for him. He had been saved by a second quirk of fate. Maybe he would survive after all—a thought that was reinforced when a man without a life jacket waved good-bye and shouted from the deck, "So long, boys. Good luck!"

Once more, the voice of Chaplain Fox.

8

David Labadie could not shake the image from his mind: a fist clinging to the railing on deck, near the stern. As he had been about to shinny down a rope into the lifeboat waiting in the water below, he saw the fist, though in the dark he could not tell who the man was, only that he was wearing an officer's cap.

"Come on!" David pleaded. "It's the last boat. Save yourself!"

But the man was silent, and his fist continued to grip the railing. He was the only person David could see this near the stern, which, it seemed, would submerge first. He somehow felt responsible for the life of this lone stranger.

"Please come!" he pleaded.

Still no response. No sobbing, no wailing, no quiet cursing—the earmarks of those frozen with fear. Just silence. The silence of a man resigned to death. David tried to tear the man's fingers free of the railing, but in vain. He finally gave up and slid down into lifeboat number 13. Who was the man who wouldn't leave? Instinctively, David was convinced that this ghostly figure was one of the chaplains. And he would be haunted by the thought even as his own survival appeared questionable.

In fact, David, who had toughened himself as a shipfitter and a woolen mill worker near Boston, was a strong swimmer and had spent much time swimming and boating along the beaches and rivers of Massachusetts. He thus had "great respect" for water and felt he could calmly handle its fiercest challenges. He remembered the sign his mother had pasted on the refrigerator at home, "Worry is like a rocking chair—it'll keep on moving, but get you nowhere."

But how could he purge that unyielding fist from his mind? How could he have failed to save one of the four men who were saving so many others? Men whose actions another survivor, Pfc John Ladd, would call "the finest thing I have seen or hope to see this side of heaven."

9

For about ten minutes after the *Dorchester* was hit, Michael Warish remained trapped in the stateroom he was visiting, his right foot pinned under a bunk rail, his mind reeling from a blow in the head from falling debris.

"I tried to lift the bunk up," he recounted, "but I couldn't do it. I knew my head was pretty well banged: it was bleeding, and my back hurt, too. I had to talk to myself to fight off the panic."

Michael felt he was doomed, and waited for a second torpedo to finish off the ship, though it would never come. Finally, he managed to free his foot, which he realized was broken, and, in great pain, crawled to the door and down the corridor, over piles of debris, to the exit leading to the deck.

"That was the longest thirty feet I ever crawled out of in my life," Michael said. "You couldn't see, it was so dark."

When he reached the deck, he crept out and removed a shoe to ease the pain in his swollen foot. But as he was wearing only a thin shirt on this frigid night, nothing could relieve him from the chills that shot through his body. Now he needed someone to help him leave the ship. He figured the more people he could find to join him, the greater would be his chance to make it. "The coast guard sees a group of lights," he noted, "that's where they're going first."

Most other men in his situation, he felt, would probably die. His view would be reflected in Private James Eardley's lament: "They said if anything happens when you're in the water, turn your red light on so we can find you. That was laughable. You know, you're in rough, heavy seas and you got two or three boats picking you up, and they're going to find maybe nine hundred men floating around in the water?"

In any case, Michael wanted company; he had never felt so lonely. He scanned the stern area on the port side of the sloping, water-washed deck, from where he wanted to jump, but all he could see were corpses, the red lights on their life jackets still blinking for help. He was, it seemed to him, alone on the ship, with only the desperate cries from the dark, foaming sea to confirm that there still was life in the world.

He did not see the men who lined the railing on the starboard side of the ship, staring into the great black void swirling ever closer, with white, fingertipped waves beckoning them to extinction—men so paralyzed with fear that even the four chaplains could not move them.

How terrible to die, Michael thought, with only the dead as company.

CHAPTER XVIII

IN SEARCH
OF BUTTERED PANCAKES

I

James McAtamney, who, like Daniel O'Keeffe, had missed his boat and landed in the water, was praying for good luck as he swam frantically to another craft. "I was only in the water a few minutes," he said, "and was close enough to the jam-packed boat to hang onto it."

But then he heard the shrill voices of men arguing pro and con.

"There's no room. We'll sink!" one cried.

"Hey, one more won't hurt!" another answered.

James was distraught. They were deciding whether he would live or die! And he couldn't, like Daniel, argue that he was an experienced seaman. It wasn't fair. Why should a soldier trained to fight on solid ground have to drown in icy water—like some sailor? Better a foxhole.

2

When Ben Epstein had slid down a rope into a boat, he found it waiting, but probably only because the seamen who had lowered it into the water had not yet released it from the cables. The boat, seething with more than fifty people, was so overcrowded that Ben had to lie on top of a "mass of humanity." Occupants were crying for the boat to be released, but Ben cried for his friend. Where was Vince? He had promised to follow him down the rope. Had his friend succumbed to fear?

Maybe he would still come down. . . . But would the boat remain stuck here long enough to give him time?

It wouldn't. The jammed boat capsized and, Ben recalled, "practically everybody was caught underneath and died."

Ben, however, was thrown clear into the sea. When he bubbled up, he felt he would somehow survive, but would Vince? In the confusion, had Vince jumped into the boat before it capsized?

"Vince! Vince!" he called out. "Where are you?"

If there was a reply, it did not filter through the pandemonium and the prayers.

Finding himself only a few feet from the sinking ship, Ben remembered reading that "when a large ship goes down, it creates a suction and takes everything around it down with it. And so off I went. I didn't know where I was going; I was just swimming away from the ship."

Ben was determined to keep swimming until he froze to death or drowned, since every moment of borrowed time was exquisitely precious. Anyway, why worry about the uncontrollable? Even a nightmare sometimes came to a happy end.

3

After helping two chaplains subdue a soldier they were trying to coax into leaving the ship, Roy Summers climbed down a rope into the water and swam to a nearby lifeboat. But he didn't stay in it long. For like Ben Epstein, he found himself in a boat overflowing with writhing flesh. And in minutes, his boat, like Ben's, capsized.

But Roy and the other occupants managed to turn it upright and crawl into it again. The craft, however, overturned once more and again was set upright, but this time Roy was unable to climb back in—because of an oar. An oar had several uses. It could be used to move and steer the boat, to strike a comrade's near-frozen legs and bring back blood circulation, or to keep people off the craft. Now a crazed person already aboard had grabbed an oar and was swinging it around, targeting Roy and others he felt were "excess" passengers.

"Stay offa here," he shouted, and he knocked some men back into the water.

Roy escaped and paddled away. Where the hell was that cutter?

Well, if he had to die, he felt, it was better to drown than to be whacked to death.

4

As the survivors of the *Dorchester* floundered in the glittery sea, many coast guard sailors were still outraged about the delay in rescuing their brothers. At least one of the three cutters, it seemed, could be sent to save them. But instead, though the minutes were ticking away during one of the most lethal twenty minutes of the war, all three escorts were ordered to search for the submarine.

To find it in case it had surfaced, the *Comanche* at 1:12 A.M., the *Tampa* at 1:28, and the *Escanaba* at 1:33 were ordered to fire a fusillade of star shells, which would, in one writer's words, "illuminate the scene in a ghostly white light." Ironically, this light, which was intended to find the submarine and deter a further attack on the convoy, actually, as one sailor later pointed out, made the cutters "sitting ducks."

In any event, no sign of the U-boat could be found, and at 1:35 the star shells no longer cast their eerie glow. The *Dorchester*'s men had already been in the freezing ocean for forty minutes, the lucky ones in leaky boats or rafts. Most of the others had likely died in half that time.

And the order had still not come to look for survivors.

5

When Walter Boeckholt had climbed down a rope, jumped, and plunged ever deeper into the sea, he didn't expect to be saved, especially since he couldn't swim. His life jacket, however, propelled his numbed body back to the surface seconds before he would have drowned. He floated a short distance and grabbed on to a large ball of rope. As his icy hands were about to loosen their grip, his life "flashed" before him.

"The first thoughts that go through your mind," he later said, "are all the bad things you've done."

But they weren't bad enough for God to whisk him from this world. In fact, God, it seemed, was helping him stay—by sending an empty doughnut raft directly toward him.

In ecstatic disbelief, Boeckholt climbed in, and shortly he was shar-ing the gift with three other soldiers who had been floating, barely alive, among hundreds of corpses. But the raft was no refuge from death. The sea, it seemed, was determined to overrule God's will, turning into a soaring roller coaster of waves.

When one of the men aboard died, the others, hoping to cheat the sea, tried to throw his body overboard to keep the raft from capsizing. But they couldn't move it. The man was frozen to the side of the doughnut.

And as the survivors contemplated the fate of their companion, they shuddered at the thought that the freezing water cascading into the raft now seemed almost certain to tip them, too, into eternity.

6

In another raft, the problem was not getting rid of one corpse but of di-vesting the craft of at least five or six survivors who were piled one on top of another, crushing bones and smothering passengers to death, even as it seemed the craft would overturn with every monstrous wave. And at the bottom of the pile lay Leander Thomas, who had already evaded death more than once.

Early during the trip from the United States, Leander was given the choice of two jobs: guard duty or K.P. He chose walking the decks over peeling potatoes, and was assigned to march along the starboard side of the *Dorchester* from midnight to 1:00 A.M. But with the weather grow-ing ever colder as the ship sailed northward, he asked to be switched to the kitchen, where he could at least bask in warmth while wielding the knife.

A most timely decision. For if he had not switched jobs just then, he would have been in the area blasted by the torpedo. After the explosion, Leander had another close call. While he was leaning over the railing on a lower deck, a doughnut raft someone dropped from above struck him on the neck and nearly knocked him overboard.

In a daze, Leander managed to slide down a rope and swim over to the raft, then to clamber in with two others. Within two minutes, the raft was piled high with more than twenty men who, in the words of one survivor, "looked like a bunch of old wet rags." Since Leander had been one of the first to jump in, he lay sprawled on the floor virtually under their combined weight, with fountains of water splashing in and threatening to drown him.

"I couldn't move, I couldn't breathe," Leander said later. "Boy, I thought I was a goner."

And then he lost consciousness.

7

Others in the water or on some craft might have been "goners" without the encouragement of the four chaplains, even as it emanated from the ship. In fact, many found the voices of the chaplains as perhaps their last source of hope. Pfc William B. Bednar, who had floated in oily water littered with dead bodies and debris, recalled, "I could hear men crying, pleading, praying. I could also hear the chaplains preaching courage. Their voices were the only thing that kept me going."

Meanwhile, Ben Epstein, propelled in part by their contagious spirit, continued to swim blindly in the black night toward nowhere. He bounced from wave to wave, protected from almost immediate death by the fuel oil that covered his heavy clothes and served as a kind of insulator, and sustained by his steel will and armor of optimism. A strong swimmer endowed with great energy, Ben was determined to keep going until he ran into some conveyance or, in an unlikely worst-case scenario, met his Maker prematurely. After this earthly hell, heaven might even be relaxing, if not joyous. That seemed to be part of the chaplains' message to the men as they faced death. And if they themselves were still alive, he knew, that's what they would still be preaching to those around them.

Suddenly, Ben's glazed eyes glimpsed an approaching lifeboat. He stopped swimming and hailed it as if he were flagging down a bus. The crowded craft splashed to a halt, and Ben tried to lift his foot over the side to get in. But at this critical moment, his strength failed him. Impeded by his heavy wet clothing, he couldn't raise his leg high enough, and nobody tried to help him. Though an oarsman had stopped the boat, many of the occupants didn't want another body, which could tip it over—a panicky attitude prevalent on almost every other boat or raft

as well. The men on this lifeboat had already agreed, however reluc-
tantly, to let Daniel O'Keeffe and James McAtamney climb aboard. No,
not another guy!

"I was so cold, I was so wet, I was so frightened," Ben recalled. "I
tried climbing up, and it was impossible."

For the first time since he had been awakened from a peaceful sleep
by the explosion, Ben's optimistic perspective began to blur.

"If you're not gonna help me get up," he moaned, "I'm going down.
I can't hold on."

Suddenly, a picture of his mother, father, and brothers flashed
through his mind. As did a vision of Vince, who might not have gotten
off the ship. He could soon be joining his friend, it seemed, if, as now
appeared likely, he would have to settle for the worst-case scenario. He
could live with it—even as he died with it.

8

Roy Summers, who had been driven from his lifeboat by an oar-
swinging survivor after the boat had capsized twice, was also facing a
fateful moment. Was drowning the only alternative to being murdered?
To Roy's great relief, he soon found another. There ahead of him was a
large, half-wrecked wooden raft. A few men occupied the seats at the
two ends; there was no floor between them.

Roy joined more than thirty others who clung to the sides of the
raft. He would find that "men were all around me with the red lights on
their life jackets on, drifting and bobbing in the water. It kinda looked
like a wheat field with a lot of lightning bugs on top."

The man holding on to a rope next to him, Roy found, was a young
member of his gun crew named Red, who, weak and in pain, was about
to let go.

"Can you hang on?" Roy asked.

"I think so," the youth replied.

But when Red started swallowing salt water and muttering unintel-
ligibly, Roy, as the waves leaped higher, wrapped one arm around his
crewman and tightened his grip on the side of the raft with the other.
"Hang on!" Roy urged. "They'll pick us up soon."

Shortly he felt the boy's wrist; it had turned cold and clammy and had no pulse. Dead! Roy then let the waves carry off the corpse. Whom would *he* cling to in ten or fifteen minutes, when his body would be frozen almost solid?

9

At the same time, Roy's superior, Lieutenant William Arpaia, and three of his men floated in their doughnut, finding that the raft, with its rope bottom and shallow rubber walls, offered little protection from the freezing sea; water rushed in with every lurch from wave to wave. One of his men died from exposure after he had "lost his mind," apparently from swallowing salt water.

Arpaia himself felt he was dying, but he had an antidote to hypothermia that few other persons on the ship apparently had. He would recall:

"The thing that saved my life was the morphine syrette that comes in our first aid kits. My hands were frozen so I couldn't give myself the shot, but one of the seamen managed to help me. I believe that the effects of morphine kept us alive and made it possible for us to resist the severity of the weather"—though it was too late to save the crewman who died.

Arpaia could not know that his best gunner, Roy Summers, might be in even greater peril than those who at least had a rope under their feet.

10

Exhausted, his mind reeling, Ben Epstein was about to surrender to the sea when two men reached down and pulled him into their boat, despite the protests of others. And as the craft pitched ahead with more than thirty passengers, he looked back and "saw a sight that will live forever with me. It was the *Dorchester* making its last lurch into the water."

The ship rolled to starboard stern first, then slowly descended into the sea at 1:20 A.M., twenty-five minutes after the explosion, with men still lining the railing on some parts of the main deck. Why had they waited so long? Ben agonizingly asked himself. Why hadn't they jumped? Yet he knew why.

"What are you jumping into?" he later mused. "The freezing water, the dark waves? They became so terrified that they just held on to the railing and went down with the ship. It was a horrifying thing to see."

His horror intensified when the image of Vince flashed before him once more. And where, he still wondered, were the chaplains, to whom the men had grown so close? He could only guess the worst, though he did not lose hope that they had somehow survived. Were they on one of the boats or rafts . . . ?

II

At 1:35 A.M., fifteen minutes after the *Dorchester* plunged into the depths, Theresa Goode, asleep in the home of her in-laws in Washington, D.C., while her own house was being refurbished, awoke with a start.

"It was as if someone had dropped me in ice water and I was just frozen," she would say. "It seemed to me that the whole room had become illuminated, and Alex's picture on the dresser just seemed to glow. I felt as if he was trying to reach me. I was just so frightened."

The last message Theresa had received from her husband was a cable apparently sent from St. John's. But since then there had been no word. Theresa remembered her premonition. Had Alex been trying to reach her—perhaps to say good-bye? Was this God's way of telling her . . . ?

12

Even as Theresa pondered the meaning of the mysterious light bathing her room, the little red lights gaily blinking in the North Atlantic night and reflected in the glistening oil slick surrounding the *Dorchester*'s bubbly grave served as a kind of theater setting for a ghastly cacophony of clashing sounds.

"One could hear men crying, praying, moaning in the freezing cold," Ben recounted. "I couldn't take it any longer."

Soon the panic-fueled sounds on his lifeboat gave way to the desperate cries of one man: "Somebody help me up! I've got to pee!"

"Pee in your pants!" replied William Kramer, the man next to him.

The man did, then muttered almost ecstatically, "Oh, that was nice and warm!"

The others were envious. They could hardly wait for *their* kidneys to function. Still, William found greater comfort in prayer than in the prospect of urination. He had gone to services conducted by Chaplain Goode aboard the *Dorchester* and left feeling that "the good Lord would watch over" him. And so, he felt, he had special heavenly protection. How fortunate that he had with him the small Bible that Rabbi Goode had given him so he could reinforce his bond with the Lord. Perhaps one day he would attend the chaplain's services again—if they both survived.

Discussion now turned to a more serious leak—in the bottom of the boat. It was growing into a stream, and it appeared that the craft would soon be flooded. Ben removed his parka and, kneeling in the rising water, covered the crack, but in vain. He and others then took off their shoes and began bailing the water, but not fast enough. With only a few inches of the boat now visible above the waterline, the craft, it appeared, would sink within minutes.

Ben had almost no feeling in his frozen feet and could barely use his hands, but he was still fuzzily optimistic. After all, he later pointed out, he came from an ancient people who had miraculously survived many catastrophes. Maybe it was time for another miracle.

13

Roy Summers, who had been hanging on to the side of a battered raft, managed to climb on it and sat at one end of the watery floor. He replaced one of the men who either had frozen to death or had gone mad and stepped overboard to drift to his death.

"I see the sun coming up," one of these men had muttered. "It's melting the butter on the pancakes. I'm going over there to get some of them." And he disappeared in the blackness of night.

Another man, shaking with chills, had said he was "going to ask Mom to bring me another blanket." He, also, dropped into the water and vanished.

Finally, of the eight or ten men originally on the raft, only Roy and three others remained aboard, and all the thirty or so men who had been hanging on were gone.

"One boy kept slipping down," Roy recalled. "We told him to sit up on the seat and we picked this boy up—he had no legs. It wasn't long till he was gone."

Roy did not have the vigor to restrain others from leaving for hallucinatory lands. "It's hard to hold a panicked man," he explained later. "They are strong and they got strength untold if you try to hold one. And they'll just pull you with them."

He remembered coming to the aid of one of the chaplains when a crazed soldier had grabbed the man by the throat for trying to save his life. Only God knew if the chaplains were still alive or had died while saving others. As he himself had been trying to do, but with little success.

As his limbs grew numb, Roy expected his turn to come at any time, though he was sure he would never go mad. He later claimed, "I wasn't scared. I don't know why. I thought about what I read in the Bible: 'Not my will be done, but thine.' "

Wasn't this the message of the four chaplains?

14

Two or three hours after Leander Thomas lost consciousness, he awoke with a start. Where was he? As his mind cleared, he realized he was still on the raft. What had happened to the more than twenty men lying on top of him? He could now breathe the frigid air freely. He looked around. Only three other survivors! The others had all been flung into the sea by the waves and the wind. Lucky again. The ones on top of him had gone first.

Suddenly, as he sat in the raft, Leander felt someone trying, it seemed, to drag him into the water. A man had swum up to the craft and, reaching up to him, put his arm inside Leander's life jacket and was hanging on to him. Leander turned to a raftmate and urged him to "tell that guy to get loose from me."

"No, no, you do it!" the raftmate replied. He would not condemn the man in the water to death.

Leander agreed, but in vain. Finally, he removed his life jacket and let it go. And the man who had been hanging on to him soon vanished in the darkness.

"Boy, it was a relief!" Leander said later.

It was after all, either the other guy or him. Pressing his hands under his armpits to keep them warm, he wondered whose turn would come next.

CHAPTER XIX

PLUCKED FROM
A FESTIVE GRAVEYARD

I

The brilliant glow of star shells soaring into the sky bathed the sea like stadium lights at a night baseball game. But after about twenty minutes the lights went off, having revealed no sign of a submarine. So at 1:43 A.M., forty-eight minutes after the explosion, Captain Greenspun finally ordered the *Escanaba* to start picking up survivors, though few who were not in a boat or on a raft could still be alive in the deadly cold water. Since the *Escanaba,* unlike the other two cutters, did not have radar, it could not in any case be used for screening.

The *Tampa* now screened the *Escanaba* as this cutter started to seek survivors, and the *Comanche* headed toward Greenland, escorting the two freighters, *Biscaya* and *Lutz.* But the *Comanche,* en route to that island, was, to the puzzlement of its crew, ordered to return to the scene of the sinking, where it arrived at 3:19 A.M. Captain Greenspun had decided to have the *Tampa,* his commodore ship, switch places with the *Comanche,* which would now screen the *Escanaba* while the *Tampa* escorted the two freighters to Greenland. It is unclear why Greenspun ordered this switch in roles.

"Those of us on deck," John Pearse later commented, "could not understand leaving, and I am sure the [convoy leader] would have preferred staying, but he was bound by sometimes harsh convoy law—you protect the surviving ships." Also, the *Tampa* had more firepower than the *Comanche*.

On the other hand, did the switch really protect the freighters? Since they had stopped near Greenland, planes based there gave these craft air cover, but they were left unprotected by an escort vessel for about five hours, the time that passed between the departure of the *Comanche* and the arrival of the *Tampa*.

This breach in security was especially surprising since Greenspun had been so careful about security while the survivors of the *Dorchester* were in the water dying. The captain did not equivocate when he told the *Comanche* what to do: Its objective was *solely* to protect the *Escanaba* from a U-boat attack, *not* to join the *Escanaba* in rescuing survivors.

Lieutenant Commander Curry, the *Comanche* skipper, was distraught. He would have to ignore the few survivors he might encounter. But what choice did he have? He had to obey orders or risk being court-martialed, especially if the *Escanaba* were attacked while he was picking up people. At the least, such disobedience could end his career and all his dreams for the future. Sometimes a warrior had to dehumanize himself for the common good.

2

When the *Escanaba* finally received the long-awaited order, "Pick up the survivors and bring them aboard," the men reacted with joy. But the elation was short lived. Who would be alive, they wondered, after freezing in the icy sea about a half hour longer than anyone thought a person could live in such water?

In minutes, the *Escanaba* was drifting through waves of blinking red lights just fast enough, it was hoped, to thwart a torpedo man's aim. What a cheerful, even spectacular sight—like a stage set in an Esther Williams musical. Fantasy then dissolved into reality, with the hard, terrible realization that most of the lights were attached to dead men. There was silence at first, the silence of shock and dismay.

Many of the men had been on other rescue missions. In fact, the *Escanaba,* which had spent the prewar years breaking ice on the Great

Lakes, had been on escort duty with the Greenland Patrol since it was formed in 1941. During the next year and a half, the cutter, with Boston as its home port, escorted numerous small convoys between U.S. and Canadian ports and Greenland, and rescued more than 150 survivors who had abandoned ships that had sunk. But never had they encountered anything resembling this vast, glittering graveyard that extended almost as far as the eye could see. Richard Swanson captured the mood decades later, saying, "I've had nightmares about it for years afterwards, seeing those dead bodies and those lights and going through and not being able to do anything."

The silence was soon broken by the shouts of some to get moving and save those who could be saved, though the wind whistled ever louder and the waves swelled ever higher, making operations increasingly hazardous. Nor were the cutters permitted to lower their lifeboats to facilitate rescue because of the submarine danger. But the *Escanaba* did have one great advantage—its gung ho "retrievers," a group of three men who would experiment with a new way of picking up survivors that had been conceived by the executive officer, Lieutenant Robert H. Prause.

Experience had shown that most drowning men, especially in a frigid sea, were helpless from exposure and shock and could not climb up sea ladders or cargo nets. It was futile, as well, to throw them bowlines so they could pull themselves on board, because they were too frozen or weak even to hang on to the lines with enough strength or to secure them under their arms.

So the retrievers—Ensign Richard A. Arrighi; Forrest O. Rednour, ship's cook; and Warren T. Dyampert, steward's mate—put on heavy rubber wet suits, which permitted their body heat to warm trapped water, and leaped into the sea with lines around their waists to examine fleetingly whether a man was dead or alive. They gave priority to individuals afloat, who were far more at risk than those in boats or on rafts.

Most of the red lights designated corpses, which were left behind. Other men were unconscious and were lifted into the cutter, as were some who "looked dead" but, it was felt, might not be. Others were thought to be unconscious, though they were actually dead. Only a relatively few men, almost all from rafts or from lifeboat number 6, were found to be alive.

Could some men have been unconscious but taken for dead and therefore left to float? The men had been in the water for almost an hour before the *Escanaba* started picking up survivors—some forty minutes beyond the period thought to be the maximum time a person could remain immersed and live. But no one can be certain that there weren't more exceptions to the "deadline."

3

Among the survivors picked up by the *Escanaba* was Edward Dionne, the acting first sergeant who had been the mother hen to guards on the *Dorchester* when they were relieved from duty. The man who pulled Edward from his raft into the ship turned out to be a high school classmate of his.

"What are you doing here?" the shocked survivor asked.

"I don't know," his old friend replied, "but I guess maybe I came here to help you."

However joyous Edward felt on being rescued, this rapturous moment could not ease his nausea, caused by the witch's brew of salt water and oil he had swallowed. Still, the brew had in a way helped to abate his suffering, for, he reported, "it gets warm to have it come up."

Now, at last, he would get a lot warmer. And he did, almost as soon as his boyhood comrade pulled him aboard the cutter, when he gulped down three or four bowls of pea soup "so thick that you could eat it with a fork." He said of his rescue:

"They sent a man over with a rubber suit tied to a rope. And he put a rope around us, and as the raft rose with the waves they would snatch that guy off, and he would be down there on the raft putting another man on the ropes. There were sixteen of us on the raft, but only thirteen of us were alive. We didn't realize the other three had died. We started out with a lot more than that, but they fell off the side and couldn't hang on."

4

Among others found were Walter Boeckholt and a raftmate who had been riding the waves on a barely stable doughnut with a dead body that was frozen to the rope floor. Walter remembered the rescue clearly:

"As the *Escanaba* pulled up beside us and saw that we were still alive, they lassoed each of us from the raft, leaving the dead one in the raft. As my body hit the deck of the cutter, it really did sound like a bag of frozen bones. They carried me below, cut my clothes from my body with a large knife, and started massaging my body, trying to get circulation moving in my legs and arms. My body was almost completely frozen. I was still conscious and was able to take a shot of whiskey for stimulation, and it was greatly enjoyed."

Most of the men on lifeboat number 6, less dazed than the barely conscious two on the doughnut, wouldn't need a shot of whiskey to be stimulated after seeing the outline of a vessel churning toward them. Someone cried out, "Look, a submarine! A submarine."

But another man shouted, "No, it's a cutter! We're saved!"

Among the most grateful men on the lifeboat was Ben Epstein. The miracle was happening. Hadn't he said that despite all the horrors and his flirtation with death, he would survive? The oarsmen on his craft, with renewed strength, headed toward the ship—or, some feared, the submarine. It was too dark to tell which.

As the vessel drew near, Ben realized that it was the *Escanaba*. Perception, however, can sometimes distort reality. It was a small cutter, but from the lifeboat it looked huge. And it had come quickly—so it seemed. All the horrors the men had experienced after the torpedo hit had been somehow compressed into an imagined time frame of a few minutes. Everything had happened so quickly. The cutter couldn't have taken almost an hour to pick them up! Why would they have been left in the freezing water for so long when this delay would be a guaranteed death sentence for most of the men from the *Dorchester*?

Only one man on the lifeboat, it seems, showed no signs of hypothermia. He was lucky enough to have lain on top of the pile of humanity cramming the boat; he never even got his feet wet.

The rescue effort did not have an auspicious start, however, especially since the cutters were ordered not to launch their own boats for fear that a submarine might attack them. The loudspeaker on the *Escanaba* warned the men on lifeboat number 6 to ride a wave to its highest point, then take turns jumping onto a cargo net hanging from the deck; this way no one would be crushed between the lifeboat and the cutter as the wave smashed them together.

But one survivor did fall into the water between the two craft. The man, covered with oil, was so slippery that the rescue crew, after lowering themselves into the lifeboat, could not grasp him and pull him back into the boat. Ensign Arrighi then jumped into the water and brought the man back alive, though he risked being crushed himself, as the roaring sea kept slamming the vessels into each other.

Leaks began to develop in Arrighi's rubber suit, but he ignored the danger and continued the rescue work until a medical officer forced him to come aboard. Although Arrighi was suffering from exposure, he refused first aid and rushed below to help treat the survivors. Meanwhile, the other two rubber-suited retrievers, Rednour and Dyampert, worked frantically to prevent floating survivors and those on rafts from being swept into the suction of the cutter's propeller. One time, Rednour swam under the counter of the vessel, though he could have been struck by a propeller blade if the ship had moved, and rescued the men loaded on a raft that had headed toward this dangerous spot.

5

Ben Epstein was one of the survivors on lifeboat 6 who found himself in a predicament. He heard someone call out from the cutter that the men should climb up the rope ladder hanging from the deck, and some who had boarded the boat directly from the *Dorchester,* without first drifting in the water were able to do so. But Ben was not among them.

"I was completely frozen," he said. "I just couldn't do it. And those great coast guard guys, they were my buddies, my saviors. They came down, picked me up, and carried me on board. And they brought me down to the galley and put me on a hard table, and there was a doctor there, Dr. [Ralph] Nix. They cut off my oil-soaked clothes, and the doctor put five men on my body—one on each hand, one on my torso, and one on each leg and foot. And he said to them, 'Rub, rub, rub, and don't stop!'

"I was conscious, and he took a flask of liquor out of his pocket—and I'm no drinker—and he poured liquor down my throat. And he said, 'Do you feel it!'

"And I said, 'I don't feel a thing.'

"And they kept rubbing and rubbing and rubbing, and the first tingling sensation I had was in my body, then my arms, then, eventually, my fingers. The only thing that didn't respond were my feet. And, I gathered, they were worried about amputation. But they kept rubbing. And the doctor ordered, 'Don't you dare stop!'

"And when I got that tingling sensation in my feet, it was incredible. And when I told Dr. Nix I got the feeling, he grabbed me and hugged me. It was incredible."

Ben could finally relax, knowing that he would remain in one piece. Relax, but not sleep. How could he, not knowing who else was being pulled from the boats and rafts? Perhaps Vince. Perhaps the chaplains. Wouldn't God save *them*? In any case, Ben, who, like the other survivors, was in the care of three to five men, was forced to stay awake in order to stay alive; he was instructed to maintain some body movement until he was deemed out of danger. The survivors were placed in bunks after their rubdown, and the men in the lower ones were each asked to keep kicking the man above him to keep him awake.

James Eardley, who lay on another table, also had frozen feet. He wondered if he would ever walk again, though he was one of the few survivors who had managed to climb up the rope ladder unassisted when his raft edged alongside the cutter. But the muscles in his arms ached from a valiant effort he had made to save the life of another man. On a crammed raft, he, like Roy Summers on another craft, had dragged along a man in the water until he finally realized the man had died. Now that he was rescued, he hoped he would never have to see another corpse again.

After the treatment he was receiving—therapy, blankets, pea soup, a good stiff drink—James was so comfortable that he told one of the sailors that he would like to lie there "forever."

"No, you wouldn't," the sailor replied.

"Why not?"

The man, James recalled, "nodded his head behind the table where there were eight or ten bodies all naked, all piled up, all dead, all G.I.s." Perhaps among them was the man he had tried to save.

"You're right," he replied. "I wouldn't."

In some life-threatening cases, the doctor advised amputation of one leg or both. When one man was given such advice, he vigorously protested, arguing that he was a bootlegger and couldn't drive a car with a wooden leg. And when a man lying on a nearby table was offered the same option, he also refused. Why? Well, he drove the guy's other car.

6

Leander Thomas's raft had been floating around in circles for about two hours with only four men left on board when suddenly, in delirium, he saw a cutter heading his way. Minutes later, he was thrown a bowline. But this rescue effort seemed a cruel joke, for his hands were so frozen he couldn't grab hold of it, and the men on the ship didn't have time to help. They moved on to save individual swimmers who might still be alive—before a submarine perhaps lurking nearby could frame the cutter in its sight.

"Hang on," someone yelled from the cutter. "We'll be back."

"Oh boy," Leander said later. "I figured I lost my chance there. I really blew it. I said I've got to get my hands warm. So I started giving it the old under-the-arm treatment and hanging on with the other hand while trying to wiggle my fingers. I said, I'll be ready this time, if they come again."

But with all those hundreds of red lights out there, and with his body a virtual icicle, it didn't seem likely they'd come back in time, or that he would be ready if they did. Well, what the hell. He had lasted longer than most of the guys on his raft.

The *Escanaba,* however, did return, and his desperate exercises paid off. This time he was able to put the loop of the rope under his arms and hang on. And shortly a man in a rubber suit helped carry him and his raftmates aboard. He was stripped, given chicken soup, and then coffee to keep him awake.

Anyway, who wanted to sleep and maybe have nightmares about being crushed under a pile of guys while drowning at the same time? Or about those poor guys on top—whom God, for some unearthly reason, had suddenly whisked into the Hereafter, permitting Leander Thomas to live.

CHAPTER XX

THE RISK
OF BEING HUMAN

I

While the *Escanaba* chugged slowly from one red light to another, seeking what was left of a once-vibrant humanity, the *Comanche,* after having escorted the two freighters partway to Greenland, patrolled the periphery of the area of the *Dorchester*'s sinking, as ordered by Captain Greenspun. But Lieutenant Commander Curry, though bowing to the reality of command discipline, was still irate about having to ignore any cries for help from a survivor who might still be alive.

Every military man, he realized, was bound by an order from his superior, and Curry was no exception. If one of his own men deliberately disobeyed *his* order, he would probably court-martial him. In any event, the question of obedience seemed now, to his relief, academic, for about two hours had passed since the explosion, and it was unlikely that anyone still floating remained alive. Thus, it appeared there was no one left to save anyway—until Curry spotted from the bridge the shadowy outlines of a lifeboat and a raft emerging from the mist. And he saw people, live people.

Curry suddenly found himself caught in a quandary. It was one thing to vow obedience to the service, but those were human beings out there. And the *Escanaba* alone couldn't possibly check on whether all those hundreds of lights were attached to dead or live bodies and rescue the living. Was his obligation to the navy greater than that to the people the navy had sworn to protect? He finally answered this question, explaining later, "I couldn't let those people go. I was supposed to screen, but I couldn't let those people go."

He added, "I took it upon myself to do some picking up, and I did. I was violating orders. If the *Escanaba* had been sunk, there was no question about it, I could've been court-martialed. They would've said, 'Mr. Curry, what were you doing at that time?'

" 'Oh, I was out picking up some people.'

" 'Well, you were supposed to be screening.'

" 'Well, that's right, Captain, that's right.'

"That's not a good process to advocate," he concluded. "I think the service needs to obey orders. . . . [But] you had to make some tough decisions."

And one of them was to save lives.

Lieutenant Commander Curry would later write in an official report, "It was realized that this was dangerous to have both vessels picking up survivors at the same time [with neither screening the other]. However, conditions were such that it was felt that chance should be taken."

The *Comanche* crewmen were gratified by this decision. Like their *Escanaba* cousins, they viewed with horror the undulating "acres" of blinking red lights. Some of the bodies had already sunk or were sinking as their waterlogged life preservers became too heavy to float after a long period in the water. Lieutenant Commander Curry later reported to headquarters:

"Many of the crew were green and were so shocked at seeing numerous bodies of men who had perished, mixed with those still alive, that they were helpless to do anything but stare until snapped out of their daze by . . . acts of courage and leadership" performed by more senior men.

Still, Richard Swanson and the other sailors persevered as the ship crawled along, stopping every so often to check on the status of a body. They stood on the bow calling out for survivors and training beams of light on each shadowy human form, despite the danger of being targeted by the enemy. And they pulled some bodies toward the ship with boat hooks to observe whether they showed any sign of life. Was the man dead or merely unconscious?

As with the *Escanaba* crew, no one on the *Comanche* could be a hundred percent certain. *Comanche* crew members were not, like some men on the *Escanaba,* trained to jump into the water to check on the condition of survivors more thoroughly. Thus, a glance at a body and at a wristwatch served as indicators of life and of death. And these indicators led to the judgment that none of the men in the water were alive.

Under the tremendous pressures of battle, should *every* presumed corpse found by the *Escanaba* and the *Comanche* have been examined more thoroughly before a final judgment was reached, in order to erase all possible doubt? That is a question that only one's conscience could have answered. Whatever the answer, the tremendous courage and dedication of the crews in saving lives under extraordinarily difficult circumstances were surely a highlight of the Greenland campaign. As one survivor, Pfc Joseph G. Archer, would say of the *Comanche* crewmen who had saved him, reflecting the sentiments of men picked up by the *Escanaba* as well:

"I remember blurting out 'God bless you fellas' to the coast guardsmen who pulled me aboard. Those guys were absolutely wonderful— cheerful, supportive, sympathetic, and completely upbeat. They ushered us belowdecks where the ship's doctor was and then berthed us in their own bunks. . . . They were just priceless to guys who were still dazed and shocked."

"Those guys" reminded many survivors of the four chaplains. They, too, had been mother and father to them, perhaps even dying in an effort to save them. How many more would have gone down with the ship but for those men of God? And their possible fate was pondered apprehensively by almost every man when he had recovered sufficiently to converse with others.

The *Comanche* moved on. It could perhaps save those on lifeboats and rafts that might be adrift amid the flotsam strewn over the gaily blinking graveyard.

2

"I don't think this guy is alive," said a crewman as he manipulated a bowline that dangled down onto a partially destroyed raft.

Only four of the eight or ten men who had crowded aboard the raft had escaped the clutches of the sea, and only one of them had not yet been pulled into the *Comanche*—Roy Summers. Sprawled at one end of the raft, his body almost completely numb, each leg swollen almost to the width of his torso, he could barely move. It was not surprising that in the darkness he was taken for dead.

Traumatized, Roy heard the sailor, but his vocal cords had nearly frozen and he could not speak. His mind reeled as fear gripped him. The ship was going to leave him there and he would die alone. Was this really the end God ordained for him? Summoning an almost superhuman strength born of sheer desperation, he managed to catch the bowline in his bone-chilled hands and loop it under his arms. And with the help of two crewmen, he was hoisted onto the cutter.

Roy was carried down through a hatch to the kitchen, stripped, and wrapped in a blanket. His mind then went blank; he would not regain consciousness until the ship reached Greenland.

God's will, as Roy had expected, was done.

The *Comanche* crawled on with its dual aim of screening the *Escanaba* and searching for survivors. It encountered raft after raft with statue-stiff men crying for the cutter to pick them up and others who were too frozen or weak to speak, pleading for rescue with ghastly silence. As the *Comanche* pulled up to each craft, the few men who were nimble enough caught hold of a large cargo net hanging from the deck and climbed onto the ship. Most were pulled up by crewmen who, steeped waist-deep in the freezing water, clung to the net with one arm.

But many, like Roy Summers, had to be pulled up with a looped rope, sometimes after having toppled into the sea. And among the bravest of the rescuers were two fast friends, Richard Swanson, the sonar operator, and Charles David Jr., a mess attendant, first class.

"I had an alto sax on board and he had a harmonica," Richard recalled. "We used to play the blues. We called it the *Comanche* blues."

And the blues were very real for them when they weren't on the ship. For Charles was black, and in those days of segregation he wasn't welcome in white company. But the two men, who were among ten retrievers, enjoyed each other's company, especially when at great risk they jointly helped to save lives.

On one occasion, Charles, though untrained for the task, dove into the frigid water to assist another retriever whom a drowning man had pulled below the surface. In a dazzling display of strength and will, he broke the stranglehold of the drowning survivor and brought both him and his rescuer to safety. And once, so exhausted did Richard Swanson become from lifting men into the ship that he himself could climb only halfway up the cargo net. He heard Charles calling from above, "Come on, Swannie! Get on board!"

Charles and another crewman then pulled Richard up, mocking the rule forbidding his friend, as heroic and selfless as anyone on the ship, from joining him for a drink when they were ashore.

If Richard was happy that Charles had shown up those who would humiliate him because of his color, he was shattered a few days later when his dear shipmate caught pneumonia from his exposure to the freezing water and died. But he was proud that Charles and he had helped to enhance the reputation of the coast guard in the eyes of the navy, which had regarded it as a second-rate arm.

"It's funny," Richard mused years later, "the navy fellas called us the Hooligan Navy. That was our name. . . . But the coast guard has been involved in so many things that people have probably never heard of. . . . I've had these fellas come up to me, survivors of the *Dorchester*, . . . and they . . . thank me for saving their life. I say I did not save your life. It was our job. It was the ship that saved your life. . . . Anyway, it was nice of them to come up and say that."

3

Richard and Charles were amazed to find only one lifeboat limping over the waves—number 13. Sitting among the survivors was Walter Miller, who could not swim and wore no life jacket but had had the good fortune to be picked up—just before the waves would have overwhelmed him—by the same boat that had left him behind while he was climbing down a rope. Henry Geoguen was also in the boat, sensing, correctly, that he would never finish the game of cribbage he had been playing with his four buddies who had refused to leave the *Dorchester* with him. They had gone down with the ship.

Another passenger was the young boy who had helped his uncle board with his baggage and then remained on the ship. He had become a cabin boy and, unlike his uncle, had managed to survive. He had wanted to face the enemy in the war, and he did.

The lifeboat was so overcrowded that it floated only about eight inches above the waterline—partly due to the humanity of David Labadie. Still feeling guilty for having failed to persuade the man he assumed was a chaplain to save himself, he had challenged those who tried to keep swimmers off the boat, as that chaplain and the three others would have done—if they were still alive.

While others cried, "Don't let them on or we'll sink!" David shot back, "Pull 'em in, pull 'em in!" And of the half dozen men who tried to board the boat, he pulled in three, including the "biggest guy in the outfit."

"The more men you have in here," he argued ingeniously, "the more they'll block the splashing of the waves, so the boat won't fill up with water so quick."

The men on this boat, more than on most other craft, fought bitterly over whether to pick up swimmers, facing the horrendous dilemma that tested the conscience of those lucky enough to have originally crowded aboard. Should they risk their own death by letting their less fortunate fellows join them, or should they let these men turn into ice statues? No one was more passionate about saving these people than David Labadie.

"It was better to risk the lives of everybody on the boat and to go down together," he later explained, "than to choose who should die and who should not. We were all on the same side, weren't we? It would have been inhuman not to take the risk."

David would not bend, making a moral choice similar to that of Lieutenant Commander Curry of the *Comanche,* who disobeyed orders and jeopardized the safety of the *Escanaba,* as well as of his own cutter, to save survivors like—David. Unlike the skipper, of course, David could command no one, but his lifeboat had a rudder, and since he had spent much of his youth on boats, he took over the steering. He chose to steer toward the red lights bobbing in the water.

But this effort bound David more tightly to the boat than he might have wished. Since he had to keep a hand in the water in order to operate the rudder as he leaned over the stern, he was soon unable to remove it from the rudder stick. His hand was frozen to it.

And he couldn't get much help from the other men, who knew little about handling a boat—surely not from a barely conscious man whom David had picked up: Michael Warish. David had seen him as he had drifted in the waves half alive after having experienced an exalting moment just before the *Dorchester* rolled over to its death—a moment that continued to haunt him even as his mind spiraled through some distant ethereal world. . . .

CHAPTER XXI

THE BOOTLACES
OF SUBLIMITY

Inch by inch, Michael had limped from the high, deserted port side of the ship around the bow to the more swiftly sinking starboard side, clinging to the railing for support to ease the pain in his broken foot. He was still trying to find two or three other men to join him in abandoning ship.

As Michael hobbled along the starboard side, he suddenly saw a group of several people, among them the four chaplains. Two were emerging from a doorway that led to the hold and were carrying a wounded man, whom they placed on the deck against a bulkhead. Three of the chaplains had already given their life jackets to others, and Father Washington, one of them, was not wearing his glasses, apparently feeling he would no longer need them.

Rabbi Goode, the fourth chaplain, now removed *his* life jacket and knelt beside the injured man. Michael recognized the victim as one of the three men who had been severely wounded during the storm that had raged after the *Dorchester* left St. John's.

Mesmerized by the scene, Michael watched from about five yards away as the rabbi then unlaced his boots and, after putting the man's unaffected arm through an armhole in the jacket, tied the other side of the jacket around the wounded shoulder with the bootlaces. When the ship went down, perhaps this improvised life preserver would permit the soldier to float in the water. Alex then joined his three companions, who were standing against a bulkhead facing eight or nine people, some wearing life jackets, some not.

All then started praying together in what sounded like a babble of English, Hebrew, and Latin. In the darkness, Michael did not note whether they linked arms, but other witnesses say they did. As water splashed ever more heavily on the tilting deck, he saw that "the chaplains were not going overboard. They were not gonna abandon ship."

Though unreligious, he began praying to himself while weeping. Rabbi Goode's effort to save the wounded man with bootlaces seemed more than an attempt to rescue one last person. Though Michael didn't realize it, he was witnessing an act right out of the Talmud, which proclaims, "Whoever saves one life is as if he saves the entire world."

The act symbolized the essence of these chaplains of different faiths, reflecting their aim of saving humanity by ridding it of its inhumanity.

Perhaps the last man to see the chaplains alive was James Eardley, who later stated, "I was on a life raft and . . . when [the ship] rolled over, . . . that's when I saw the four chaplains, [who] had climbed up on the keel, and they were standing arm in arm. . . . And then . . . she nosed down [and] they slid off . . . into the water."

Minutes earlier, Michael, feeling that he couldn't drag anyone from prayer to join him in abandoning ship, had decided to jump into the sea alone. But since the bow was too high, he limped back around the bow, struggling toward the stern, from where he could virtually walk into the water. When he reached the stern, he climbed over the railing and dropped about two feet into the sea, riding a wave that pulled him away from the ship.

Michael now lost hope of surviving and even the desire to survive. All around him, hundreds of red lights bobbed and blinked like fireflies in the night. Who would come for him in the twenty minutes he had to live? And the more benumbed he became in the icy water, the easier it seemed to die. The chaplains weren't afraid to die, so why should he be? What was so bad about going to heaven? He would simply fall asleep when his twenty minutes were up—if he didn't choke to death first from the oil and salt that stuffed his nose and burned his throat.

As Michael drifted toward oblivion, he vaguely heard a voice shouting, "Pull him up!"

"No, no, no!" Michael groaned.

He was already halfway to heaven—too close now to turn back. He was becoming more and more comfortable. "Let me go to sleep and die," he thought.

But David Labadie, who had finally managed to pull his frozen hand loose from the rudder, would have none of it. Not while he was steering the lifeboat!

"They used a boat hook on me and pulled me up," Michael reminisced. "I then started losing my mind."

Had he finally reached heaven? He wasn't sure. As the boat moved on, his eyes suddenly captured a blurred image that seemed to spark him to life, at least momentarily. A few seats away sat the young boy whom he had permitted to stow away on the *Dorchester* before it sailed. The drummer boy was alive! Or were they reunited in heaven? Was life still going on with all the dead around?

Suddenly, Michael heard a man on the cutter roar through a loudspeaker: "We can't stop. We're going to make another pass. Get ready to grab the cargo net and climb aboard."

As the cutter nudged up to the lifeboat, Michael raised his hands, trying to indicate that they were frozen. "I just couldn't take hold of the net," he remembered.

But someone behind him in the boat pushed him toward the ship, and he desperately tried to grasp the net so he wouldn't fall between the two craft. At that moment, Michael lost consciousness. Someone caught him, however, and two crewmen climbed down the net and carried him into the cutter. Like the survivors rescued by the *Escanaba,* he was stripped of his clothing, placed on a table, and given the same life-saving treatment.

Lieutenant Commander Curry wrote in his report: "Not one man was picked up from the water itself, indicating . . . that one could not long survive in it. Furthermore, after the first boatload was saved there was not a man who was capable of climbing the cargo net himself, and all had to be hoisted aboard by bowlines and lifted aboard by our men."

Curry didn't know it, but he didn't have to worry that he might be court-martialed for disobeying Captain Greenspun's order to screen the *Escanaba* and not stop to pick up survivors. For the captain, apparently feeling that his judgment might be questioned if he punished a man for saving lives, straight-facedly reported to headquarters on February 6 that he had "directed" the *Comanche* "to join the *Escanaba* in the rescue work, one of them screening." He failed to mention that the *Escanaba,* being unequipped with radar, could not be used for screening and that the *Comanche* would therefore perform *both* tasks—as desired by Curry.

2

While the *Escanaba* and the *Comanche* crept through the swirl of dancing red lights searching for survivors and warily scanning for a periscope, *U-223* lay like a dead whale more than 500 feet below the surface, with the crew quietly expecting to die.

According to *U-223* crew members, soon after the *Dorchester* sank, their submarine trembled from the impact of depth charges exploding nearby, just as they had feared. But cutter crewmen would deny they had fired any charges, saying they would not have risked killing the men floating in the water. And the logs of the three cutters do not mention that such bombs were fired after the sinking.

It is unclear how these conflicting claims can be reconciled, but one expert opinion is that the Germans may have mistaken the thunderous underwater sounds emanating from the sinking of the *Dorchester* for those of depth-charge explosions.

Regardless, when Lieutenant Commander Wächter reported the sinking to U-boat Control, his details were vague. *U-223* had hit its target, he said, and he estimated its tonnage, though he couldn't identify its class. Wächter glowed with delight. He had registered a hit on *U-223*'s very first mission. And he had done this without the support of any other submarine.

His joy and that of his men, however, were diluted by the fear that other ships in the convoy would retaliate with their technically superior equipment. They felt they would be fortunate indeed to reach home alive to enjoy the acclaim. Kurt Röser related, "At first we had a feeling of relief or luck because we hit our target. But at the same time we understood that now we were the ones who were hunted, and that we had to face the same destiny as those on the ship had faced. It was a feeling of deep fear and uncertainty among us, especially when we listened to the sound of the sonar and when we heard the depth charges being dropped and listened to the engines of the ships that dropped them. . . . Each time these bombs exploded in the water there was a feeling of strong tension. It was very hard for us."

Finally, after the Germans had endured the tension for about eight hours, their sonar signaled that the rescue ships were leaving the scene of the sinking. The crew surfaced and sailed off to meet its wolf pack several hours away.

One of the ships leaving the disaster area was the *Escanaba,* which had continued to search for living persons until 9:20 A.M. It had picked up a total of 132, one of whom died soon after being taken aboard, and had also plucked thirteen bodies from boats or rafts. The *Comanche* gave up its search at about the same time after pulling aboard ninety-four persons, one of whom also died later. Among the missing were the four chaplains and Captain Danielsen.

The two cutters, with survivors stretched out in all available space amid organized chaos, then left for Narsarssuak, Greenland, arriving at three A.M. the following morning, February 4. Near dawn, the survivors were tucked away in hospital beds—though Michael Warish, against doctor's orders, was soon on his way to the boiler room of his unit's barracks to ponder the meaning of heaven and hell, as filtered through the spirit of the four chaplains.

EPILOGUE

I

The *Tampa,* after escorting the two freighters to Greenland, returned to the scene of the sinking later that morning and joined several other ships continuing to search the sea for men who might possibly still be alive, this time with the help of low-flying aircraft. But, as expected, none were found.

Many bodies had sunk when their life jackets became waterlogged, the weight dragging the wearer down. When a craft with dead aboard was sighted, marksmen reportedly sank it with bursts of fire in an informal sea burial. A cable from the *Tampa* and another ship to their headquarters reported on the morning of February 6 that they were abandoning their search:

"Regret to report no additional *Dorchester* survivors found. Saw 2 swamped boats, about 8 rafts, at least 100 bodies. Limited daylight hours and urgency of search for survivors precluded taking time to recover bodies."

Four months later, on the morning of June 3, 1943, there would be still more bodies to recover—this time those of the *Escanaba* crew, which, at great risk, had saved the lives of many *Dorchester* survivors. The *Escanaba* was escorting a convoy from Greenland to St. John's when it blew up and sank immediately, killing all but two of the 103 people aboard, including the men who had devised the new method of rescue. What caused the explosion? No one knows; the Germans later claimed that the nearest U-boat was 150 miles away and that they had laid no mines in the area. In any event, the disaster sent the *Dorchester* survivors into new mourning.

They were already trying to face the reality of the little red lights that had merrily bobbed in the waves until they sank with the corpses into the cruel but heroic history of the *Dorchester;* Christmas was finally over. But in a sense, the lights will glow eternally over their graves, apparently including those of the four unknown recipients of the life jackets that might have permitted the chaplains to live.

Actually, they do live, and always shall—in the hearts of all people who yearn for a world basking in the light of brotherhood and peace, the brightest light of all.

2

On February 13, 1943, Isadore Fox and her niece were at home recording funny stories that were to be sent to George to cheer him up. But these stories would never reach him. Before the record was completed, there was a knock on the door, and Isadore, answering it, was handed a telegram "that bore that dreadful message, 'We regret to inform you . . .'"

In shock, she collapsed on her bed. She had just received a letter from him, apparently delayed, saying, "I am feeling fine in case you are wondering. I know you were anxious to hear from me. I haven't a trace of a cold any longer and am seldom bothered with anything else. . . . Many men come for counsel. This is the reason I am here and I am glad."

Isadore was sure he was trying to tell her that he had arrived at his destination safely. She wrote to a War Department official that she "felt deep within my heart as though a voice was saying, 'On land, on land, on land,' and I have not ceased to hear those same words, also the words 'safe and well,' time and again. . . . I cannot doubt but [God] has spoken to me. . . . I beg you in the name of my husband . . . and in the name of our Eternal God and Heavenly Father to see to it that the War

Department make a further search for my husband to ascertain if he may not possibly be a German prisoner, or on some island in confinement where he cannot write or get a word to me."

Finally, Isadore had to accept the reality that George was not hiding behind someone this time, waiting to fling himself into her arms. Her Methodist minister came over and tried to comfort her, telling her that she should be very proud of George, whom the newspapers were calling a great hero.

"I do not want a hero," Isadore sobbed. "I want my husband. I always knew he was a hero, the way he worked in those small churches and never complained, even when the pay was so small he could not get proper food for his children."

Isadore later wrote that she "did not want to live without George." When friends and relatives reminded her that her children needed her, she replied, "Although I love my children dearly, with George gone there seems to be a gap of a million miles between the children and me."

She had never realized so clearly that "he was nearly my whole life. I felt only a shadow without him."

A letter from her son, Wyatt, however, offered her some solace. He wrote, "I've just got to be the kind of a man that my father was."

Wyatt surely realized how happy his father would have been to hear these words—words George was never able to utter as a boy in his earlier wretched life. As for George's daughter, Mary, she would treasure the last words he wrote her: "I want you to know how proud I am of you that your marks in school are so high, but always remember that kindness and charity and courtesy are much more important."

Isadore would now do what she knew her husband would want her to do. She took special courses at the Boston University School of Theology and in 1955 became an ordained minister. She was appointed to several parishes in New Hampshire and Vermont and served as chaplain of the American Legion Auxiliary in Vermont.

"I have never felt," she said, "that I am carrying on George's work. His work never left off, and his spirit continues in the lives of the thousands he has inspired. But I do feel that I am doing good, and that he is pleased and proud."

3

Theresa Goode grew desperate when her brother-in-law reported to her that he had sought information about Alex from the War Department, senators, and congressmen, but without success. And she wasn't soothed by their replies that if a catastrophe had occurred, many passengers may have survived.

"I waited and waited," Theresa recounted, "and one Saturday morning I was getting Rosalie ready to take her downtown to buy her leggings and a winter coat. I tried so hard not to cry, but the telephone rang and it was my sister. And she said, 'I just received a telegram.'

"She didn't have to tell me any more. I said, 'For God's sake, open it!' And I knew immediately what it was—that he was missing in action."

Though shattered by the news, Theresa reacted like a robot, stripped for the moment of any feeling. She drove Rosalie downtown and bought her winter clothes as she had intended to do.

"I think it was days before I could cry," she recalled. "I just refused to believe it. I was in a state of shock. And for a long, long time I would never discuss it with anyone. I just kept looking in the faces of people when I was on the bus or a streetcar and thought that they looked just like Alex. I kept hoping against hope that perhaps he was saved and he was lost and would be coming back."

But then, a call from the War Department. The ship had gone down and Alex wasn't one of the survivors. Theresa still refused to believe it. She needed him. The world needed him. He must be alive somewhere. Maybe that was the message he had sent her that night minutes after the ship went down.

Even after Theresa realized that Alex would not return, he never really left her. When she wasn't busy bringing up Rosalie, she spent much of her time over the next years building a home archive of letters and other documents telling the story of Alex's life. Fourteen years after his death, she married another brilliant rabbi, Harry Kaplan, but once more, tragedy. He died eleven years later.

Rosalie, now grown up, married a science teacher, Paul Fried, and had two children, Alex and Sarah. She dedicated herself to spreading the interfaith message that her father and the other three chaplains had delivered to the world. She spoke in churches and synagogues and, together with David Fox, a nephew of Chaplain Fox, founded in 1997 the Immortal Chaplains Foundation in St. Paul, Minnesota, to institutionalize the message. Two years later, in February 1999, Rosalie died in a car accident.

Theresa, who had seen her daughter as the living spirit of Alex, was crushed by this new tragedy and fell gravely ill. But exhibiting extraordinary strength and courage, she has managed to survive, perceiving images of her husband in her grandchildren and sometimes unlocking her archive to reread Alex's letters and relive the joyous past.

4

On February 11, 1943, Betty Poling was anxiously waiting at home in Schenectady for word from her husband that he had arrived safely in Greenland, where he had told her he would be going. Valentine's Day was only three days away, and what a gift it would be to hear that news.

And she expected to hear it when a messenger handed her a telegram. But it was not the message she expected. It was from the adjutant general's office in Washington. Clark, it said, was missing in action in the North African area.

Betty was devastated. But she was sure there was a mistake. Clark had told her he was heading for Greenland, not North Africa. Maybe the telegram was intended for someone else.

She immediately telephoned Dr. Poling. He agreed that the notice must be a mistake. "Clark's ship could not have reached North African waters," he said. "There had not been time." Anyway, he knew that Clark had been heading to Greenland.

Shortly they would learn that the message was indeed erroneous. He was missing not in North African waters but in the North Atlantic. Finally, on April 10, the family was told that Clark was officially considered "lost in action."

Soon afterward, Betty would receive her valentine gift, if a bit delayed. She gave birth to a little girl, Susan, or Thumper, as Clark had nicknamed his unborn child before he had gone off to turn the world into a place where all children could romp with Bambis and bunnies and never have to recoil from the blast of a bomb, especially one triggered by racial hatred.

Clark Poling Jr., whose only memory of his father was as the captain of a carpet sweeper on which he was the passenger, would embrace the interfaith principles that Clark Sr. had followed even unto death. The son, however, chose not to follow his father into the ministry but became a professor at Emory University in Atlanta, where he would serve as chairman of the Art History Department. He married Eve Corey, a noted psychologist who happened to be Jewish.

5

One day in early February, Marge Kolosek, a sister-in-law of Father Washington's, heard a terrible shriek emanating from the house next door. It was her grandmother Mary. Marge rushed over to the house, where she found Mary, a short, stout woman, holding the telephone receiver and screaming, "John's gone! Oh, my God, John's gone!"

Marge grabbed the receiver with one hand and held on to Mary with the other to keep her from tipping over in her chair as she continued to wail uncontrollably. The War Department official on the other end of the line repeated his message to Marge: Chaplain Washington was missing.

Marge put down the receiver and assured her grandmother, "Don't worry, they'll find him. You've got to think positively."

But Marge was not sure she could follow her own advice—especially since she had had a frightening dream about John.

"I dreamt I saw him and grabbed him by the arm," she recalled. In the dream, she said, "Oh, you're home!"

But John replied, "Don't look for me, Marge. I'm not coming home."

The scene seemed so real. And it turned out to be.

Nor would Mary's tortured cries stop for long. A few months later, the telephone would ring again. And another voice would repeat in her ear a grotesquely familiar message. Her second son, Francis, an Army Air Forces bombardier, had been killed in the Pacific. How much pain could a mother bear? Even more. Her third son, Leo, was missing in

France, though he would turn up wounded in a British hospital. But shortly after he returned home, he, too, would die from his wounds.

Mary now had only memories of three of her beloved sons. And surely one of her most cherished ones was of that Sunday afternoon she had spent with John watching a movie and dining in a fine restaurant. A wonderful sunny afternoon—that would lead to a lifetime of agonized mourning. Mourning so intense that after she learned of John's death she sealed herself off from the world and refused to leave home for any reason. She died there several years later.

6

Since the end of World War II, numerous honors have been posthumously conferred upon the four chaplains. In 1961, a unique, specially designed Congressional Medal of Valor, equivalent to the Congressional Medal of Honor, was awarded to each of them. (Many military officials argued that they should have received the Medal of Honor, but their superiors claimed that it could be awarded only for extraordinary courage in combat, somehow feeling that a submarine attack on a ship was not combat!) Earlier, in 1944, the chaplains had been awarded the Purple Heart and the Distinguished Service Cross; the medals were given to Theresa Goode, Isadore Fox, Betty Poling, and Anna Schwoebel, John Washington's sister. Mary Washington, John's mother, sent her regrets to the War Department, explaining that she "could not attend as I have not left my home for any affairs since hearing of my son's death."

Although no postage stamp memorializing an individual (except for a U.S. president) can normally be issued until ten years after the person's death, a congressional waiver on this limitation permitted the issue in 1948 of a three-cent stamp with the heading "These Immortal Chaplains" and an illustration of the four men above a sinking ship. And in 1998, Senators Orrin Hatch and Red Grams pushed through the Senate a unanimous resolution, concurred in the House, to designate February 3 as Four Chaplains Day. Legislatures in some states have passed similar resolutions.

Other honors, too, have been heaped on the four heroes, with monuments to them springing up in many cities and towns. The Pentagon and the Washington National Cathedral each has a stained-glass window featuring the chaplains. A wax tableau depicting their last minutes aboard the *Dorchester* has been featured in the National Historical Wax Museum in the capital. A fountain dedicated to them spouts water in the National Memorial Cemetery outside the city. A Four Chaplains Memorial Viaduct, a major flood-control project, is the pride of Massillon, Ohio.

A public school has been named for Alex Goode in York, Pennsylvania, where he presided as a rabbi. In the lobby of the school a ceramic tile mural bears the likeness of all four chaplains, with an identical inscription from Malachi 2:10 under each, in Hebrew (Goode), in Latin (Washington), and in English (Fox and Poling):

> *Have we not all one Father?*
> *Hath not one God created us?*
> *Why do we deal treacherously every man against his brother,*
> *by profaning the covenant of our fathers?*

A stained-glass window in St. Stephen's Church in Kearny, New Jersey, where John Washington served as a priest, portrays him flanked by saints. A permanent scholarship fund honoring Clark Poling's memory has been established at Yale University, while a children's school in Clark's honor has been added to a newly rebuilt Dutch Reformed Church in Schenectady; the previous historic church burned down in 1948. And an oil painting of George Fox hangs in the Vermont State House.

Further spreading the four chaplains' message of brotherhood and peace are the many churches, synagogues, veterans' organizations, and civic groups that hold special memorial ceremonies on the anniversary of the *Dorchester*'s sinking.

Such activities are energetically supported by the Immortal Chaplains Foundation established in 1997 by Rosalie Goode Fried and David Fox, with a board honorarily headed by Theresa Goode Kaplan and former Vice President Walter Mondale. Located on the campus of Hamline University, in St. Paul, Minnesota, which sponsors many of its activities, this institution is a true keeper of the flame, with a motto that asks, "If we can die together, why can't we live together?"

The foundation spreads the story of the four chaplains and their ecumenical message through speakers, school curricula, radio and television documentaries, and other media outlets. It initiated the movement to have Congress and individual states designate February 3 as Four Chaplains Day. And David Fox has interviewed for its archives more than thirty survivors, relatives and friends of the chaplains, and *U-223* crew members. The institution's principal purpose is "to tell their uplifting story and the stories of people who have also risked everything to save [or seek reconciliation with] others of another faith or ethnicity and to remind us of the capacity for compassion we all have in us."

This campaign is highlighted by the anniversary ceremonies, at which an Immortal Chaplains Prize for Humanity is given to persons who, in the spirit of the chaplains, have taken this risk. Archbishop Desmond Tutu of South Africa movingly mused on receiving the honor:

"It is the wonder of human beings. They [the chaplains] did what they did almost instinctively. It makes us proud to be a human being. You hope you would respond in a similar way. Human beings are made for goodness, for love. That's the way God made us."

Others who have won the award, some posthumously, include the German pastor Martin Niemoeller, who was sent to a concentration camp for protesting Nazi atrocities against the Jews; Hugh C. Thompson Jr., the U.S. helicopter pilot who intervened to stop the My Lai massacre during the Vietnam War; Amy Biehl, who was killed in South Africa in the struggle against apartheid; Chiune Sugihara, the Japanese consul in Lithuania, who saved the lives of many Jews in World War II; Omri Abdel-Halim Al-Jada, a Palestinian youth who drowned in Lake Tiberias while saving the lives of two Israeli children; and Charles W. David Jr., the black *Comanche* mess attendant who died from pneumonia after rescuing *Dorchester* survivors in the icy water. (Charles's shipmate Richard Swanson is holding the award until some member of the honoree's family can be located.)

One of the foundation's most memorable moves was to bring over four guests from Germany: Kurt Röser; Gerhard Buske, first officer of the *U-223* submarine crew; and their wives. They attended the 2000 anniversary ceremony held in Washington to reflect the foundation's view that former foes must be included in a world of peace and brotherhood. About a year after the *Dorchester* went down, *U-223* suffered a similar fate when British destroyers attacked it, killing most of the crew. Röser was captured and sent to a prisoner-of-war camp in Mississippi, where he picked cotton and helped to sandbag the levee against flooding. Buske was sent to an officers' prisoner camp in Canada.

In Washington, the Germans toured the United States Holocaust Memorial Museum, where they appeared visibly shocked to see the horrors of the boxcars and gas chambers; one of the wives almost fainted. The next stop was Theresa Goode Kaplan's apartment in Chevy Chase, Maryland, which they visited only after her grandson, Alex, persuaded the widow to overcome her revulsion at the thought of welcoming members of a submarine crew responsible for her husband's death.

Despite her torment, Theresa shook the Germans' hands and silently accepted their expressions of respect for her husband and of sorrow for her suffering. Buske helped to ease the tension by removing a harmonica from his pocket and playing a slow, moving rendition of "Amazing Grace." Everyone applauded, then sank into a silence electric with mixed emotions.

Three years later, Buske took out his harmonica again and played the same song at the foundation's sixtieth-anniversary remembrance ceremony, where he urged the audience to pursue the dream of the four chaplains. Like them, he said, "we ought to love when others hate; . . . we can bring faith where doubt threatens; we can awaken hope where despair exists; we can light up a light where darkness reigns; we can bring joy where sorrow dominates."

The Immortal Chaplains Foundation is complementary to another institution, the Chapel of the Four Chaplains, which was founded in 1951 in Philadelphia by Dr. Daniel Poling in honor of his son and the three other chaplains. At the dedication ceremony, President Truman delivered an address lauding the sacrifice of the four chaplains as reflecting the fact that "the unity of our country is a unity under God."

Under Dr. Poling, the chapel thrived as visitors of all faiths stopped to pray there. But after his death in 1968, it fell into gradual decline and in 1997 some survivors and relatives of the four chaplains and their supporters, led by David Fox and Rosalie Goode Fried, formed the Immortal Chaplains Foundation.

The future of this dedicated institute, however, depends on contributions from people who believe in the message. Such contributions can be sent to The Immortal Chaplains Foundation, Hamline University, Box 48, 1536 Hewitt Avenue, St. Paul, Minnesota 55104. The Web site is www.immortalchaplains.org.

7

In Greenland, most of the survivors aboard the coast guard cutters *Escanaba* and *Comanche* were, like Michael Warish, taken to the army hospital, where some remained for weeks "thawing out" from their ordeal before being assigned to their tasks in Greenland. Others too disabled to serve, at least in this environment, were sent home.

Actually, the ordeal of most survivors did not soon end. They were often in pain and many could not easily walk, for their feet did not fully recover from their near-frozen condition. Many also had recurring nightmares and frayed nerves. Yet most tried and succeeded to live normal lives.

Ben Epstein married Miriam Burg, whom he had met after returning home, and resumed his accounting career, then went into the fabric and construction businesses in the New York area. But though life, despite his war-related injuries, returned to normal, not a day has gone by, he says, when he hasn't thought of his friend, Vince Frucelli, and the four chaplains. Ben retired in 1984, and the couple moved to Florida, where the survivor finally found relief from the cold winter that had constantly tormented and even crippled him.

But Ben has remained tormented in another way. When he learned of the evidence I unearthed indicating that many of the hundreds of his comrades had needlessly been left to die in the water, he wrote to me: "I am overwhelmed with rage by the revelation that the coast guard cutters, *Escanaba* and *Comanche,* were directed by the coast guard officer in command to seek out the submarine that torpedoed the *Dorchester* before saving my fellow soldiers, thus assuring the death of most of them. The decision was morally reprehensible."

Ben's rage reflects the passion consuming him even today when he lectures or gives interviews on the four chaplains and the *Dorchester*'s sinking. Speaking of the chaplains, he told one audience:

"I ask myself, could I do it? Take off my life preserver and give it to someone else? Absolutely not. I don't think I could do it. I didn't do it. And I ask you in the audience, how many of you could do it? And I don't want an answer. That's why I say their bravery, their heroism is beyond belief. That is one of the reasons why we must tell the world what these people did."

8

Roy Summers, whose swollen legs had to remain in slings for weeks, was sent home to Murphysboro, Illinois, where he was cared for by his wife, since, with his legs "like rubber," he says, he "couldn't even walk to the toilet." His right arm and back also gave him continuous pain. When he had at least partially recovered, he began work for a power company and then, after six years, as a traveling salesman. Though he found it difficult to climb stairs, which he often had to do, he stayed on the job for forty years.

David Labadie has also had a perpetual problem with his feet, having been in the freezing water without shoes. After his discharge from the service, he worked as an automobile mechanic, then as a maintenance mechanic for the Weymouth Housing Authority in his hometown of South Weymouth, Massachusetts, retiring in 1978.

The nightmares David experienced occurred not only in his sleep. Though he had helped to save so many men, the curse of the *Dorchester* seemed to pursue him. He has been seriously hurt in three car accidents in the last twenty years, though he was blameless. His wife died in 2001, and he was afflicted with lung cancer the following year.

9

Walter Boeckholt spent seven weeks in the Greenland hospital learning to walk again, for his feet were so numb that he never knew when they were on the floor. He still found it hard to believe that he had survived his nine-hour ride from wave to towering wave in a doughnut with a dead body frozen to it and tipping it to one side. And he realized how lucky he was as he gazed out the window from his hospital bed at dozens of bodies being buried in a field of crusty snow.

When released from the hospital, Walter served in Greenland for two more years, though his nervous system, as well as his body, was never to recover completely. After the war, he worked for a furniture company in Algona, Iowa, his hometown, retiring after thirty-seven years of intermittent pain to find relief watching his two grandchildren at play.

10

Michael Warish returned home with 90 percent disability pay but decided to remain in the army, though he suffered almost constant pain in his arms, legs, and shoulders. His mind was also affected; he was sometimes unable to separate fantasy from reality, thinking, as he did in the water, that he was no longer alive. He nevertheless rose to the rank of sergeant major as an adviser to the national guard, retiring from the army in 1963. At last he could relax with his wife and six children.

But in 2002, misfortune struck again when he was injured in a car crash, and he could move around only with a walker. His hands, which were once almost frozen, now had no feeling at all, and he could not even hold a fork.

Michael was comforted, however, by the love and attention of his family, and also by the spiritual strength that stemmed from his experience with the four chaplains. He thought of them often, especially of that moment when he had seen them join in common prayer as the *Dorchester* was going down. They showed him the true meaning of what God stands for, in whatever form He is seen. Maybe he would see them again in heaven—where at times he still thought he was.

In September 2003, fantasy became reality. Presumably, Michael Warish has joined his heroes.

NOTES

1

First Sergeant Michael Warish's experience after arriving in Greenland is based on several interviews with him, as is all material involving him in this book.

2

Description of the *Dorchester* was found in *Troopships of World War II* by Roland W. Charles, p. 180; *The Daily Press,* Newport News, Va., June 22, 1986; "The Queen of Sea Routes: Merchants and Miners Transportation Co." by Edward A. Mueller, http://www.catskill.net/purple/queen.htm. Chester J. Szymczak's remark about the *Dorchester*'s mishaps is from his book *The Men, the Ship,* p. 11.

The story of the *Chatham* appears in Mueller, and was described in interviews with Roy Summers, who survived both the *Chatham* and the *Dorchester* sinkings.

James McAtamney's quotation regarding first impressions of the *Dorchester* is from a videotaped interview conducted for the Immortal Chaplains Foundation (ICF) by David Fox, its head. The story about a soldier's false teeth was told to the author by several survivors.

3

Benjamin Epstein's initial experience on boarding the ship is based on a personal interview.

Onboard and survivor figures are contained in a U.S. Army Department memorandum report to the chief of the casualty branch, April 14, 1943. Other reports indicate varied numbers, with the onboard figure ranging from 900 to 904.

Survivor David J. Labadie related in a personal interview how the chaplains welcomed the passengers aboard.

CHAPTER II: A RARE KIND OF LOVE

1–2

Especially useful was the rich material about the post–Pearl Harbor days of Chaplain Fox and his family that appears in *The Immortal Chaplain* by Isadore H. Fox, the minister's widow. (This volume is the source of much of the material, including quotes, involving her.) Francis Thornton's *Sea of Glory* was also helpful.

The author interviewed David Fox, Edna Fox, Leslie Fox, Siglinda Fox, and Grace Fox Wiest. The ICF's videotaped interviews used include those of Florence Fox, Oliver Fox, Siglinda Fox, and Grace Fox Wiest. Other sources were an article in the *American Legion* magazine, "A Chaplain Is Called Home," by Wyatt Fox, February 1991 (for the quote about World War I), and, from the *Philadelphia Inquirer,* "Horror and Heroes as *Dorchester* Sank," February 2, 1993.

3

The chaplains' experience at Harvard (including quotes) is from *The Anguish and the Ecstasy* by Isaac Klein, pp. 22–27, and a personal interview with Theresa Goode Kaplan.

4

The Goodes' reaction to Pearl Harbor was described in personal and videotaped ICF interviews with Theresa Goode Kaplan. The story of Goode's trek in his childhood to the grave of the Unknown Soldier came from her as well. Personal interviews with Bryna Jaman, Goode's niece, and Edward Pinsky, his nephew, cast light on the chaplain's relationship with his mother.

5

Theresa Goode Kaplan described in personal interviews her husband's life at military posts, including his housing problem, his popularity with the troops, and his lobbying effort to be sent overseas.

6

The bonding of the four chaplains at Camp Miles Standish is based on Thornton, p. 170, Wyatt Fox's account in the *American Legion* magazine, February 1991, and personal interviews with Theresa Goode Kaplan.

7

Clark Poling's view toward peace and brotherhood is dealt with by his father, Daniel A. Poling, in his books, mainly in *Your Daddy Did Not Die* (including quotes not otherwise attributed), but also in *Faith Is Power for You,* and *Mine Eyes Have Seen.* The son's antiwar attitude in the late 1930s was expressed in the July 1939 issue of the magazine *De Omroeper.*

Dr. Poling's role in World War I is described in his book *Mine Eyes Have Seen,* pp. 89–103 (including letter from his son). Other scenes in this chapter involving Dr. Poling are from this book as well as from the other two books mentioned above, which contain similar or identical material.

In ICF interviews, Daniel Poling Jr. and his wife, Evangeline, contributed valuable insights into Clark Poling's decision to seek the chaplaincy on the battlefield and descriptions of the excitement and family anxiety generated by the decision. Thornton adds some details.

Robin Chaffee, Peter Ten Eyck, Irma Long, and Katherine Scranton Rozendaal, who knew Clark Poling well, reminisced in personal interviews about the attitude of his church toward him. Laura Linder, an official of the church, provided access to whole scrapbooks of newspaper articles and letters from Poling's friends that threw further light on the chaplain's activities and character.

8

The section on John Washington and his enlistment is based on material in Thornton and on personal interviews conducted with Father Washington's relatives, friends, and associates: niece Joanne Schwoebel Brunetti, sister-in-law Marge Kolosek, Edward Chicowski, Sister Theresa Jordan Corcoran, Father Louis Saporito, Father Paul Shalvoy, and Monsignor Edwin Sullivan. Sheila Meyer, another niece, provided some of the chaplain's speeches and other material used in this chapter. Material about Washington in the archives of St. Stephen's Church in Kearny, New Jersey, also proved extremely valuable.

CHAPTER III: COLD CHILLS AND A CAKE OF ICE

I

Colonel Frederick Gillespie described in a personal interview how he chose two of the four chaplains for overseas duty.

2

This section about George Fox's visit home is based on material from Isadore Fox's book, *The Immortal Chaplain*.

3

Theresa Goode Kaplan reminisced in a personal interview and in an ICF video-taped interview about her husband's determination to go overseas, and about the days she spent with him before he departed. She made available to the author the chaplain's farewell note to her.

4

Daniel Poling's *Your Daddy Did Not Die*, pp. 127–28, describes Clark Poling's last days before going overseas, drawing on a conversation Dr. Poling had with Betty Poling after his son's departure.

5

The account of Chaplain Washington's last days at home is based on material in Thornton, pp. 225–26, and personal interviews with Marge Kolosek and Monsignor Edwin Sullivan.

CHAPTER IV: AN ODD FOURSOME

I

All material in this chapter dealing with Michael Warish, including quotes, is based on personal interviews with him. The quote by James McAtamney regarding relations between the different faiths comes from a videotaped interview he gave to ICF.

CHAPTER V: POOR OLD GEORGE

1

The material about George's childhood is drawn from Thornton and an anonymous source. Wyatt Fox's article in the *American Legion* magazine, February 1991, describes his father's role in World War I. The *Illinois Wesleyan University Magazine,* Spring 1993, also deals with this role.

2

The story of George Fox's adoption comes from interviews with David Fox, Siglinda Fox, and Grace Fox Wiest, and from ICF videotaped interviews with the latter two and with Florence Fox and Oliver Fox.

3

The meeting and marriage of George and Isadore are recounted in Isadore's book. Also helpful was Thornton and an article in the *American Weekly,* "Widow in the Pulpit," by Booton Herndon, January 13, 1948.

CHAPTER VI: BLESSING THE BORED

1

Material involving Michael Warish in this chapter, including quotes, is based on personal interviews with him. Quotes by James McAtamney come from his videotaped ICF interview.

2

The chaplains' activities aboard the *Dorchester* were described in personal interviews with survivors. McAtamney's quotes are from the videotaped ICF interview. Charles Macli's quote is also from a videotaped ICF interview. Material involving William Kramer, including his quote, is from a personal interview. Edward Dionne recalled the story of Washington and the card players in a videotaped ICF interview. Daniel O'Keeffe described his meeting with Washington and Goode in a personal interview.

CHAPTER VII: THE PROPHET AND THE PRIZE

1–2

Alexander Goode's background and thinking were reflected in the hundreds of personal documents that were made available by his widow, Theresa—letters, memorandums, memoirs, appraisals of himself, scribbled thoughts, articles he wrote, and pages from an unpublished book, "Cavalcade of Democracy," he authored. Theresa herself contributed additional detail in personal and videotaped ICF interviews. The rabbi's grandson, Alexander; his granddaughter, Sarah; his niece, Bryna Jaman; and his nephew, Edward Pinsky, added stories they had heard from their elders. And the rabbi's daughter, Rosalie, who died in a car crash in 1999, left behind some endearing thoughts about her father in a videotaped ICF interview.

3

Details of the relationship between Alex Goode and Theresa are revealed mainly in the almost daily love letters the future rabbi wrote Theresa before and after they married, while he was away at school for several years. In these letters, he expressed not only his passion for her but his profound devotion to the ideals and dreams they would pursue together. Theresa elaborated on these dreams in her interviews.

4

Goode's experience at the temple in York, Pennsylvania, was described in about fifty pages of scrawled narrative found among his papers, which are in the personal archives of his widow, Theresa Goode Kaplan. Victoria Lyles's quotation praising Rabbi Goode for his contributions to York's educational system and its social progress comes from an interview with Francis Thornton that appears in his book *Sea of Glory*, p. 108. Ms. Lyles made a similar statement in a letter to Theresa Goode Kaplan dated March 15, 1943. Additional material was furnished in personal interviews with Theresa; Elaine Sevel Blank, a student of the rabbi, and her husband, Daniel; Betty Forner, also a temple student, and her husband, Herschel; Betty Hirschfield and Elliot Miller, temple members; and Erwin Goldenberg, the present temple rabbi. Members of the Grumbacher family and of other board families declined to answer questions about the board's relations with Rabbi Goode.

CHAPTER VIII: EN ROUTE TO A SAFE PLACE

1

Material related to Ben Epstein is based on several personal and ICF interviews. The approach to, and arrival in, St. John's was described in personal interviews with Epstein, James Eardley, Henry Geoguen, William Kramer, David Labadie, Michael Nowins, Daniel O'Keeffe, Roy Summers, and Warish. Also contributing to the description, in ICF interviews, were Edward Dionne, Eardley, Kramer, Labadie, James McAtamney, Walter Miller, and Leander Thomas. Warish told of the breakfast meeting with the four chaplains before they debarked.

2

Descriptions and references to Greenland are based on these books: *Iceland and Greenland* by Austin N. Clark; *Strangers in Greenland* by the New York American Tract Society (reference to the "season of perpetual day . . . ," p. 41); and *Greenland* by Vilhjalmur Stefansson. Epstein quoted in a personal interview the comments of people in St. John's to the troops. Washington's meeting with Father Bowdern is described in a letter Bowdern wrote to the *Church Bulletin* of St. Stephen's Church in Kearny, New Jersey, for the May 1943 issue.

CHAPTER IX: THE POET AND THE CARPET SWEEPER

1–3

Scenes involving Daniel Poling Sr. are based mainly on material from his book *Your Daddy Did Not Die*. Clark's football experience, including his quote of self-doubt, is dealt with on p. 52. His questions about God and his acceptance are from pp. 84–91.

Material on these subjects can also be found in the father's two other books, *Mine Eyes Have Seen* and *Faith Is Power for You*. Daniel Poling Jr.; Evangeline Poling, his wife; and Jack Hogan, a friend of Clark's, offered additional insights into his early years in their videotaped ICF interviews.

4–6

Description of Poling's ministerial experience in Schenectady comes from the above sources and from personal interviews with these friends and parishioners: Robin Chaffee, Peter Ten Eyck, Irma Long, and Katherine Scranton Rozendaal. Another friend, Frederick Wyatt, was interviewed by ICF.

CHAPTER X: RUNNING THE GAUNTLET

I

Criticism of the disposition of the escort cutters is found in the Report of Escort Operations, Convoy SG 19, from the Commander of Task Force 24 to the Commander in Chief, United States Fleet, February 6, 1943. In a personal interview, naval expert Franklyn Dailey Jr. compared the speeds and other capabilities of the *Dorchester* and larger troop-carrying ocean liners. The departure of the *Dorchester* from St. John's is described in a memoir by John Pearse; and in personal interviews with James Eardley, Henry Geoguen, William Kramer, David Labadie, Michael Nowins, Daniel O'Keeffe, Roy Summers, and Michael Warish.

2

Material on the U-boat campaign was based in part on *Hitler's U-boat War: The Hunted, 1942–1945* by Clay Blair, pp. 176–79; *U-boats at War* by Harold Busch; and *German U-boat Commanders of World War II* by Rainer Busch and Hans-Joachim Röll. Gerhard Buske, a member of the *U-223* crew, contributed his knowledge of his submarine's operations in a personal interview, and fellow crewmen Erich Pässler and Kurt Röser offered theirs in videotaped ICF interviews.

CHAPTER XI: THE WIND AND THE WARNING

I

The storm en route to Torpedo Junction was described in personal interviews with the survivors listed in the notes for the previous chapter, and by John Pearse in a memoir.

2

Warish told of the failed plans for an "amateur night" in a personal interview. The submarine threat and the measures taken to thwart it are detailed in a report by Lieutenant (jg) William H. Arpaia to the vice chief of naval operations, March 9, 1943. Chester Szymczak, a survivor himself, refers to the threat in *The Men, the Ship*, though it is depicted through the eyes of a fictitious character he uses to express his own observations. Several other survivors, including Warish, also described the defensive actions taken and the growing anxiety of the passengers.

3

Warish's meeting with Washington was described in a personal interview with the sergeant.

CHAPTER XII: GOD AND THE EIGHT BALL

1--2

This chapter is based on material in Thornton and on personal interviews conducted with Father Washington's relatives, friends, and associates: niece Joanne Schwoebel Brunetti, sister-in-law Marge Kolosek, Edward Chicowski, Sister Theresa Jordan Corcoran, Father Louis Saporito, Father Paul Shalvoy, and Monsignor Edwin Sullivan. Sheila Meyer, another niece, provided some of the chaplain's speeches and other material. Information about Washington in the archives of St. Stephen's Church in Kearny, New Jersey, was also very valuable.

CHAPTER XIII: TOO LATE FOR COFFEE

1

Material about Michael Warish's activities after the storm is based on personal interviews with Warish.

2

References to the party on the night of the sinking were made by Anthony Naydyhor in a videotaped ICF interview, and by Kenzel Linaweaver and Robert Williams in affidavits dealing with the last hours aboard the *Dorchester* and the heroics of the four chaplains.

3

Roy Summers described Washington's prayer service in a personal interview. Warish's walk on deck also came from a personal interview. Reference to "a vast mosaic . . . of ice pans" comes from *Greenland's Icy Fury* by Wallace Hansen.

4

James McAtamney's guard assignment was discussed in a videotaped ICF interview.

5

Material involving Daniel O'Keeffe came from a personal interview.

6

Lieutenant Commander Wächter's decision to torpedo what turned out to be the *Dorchester* was dealt with in videotaped ICF interviews with Erich Pässler and Kurt Röser.

CHAPTER XIV: COUNTDOWN TO HYPOTHERMIA

1

The scene involving Michael Warish and the torpedoing is based on a personal interview.

2

U-223's actions are from videotaped ICF interviews with Pässler and Röser.

3

Scenes involving Lieutenant Arpaia are from his report to the vice chief of naval operations, March 9, 1943. Material on Roy Summers was provided in a personal interview. The order to abandon ship was mentioned in Arpaia's report to the vice chief of naval operations and in the personal interview with Summers.

4

Attitudes of the four chaplains are highlights from their biographies, dealt with in other parts of this book.

5

Captain Greenspun, from aboard the *Tampa,* told headquarters of the sinking of the *Dorchester* in his Report of Escort Operations, SG 19, February 6, 1943. John Pearse, who also viewed it from the *Tampa,* later described it in a memoir.

6

The panic and confusion during the sinking was described by several survivors. The availability of lifesaving equipment is indicated in a memorandum from the

U.S. Army Status Finding Section to Chief, Casualty Branch, April 14, 1943. A memorandum for the file of the Navy Department, Office of the Chief of Naval Operations, summarized on March 1, 1943, the details of the attack. Lieutenant Arpaia reported on the sinking to the vice chief of naval operations. Private Felix Poche reported to his superior on how Sergeant Lloyd Phelps himself died after saving him from death, August 10, 1944. Walter Boeckholt wrote a memoir on his experience.

CHAPTER XV: THE PEN AND THE PENNILESS

1

Material related to Daniel O'Keeffe comes from a personal interview.

2

Information concerning Edward Dionne is based on a videotaped ICF interview.

3

Details dealing with Walter Miller derive from a videotaped ICF interview and a personal unpublished memoir entitled "Four Shepherds and Their Flock."

4

The story involving Henry Geoguen comes from a personal interview.

5

The description of James McAtamney's experience is based on a videotaped ICF interview.

6

Roy Summers's account comes from personal and videotaped ICF interviews.

7

Ben Epstein told of his experience in personal and videotaped interviews.

8

Walter Boeckholt's near disaster is described in his memoir.

CHAPTER XVI: A DEADLY DECISION

1

Escanaba skipper Peterson's communication with Captain Greenspun about the sinking was described in the Report to Commander, Task Unit 24.8.3, on February 5, 1943.

2

Details of Captain Greenspun's controversial decision to look for the submarine before rescuing the victims were drawn from the logs of the three cutters, from personal interviews with Richard Swanson and Franklyn Dailey Jr. (the expert quoted), and from a videotaped ICF interview with Captain Curry. The history and background of the Greenland Patrol can be found in *The United States Coast Guard in World War II* by Malcolm F. Willoughby, pp. 95–103.

CHAPTER XVII: FULFILLING DESTINY

1

Material about Roy Summers is based on personal and videotaped ICF interviews with him.

2

Charles Macli told of Washington's refusal to abandon ship in a videotaped ICF interview.

3

Walter Miller's effort to abandon ship was described in a videotaped ICF interview and in his memoir, "Four Shepherds and Their Flock."

4

References to Hugh Moffett and Chaplain Washington are from an unpublished memoir by Moffett, "The Story of the *Dorchester* and the Four Chaplains." References to Edward Dionne and Washington are from videotaped ICF interviews.

5

The story of Chaplain Goode's gloves and Lieutenant John Mahoney is from "The Heroism of the Four Chaplains" by James A. Cox, in the *Marine Corps League Magazine,* Autumn 1989.

6

Grady Clark told Dr. Daniel Poling this story, which was reported in the *Eagle* magazine (Milwaukee, Wisconsin) in its October 1950 issue.

7

Daniel O'Keeffe's escape from the sinking ship was described in a personal interview.

8

David Labadie related this account of the lone stranger in a personal interview. John Ladd's remark can be found in an article, "This Side of Heaven," in *American Legion* magazine, February 1998.

9

Michael Warish's attempt to save himself was described in a personal interview.

CHAPTER XVIII: IN SEARCH OF BUTTERED PANCAKES

1

The description of James McAtamney's experience in the water comes from his videotaped ICF interview.

2

The story of how Ben Epstein abandoned ship was told in personal and videotaped ICF interviews.

3

Roy Summers's experience was described in personal and videotaped ICF interviews.

4

The order to the three coast guard cutters to search for a submarine was found in their respective logs. Reference to "a ghostly white light" is from an article, "Untold Rescue," by Gary Turbak in the magazine *VFW*.

5

The story of Walter Boeckholt appears in his memoir.

6

Leander Thomas's misery was detailed in his videotaped ICF interview.

7

William Bednar's quotation can be found in the article "The Heroism of the Four Chaplains," in the *Marine Corps League Magazine*, Autumn 1989.

Ben Epstein's long swim is described in personal and videotaped ICF interviews.

8

The story of Roy Summers and the half-wrecked boat is from personal and videotaped ICF interviews.

9

William Arpaia's experience is detailed in his report to the vice chief of naval operations.

10

Ben Epstein's experience was described in personal and ICF interviews.

11

Theresa Goode Kaplan spoke of her vision of her husband in a personal interview.

12

William Kramer's lifeboat experience was described in a personal interview.

13

Roy Summers's account is taken from personal and videotaped ICF interviews.

14

Leander Thomas's story is from his videotaped ICF interview.

CHAPTER XIX: PLUCKED FROM A FESTIVE GRAVEYARD

1

The moral question of when to rescue was examined in personal interviews with Franklyn Dailey Jr., John Pearse, and Richard Swanson, and in a videotaped ICF interview with Ralph Curry.

2

Material about the *Escanaba* rescue effort is from a personal interview with Richard Swanson; the *Coast Guard News; Greenland Patrol, 1940–45;* the *VFW* magazine, February 1999, in "Untold Rescue" by Gary Turbak; a report from Carl U. Peterson, Commanding Officer, *Escanaba,* to Commander, Task Unit 24.8.3, February 5, 1943; *Harbor Watch,* January 29, 1999; *The Coast Guard at War: The Greenland Patrol, December 7, 1941– April 12, 1944;* and the *Escanaba*'s log, February 3, 1943, and February 4, 1943.

3

The rescue of Edward Dionne, including his meeting with an old classmate, was detailed in an ICF interview.

4

Walter Boeckholt's rescue was detailed in his memoir. The saving of the survivors of lifeboat number 6 was depicted by Ben Epstein in personal interviews and in an ICF interview.

5

Ben Epstein and James Eardley related in personal interviews how they were treated after their rescue.

6

Leander Thomas's rescue was described in a videotaped ICF interview.

CHAPTER XX: THE RISK OF BEING HUMAN

I

Ralph Curry's dilemma was examined in a videotaped ICF interview with him. His description of the *Comanche*'s rescue operation was found in his Report to Commander, Task Force 24.8.3, February 12, 1943. It was also detailed in a personal interview with Richard Swanson. Joseph Archer's expression of gratitude to the rescuers appeared in *Greenland Patrol, 1940–45,* October 1998.

2

Roy Summers's rescue was described in a personal interview. Information on the joint rescue efforts of Swanson and Charles David Jr. came from a personal interview with Swanson and an article by Michael Kelly in the *Omaha World-Herald,* February 23, 1999.

3

David Labadie's story was based on personal and videotaped ICF interviews and on the statements of Michael Warish and other survivors in personal and ICF interviews.

CHAPTER XXI: THE BOOTLACES OF SUBLIMITY

I

Material dealing with Michael Warish came from personal interviews. The statement by James Eardley about the chaplains was also given in a personal interview. Ralph Curry's statement appears in his Report to Commander, Task Force, 24.8.3, February 12, 1943.

2

The story of *U-223* was told in videotaped ICF interviews with Erich Pässler and Kurt Röser, and in a personal interview with Gerhard Buske.

I

A naval message from Commander, Task Force 24, informed the commander in chief of the Atlantic Fleet, on February 3, 1943, that ships were being sent to assist in rescue operations. A naval message from Commander, Task Unit 24.8.3, Search Group, to Commander, Task Force 24, announced on February 6, 1943, the end of the search for bodies. James Eardley and John Pearse also contributed to the account of the late-stage rescue effort. Seaman Raymond O'Malley, one of only two men to survive the sinking of the *Escanaba* in June 1943, recounted in a personal interview the details of the tragedy.

2

The material about Isadore Fox is based on her book *The Immortal Chaplain*. The quote starting "I have never felt ..." is from "Widow in the Pulpit" by Booton Herndon, which appeared in the *American Weekly*, January 13, 1948.

3

Theresa Goode Kaplan told her story in personal interviews and a videotaped ICF interview. Paul Fried, Rosalie's husband, contributed information during a personal interview.

4

How Betty Poling and Dr. Daniel Poling dealt with the news of Clark's death is described in Dr. Poling's book *Your Daddy Did Not Die*, pp. 133–35, and *Mine Eyes Have Seen*, pp. 202–03. Clark Poling Jr. offered thoughts he had gathered from his mother and other family members.

5

Material on the reaction of Chaplain Washington's mother, Mary, to her son's death was described by Marge Kolosek, the priest's sister-in-law, in a personal interview.

6

Details of the postwar honors conferred posthumously upon the four chaplains were provided by the Immortal Chaplains Foundation, the families of the chaplains, many newspapers and magazines, and Chester J. Szymczak's *The Men, the Ship*.

7

Material dealing with Ben Epstein was furnished by him in personal interviews.

8

This section is based on personal interviews with Roy Summers and David Labadie, respectively.

9

Walter Boeckholt's postsinking experiences are recorded in his memoir and in the *Messenger* (Algona, Iowa), November 27, 1980. His wife, Mildred, was helpful in providing information.

10

Michael Warish gave details about what happened to him in personal interviews.

BIBLIOGRAPHY

VIDEOTAPED INTERVIEWS

Courtesy of David Fox of the Immortal Chaplains Foundation

Joseph Archer, *Dorchester* survivor
Henry H. Arnett, *Dorchester* survivor
Robert L. Blakely, *Dorchester* survivor
Gerhard Buske, first officer, *U-223*
Charles B. Ciccia, *Dorchester* survivor
Ralph Curry, commander of *Comanche*
Edward J. Dionne, *Dorchester* survivor
James Eardley, *Dorchester* survivor
Benjamin Epstein, *Dorchester* survivor (interview and speech)
Florence Fox, sister of George Fox
Oliver Fox, brother of George Fox
Siglinda Fox, sister-in-law of George Fox
Rosalie Goode Fried, daughter of Alexander Goode
Jack Hogan, secretary of Clark Poling
Theresa Goode Kaplan, widow of Alexander Goode
William Kramer, *Dorchester* survivor
David Labadie, *Dorchester* survivor
Charles Macli, *Dorchester* survivor
James McAtamney, *Dorchester* survivor

Walter Miller, *Dorchester* survivor
Anthony J. Naydyhor, *Dorchester* survivor
Erich Pässler, torpedo man, *U-223*
John Pearse, crewman on *Tampa*
Roland Phillips, friend of Clark Poling
Clark Poling Jr., son of Clark Poling
Daniel Poling Jr., brother of Clark Poling
Evangeline Poling, sister-in-law of Clark Poling
Kurt Röser, crewman, *U-223*
Roy Nicholas Summers, *Dorchester* survivor
Leander Thomas, *Dorchester* survivor
Michael Warish, *Dorchester* survivor
Grace Fox Wiest, sister of George Fox
Frederick Wyatt, friend of Clark Poling

Additional videotapes of foundation ceremonies were provided by Paul Fried, and that of a dinner honoring the memory of Chaplain Poling was furnished by Laura Linder.

BOOKS

Abercrombie, Clarence L., III. *The Military Chaplain.* Beverly Hills, Calif.: Sage, 1977.
Ahlstrom, Sydney E. *A Religious History of the American People.* New Haven: Yale University Press, 1972.
Appelquist, A. Ray, ed. *Church, State and Chaplaincy.* Washington, D.C.: General Commission on Chaplains and Armed Forces Personnel, 1969.
Barish, Louise. *Rabbis in Uniform.* New York: Jonathan David, 1962.
Beach, Edward L. *Submarine.* New York: Henry Holt, 1946.
Bekker, C. D. *Defeat at Sea.* New York: Henry Holt, 1955.
Birch, John J. *The Pioneering Church of the Mohawk Valley.* Schenectady: Consistory, First Reformed Church, 1955.
Blair, Clay. *Hitler's U-boat War: The Hunted, 1942–1945.* New York: Modern Library, 1998.
Brooks, Geoffrey, and Wolfgang Hirschfeld. *The Story of a U-boat NCO, 1940–1946.* Annapolis: Naval Institute Press, 1996.
Brown, W. Y. *The Army Chaplain.* Philadelphia: William S. and Alfred Martien, 1863.

Burn, Alan. *The Fighting Commodores.* Annapolis: Naval Institute Press, 1999.

Busch, Harold. *U-boats at War.* New York: Ballantine, 1955.

Busch, Rainer, and Hans-Joachim Röll. *German U-boat Commanders of World War II.* Annapolis: Naval Institute Press, 1999.

Chapman, Robert. *Tell It to the Chaplain.* New York: Exposition, 1952.

Charles, Roland W. *Troopships of World War II.* Washington, D.C.: Army Transportation Association, 1947.

Clark, Austin N. *Iceland and Greenland.* No. 15. Smithsonian Institution War Background Studies, Washington, D.C.: Smithsonian Institution, 1943.

The Coast Guard at War: The Greenland Patrol, December 7, 1941–April 12, 1944. U.S. Coast Guard Headquarters.

Conn, Stetson, Rose C. Engelman, and Byron Fairchild. *United States Army in World War II: The Western Hemisphere—Guarding the United States and Its Outposts.* Washington, D.C.: Office of the Chief of Military History, Department of the Army, 1964.

Crosby, Donald F. *Battlefield Chaplains: Catholic Priests in World War II.* Lawrence: University of Kansas Press, 1994.

Cross, David. *Pride of Our People.* Garden City, N.Y.: Doubleday, 1979.

Drazin, Israel, and Cecil B. Currey. *For God and Country.* Hoboken, N.J.: KTAV Publishing, 1995.

Elkins, Dov Peretz, and Jonathan David. *God's Warriors.* New York: Middle Village, 1974.

Harris, Robert. *Enigma.* New York: Random House, 1996.

Fox, Isadore H. *The Immortal Chaplain.* New York: Exposition, 1965.

Frank, Wolfgang. *The Sea Wolves.* Translated from German. New York: Rinehart, 1955.

Germain, Aidan Henry. "Catholic Military and Naval Chaplains, 1776–1917." Dissertation, Washington, D.C., 1929.

Gersh, Harry. *These Are My People.* New York: Behrman House.

Ginsberg, Louis. *History of the Jews of Petersburg, 1789–1950.* Petersburg, Va., 1954.

Goldman, Alex J. *Giants of Faith: Great American Rabbis.* New York: Citadel, 1964.

Goode, Alexander D. "Cavalcade of Democracy." Unpublished.

Gross, David C. *Pride of Our People.* Garden City, N.Y.: Doubleday, 1979.

Gushwa, Robert L. *The Best and Worst of Times.* Washington, D.C.: Office of the Chief of Chaplains, Department of the Army, 1977.

Haskell, W. A. *Shadows on the Horizon.* Annapolis: Naval Institute Press, 1999.

An Historical Sketch of the First Reformed Church of Schenectady. New York, 1976. Pamphlet.

Honeywell, Roy J. *Chaplains of the United States Army.* Washington, D.C.: Office of the Chief of Chaplains, Department of the Army, 1958.

Howarth, David. *Sledge Patrol.* New York: Macmillan, 1957.

Jones, Michael T. *The Air Force Chaplain: Clergy or Officer?* Maxwell Air Force Base, Ala.: Air War College, Air University, April 1996.

Jorgensen, Daniel B. *The Service of Chaplains to Army Air Units, 1917–1946.* Washington, D.C.: Office of Air Force Chaplains.

Kemp, Paul. *U-boats Destroyed.* London: Arms & Armour, 2000.

Klein, Isaac. *The Anguish and the Ecstasy.* New York: Vantage, 1974.

Lev, Aryeh. "What Chaplains Preach." Thesis for promotion in army chaplaincy, 1941.

Livazer, Hersh. *The Rabbi's Blessing.* Jerusalem, 1980.

Mason, David, *U-boat: The Secret Menace.* New York: Ballantine, 1968.

The Military Chaplaincy. Report to the President by the President's Committee on Religion and Welfare in the Armed Forces, October 1, 1950.

Monsarrat, Nicholas. *The Cruel Sea.* New York: Knopf, 1951.

Moore, Deborah Dash. *Worshipping Together in Uniform: Christians and Jews in World War II.* San Francisco: University of San Francisco, September 13, 2001.

Morison, Samuel Eliot. *The Battle of the Atlantic, September 1939–May 1943.* Boston: Little, Brown, 1948.

Mulligan, Timothy P. *Neither Sharks Nor Wolves: Germany's U-boat Arm, 1939–1945.* Annapolis: Naval Institute Press, 1999.

Nave, Orville J. *Nave's Handbook on the Army Chaplaincy.* Los Angeles, 1917.

New York American Tract Society. *Strangers in Greenland.* Washington, D.C.: Office of the Chief of Chaplains, Department of the Army, 1977.

Niestlé, Axel. *German U-boat Losses During World War II.* Annapolis: Naval Institute Press, 1998.

Overy, Richard. *Why the Allies Won.* New York: Norton, 1997.

Padre [Wuest, Karl A.]. *They Told It to the Chaplain.* New York: Vantage, 1953.

Poling, Daniel A. *Faith Is Power for You.* New York: Greenberg, 1950.

———. *Mine Eyes Have Seen.* New York: McGraw-Hill, 1959.

———. *Your Daddy Did Not Die.* New York: Greenberg, 1944.

Pontius, Kathryn Sharp, Gerald F. De Jong, and J. Dean Dykstra. *Three Centuries: The History of the First Reformed Church of Schenectady, 1680–1980.* 2 vols. Schenectady: The First Reformed Church of Schenectady, 1980.

Price, Lucien. *Religion of the Soldier and Sailor.* Cambridge, Mass.: Harvard University Press, 1945.

Riesenberg, Felix, Jr. *Sea War: The Story of a U.S. Merchant Marine in World War II.* New York: Rinehart, 1956.

Rohwer, J., and G. Hummelchen. *Chronology of the War at Sea, 1939–1945.* Annapolis: Naval Institute Press, 1972.

Rössler, Eberhard, *The U-boat.* Annapolis: Naval Institute Press, 1981.

Schwartz, Charles Downer, and Ouida Davis Schwartz. *A Flame of Fire.* Rutland: Academy Books, 1982.

Sephton, John. *What the Sagas Say of Greenland.*

Showell, Jak P. Mallmann, *U-Boats Under the Swastika,* 2nd ed. Annapolis: Naval Institute Press, 1987.

Simon, Edward A. "The Influence of American Churches on the Development of the Structure and Duties of the Army Chaplaincy, 1914–1962." Thesis, Princeton Theological Seminary, 1963.

Simpson, G. W. *Manual for United States Army Chaplains.*

Slomovitz, Albert Isaac. *The Fighting Rabbis.* New York: New York University, 1999.

Stefansson, Vilhjalmur. *Greenland.* Garden City, N.Y.: Doubleday, Doran, 1942.

Student Rabbinic Association of the Hebrew Union College. "Report on the Chaplaincy of the Student Public Association." New York: Jewish Institute of Religion, 1968.

Szymczak, Chester J. *The Men, the Ship.* Milwaukee: Great Lakes, 1976.

Thornton, Francis. *Sea of Glory.* Englewood Cliffs, N.J.: Prentice Hall, 1953.

United States Bureau of Naval Personnel. *The History of the Chaplain Corps.*

The U.S. Army Chaplaincy, 1920–1945.

Veterans of Foreign Wars. *Pictorial History of the Second World War.* vol. 10. Veterans of Foreign Wars of the United States, 1949.

Von der Porter, Edward P. *The German Navy in World War II.* New York: Crowell, 1969.

Waring, George J. "Chaplain's Duties." Washington, D.C.: Government Printing Office, 1912

Werner, Herbert A. *Iron Coffins.* London: Arthur Barker, 1998.

Wiggins, Melanie. *U-boat Adventures.* Annapolis: Naval Institute Press, 1999.

Willoughby, Malcolm F. *The United States Coast Guard in World War II.* Annapolis: Naval Institute Press, 1957.

NEWSPAPERS, PERIODICALS, AND OTHER MEDIA

Albany Times-Union, February 3, 1993

American Legion, February 1989, February 1991, February 1998

The American Weekly, January 13, 1948

The Associated Press, January 30, 1993

Boston Herald, March 4, 1943

Boynton Beach Times (Fla.), January 30, 1997

Catskill On line: http://www.catskill.net/purple/queen.htm

Chicago Daily News, March 18, 1943

Chicago Herald-American, February 22, 1943

Chicago Tribune, February 22, 1943

Christian Advocate, May 20, 1943

The Church Bulletin, May 1943 (St. Stephen's, Kearny, N.J.)

Church Quarterly Review, January 1957

Coast Guard News/Harbor Watch, January 14, 2000

The Daily Gazette (Schenectady), February 3, 1993

D.A.V. Magazine, February 2000

The Day (New London, Conn.), October 9, 1936

Delray Times, vol. 27, no. 21

De Omroeper, July 1939

The Eagle (Milwaukee, Wis.), October 1950

Gazette and Daily (York, Pa.), January 30, 1939, February 24, 1942

Globe-Gazette (Algona, Ia.), April 11, 1993

Greenland Patrol, 1940–45 (Baldwin, N.Y.), ed. John S. Stamford

Harbor Watch, January 29, 1999

The Herald (Tamarac, Fla.), February 4, 2001

Hickory Daily Record (N.C.), April 19, 1988

Hollywood Citizen News, February 3, 1953

Illinois Wesleyan University Magazine, Spring 1993

International Security, Spring 1994

Interpreter, April 1997

Jewish Exponent, Philadelphia, October 19, 1951

Jewish Week (N.Y.) January 29–February 4, 1990

The Journal of Military History, April 1992

The Knickerbocker News-Union-Star (Albany, N.Y.), February 21, 1970

Lincoln Journal Star (Neb.), February 13, 1999

Marine Corps League Magazine, Autumn 1989

The Messenger (Algona, Ia.), November 27, 1980

Military Affairs, Summer, 1950

Milwaukee Journal, September 22, 1955

Milwaukee Sentinel, February 3, 1963

National Jewish Monthly, June 1939

Newark Star-Ledger, January 29, 1993

Newport News Daily Press, June 22, 1986

Newsweek, July 22, 1957

New York Daily News, March 5, 1943

The New Yorker, February 21 and 28, 2000

New York Harbor Watch, March 31, 2000

New York Herald, March 5, 1943

New York Journal-American, April 11, 1943

New York Sun, February 22, 1943, March 5, 1943

New York Times, February 24, 1943, March 5, 1943, December 3, 1944

Omaha World-Herald, Midlands Section, February 23, 1999

Patterson Morning Call (N.J.), February 27, 1960

The Philadelphia Inquirer, January 31, 1993, February 2, 1993

The Purple Heart, January–February 1990

Reader's Digest, June 1989

Reading Times (Reading, Pa.), February 27, 1942

The Record (N.J.), February 12, 1999

The Retired Officer Magazine, December 1992

Rockland County Times (N.Y.), February 14, 2001

Schenectady Gazette, May 18, 1949, February 23, 1961

Schenectady Union-Star, February 4, 1950

Sea Classics, January 1973, March 1998

Sewickley Herald (Pa.), May 29, 1986

This Week, September 11, 1955

Time, July 5, 1943, December 11, 1944

Troy Conference, 1943

VFW, February 1999

Washington Evening Star, March 5, 1943

Washington Jewish Week, February 17, 2000

WGY News (Schenectady), "Household Chats with Betty Lennox" (Betty Poling),
    October–November 1943

DOCUMENTS

Correspondence and reports involving principal characters in the book are listed here under their names.

Atlantic Fleet Anti-Submarine Warfare Officer. Report to Commander-in-Chief, U.S. Atlantic Fleet, March 10, 1943.

Boeckholt, Walter A. Memoir.

Chaffee, Robin. (Friend of Clark Poling.) Letter to author, September 30, 2002.

Chaplains. Memorandum from Chief of Chaplains to Adjutant General (re awards), January 29, 1944.

———. Monthly Report, December 1942 (each of the four chaplains).

Comanche, U.S. Coast Guard Cutter. Log, February 3, 1943.

———. Report of Assistance to Treasury Department, U.S. Coast Guard, February 1943.

———. Commanding Officer, Report to Commandant, U.S. Coast Guard, February 12, 1943.

———. Commanding Officer, Report to Commander, Task Force 24.8.3, February 12, 1943.

Commander-in-Chief, United States Atlantic Fleet. Report to Commander-in-Chief, United States Fleet, April 6, 1943.

Commander, Task Force 24. Report to Commander-in-Chief, U.S. Atlantic Fleet, February 3, 1943, February 6, 1943, and March 24, 1943.

Commander, Task Unit 24.8.3, Search Group, to Commander, Task Force 24, February 6, 1943.

Duane, U.S. Coast Guard Cutter. War Diary, February 3, 1943, and February 5, 1943.

Emery, Elsie. (Friend of Clark Poling.) Letter to author.

Escanaba, U.S. Coast Guard Cutter. Log, February 3, 1943.

———. Commanding Officer, Report to Commandant, U.S. Coast Guard, February 9, 1943.

———. Commanding Officer, Report to Commander, Task Unit 24.8.3, February 5, 1943.

———. War Diary, February 3, 1943.

———. Letter to John F. Monahan, Chief of Chaplains Office, Washington, D.C., October 2, 1942.

Fox, George. Letter to Chief of Chaplains, Washington, D.C., May 21, 1942.

Fox, Isadore. Letter to Chief of Chaplains, Washington, D.C., April 13, 1943.

———. Letter from Chief of Chaplains, William R. Arnold, Washington, D.C., August 7, 1943.

Gilman, Representative Benjamin. *Congressional Record,* February 2, 1999.

Goode, Alexander. Letter from the Headquarters First District, Army Air Forces Technical Training Command, November 4, 1942.

———. Letter from Hebrew Union College, Office of the Registrar, February 24, 1937.

———. Letter to Bernard Sevel, June 16, 1942.

———. Letter to Beth Israel Congregation, May 11, 1942.

———. Letter to Jason B. Snyder, YMCA, York, Pa., November 12, 1942.

———. Manuscript, "Ethics for Democracy."

———. Manuscript, History of Alexander Goode's Experience in York, Pa.

———. Manuscript, History of Alexander Goodkowitz.

———. Manuscript, "A Sympathetic Soul."

———. Report on Alexander Goode, Army Air Forces.

———. Report on Graduation Thesis, February 19, 1937.

Goode, Theresa. Letters from William R. Arnold, Chief of Chaplains, March 24, 1943, June 15, 1943.

———. Memoir.

Greenspun, Joseph. Report of Escort Operations, SG 19, February 6, 1943.

Miller, Walter. Memoir, "Four Shepherds and Their Flock."

Moffett, Hugh. Memoir, "The Story of the *Dorchester* and the Four Chaplains."

Monahan, John F., Chief of Chaplains Office. Letter to George Fox, October 7, 1942.

Pearse, John, Secretary of *Tampa* Reunion Committee. Letter to Head Chaplain of Chapel of the Four Chaplains, February 3, 1996.

———. Memoir, February 2, 2000, February 6, 2000.

Poling, Clark. Letter from Adjutant General, Washington, D.C., April 22, 1943.

———. Letter from Chief of Chaplains, Washington, D.C., March 24, 1943.

———. Letter from Chief of Chaplains, Washington, D.C., June 15, 1943.

———. Letter from Ernest M. Kigon, Union College.

———. Letter to his Congregation.

———. Request for Foreign Service to Chief of Chaplains, October 27, 1941.

Tampa, U.S. Coast Guard Cutter. Log, February 3, 1943.

———. Daily War Diary, February 1943.

War Department, Office of the Chief of Chaplains. Memorandum to Adjutant General, July 17, 1942 (re Alexander Goode).

Office of the Chief of Transportation, Records.

Warish, Michael. Memoir.

Washington, John. Remembrances by Frances Compton.

LIBRARIES AND ARCHIVES

American Jewish Archives, Cincinnati, Ohio.

Archdiocese of Newark Archives, Seton Hall University, South Orange, N.J.

Bureau of Naval Personnel, Washington, D.C.

Catholic War Veterans, Arlington, Va.

Center of Military History, Department of the Army, Washington, D.C.

Chief of Transportation Office, Records, Washington, D.C.

Columbia University Libraries, New York.

Dutch Reformed Church Archives, Schenectady, N.Y.

Fort Snelling Memorial Chapel Foundation, Fort Snelling State Park, Minn.

Illinois Wesleyan University Library, Bloomington, Ill.

The Immortal Chaplains Foundation, Hamline University, St. Paul, Minn.

Jewish Historical Society, New York.

Library of Congress, Washington, D.C.

Methodist Commission on Chaplains, Washington, D.C.

Military History Institute, Carlisle, Pa.

National Archives and Records Administration, College Park, Md.

National Maritime Center, Arlington, Va.

National Museum of American Jewish Military History, Washington, D.C.

National Personnel Records Center, St. Louis, Mo.

National War College, Carlisle, Pa.

Naval Historical Center, Washington, D.C.

Navy Department Library, Washington, D.C.

New York Public Library, New York.

Pennsylvania Historical and Museum Commission, Bureau of Archives and History, Harrisburg, Pa.

Schenectady Museum, Schenectady, N.Y.

Seton Hall University, Special Collection Center, Walsh Library, South Orange, N.J.

Smithsonian Institution, Washington, D.C.

St. Stephen's Church Archives, Kearny, N.J.

Troy Conference Archives, Saratoga Springs, N.Y.

United Methodist Church, General Commission on Archives and History, Madison, N.J.

United Methodist Church Information Service, Nashville, Ill.

United Methodist Conference Center, White Plains, N.Y.

United States Army Chaplain Center and School, Fort Jackson, S.C.

United States Coast Guard, Department of Transportation, Washington, D.C.

United States Island Veterans Organization, Staten Island, N.Y.

United States Merchant Marine Academy, Kings Point, N.Y.

United States Naval Institute, Annapolis, Md.

APPENDIX I

"I knew the four chaplains and saw them give up their life belts and go down on the ship without them."
—Henry H. Arnett

"I . . . witnessed the act of heroism on the part of the chaplains. . . . Up to the very last minute they continued with their mission of helping and comforting the terror stricken."
—Frank G. DiMeo

"The ship started sinking, . . . and as I left the ship, I looked back and saw the chaplains . . . with their hands clasped, praying for the boys. They never made any attempt to save themselves, but they did try to save the others. I think their names should be on the list of The Greatest Heroes of this war."
—Grady L. Clark

"I saw all four chaplains take off their life belts and give them to soldiers who had none. . . . The last I saw of them they were still praying, talking, and preaching to the soldiers."
—Thomas W. Myers Jr.

"I passed two of the four chaplains. They were passing out life preservers from boxes on deck. When these were gone, I saw them take the life preservers from their own persons and hand them out too. . . . It was common talk among the survivors that all four of the chaplains had given away their life belts and had gone down with the ship."
—Oswald R. Evans

"The four chaplains were asking the men to be calm and [saying] that every effort would be made to save them . . . , and generally attempting to maintain order. . . . At this point, I dove into the water and succeeded in getting into a lifeboat, but almost immediately it capsized. . . . So I returned to the *Dorchester* and remained on it until the water on the deck . . . was up to my knees. The chaplains were still on the deck and remained there when I dove off the ship for the second time."
—John P. O'Brien

"I saw these chaplains without life preservers kneeling on deck and praying for us."
—Kenzel L. Linaweaver

"The encouraging thoughts and remarks of the chaplains was in no small way responsible for some of the more fearful individuals going over the side and eventually being saved."
—William G. Bunkelman

"During the time I was on deck I saw the chaplains give their life preservers to soldiers who did not have one."
—Hollis Wall Jr.

"From my position as I clung to [a] lifeboat, I saw the chaplains clearly, standing at the rail of the transport minus their life jackets, urging men to leave the ship with disregard to their own safety."
—William J. Pantall

"The last I saw of the chaplains they were standing on deck praying. By that time the ship had capsized and was at a forty-five-degree angle."
—Anthony J. Povlak

"After leaving my stateroom and going out on deck, I saw at least three chaplains . . . give up their life jackets to men who were without them."
—Ernest L. Heaten

"It is impressed clearly in my mind that these chaplains demonstrated unsurpassed courage and heroism when they willingly gave their life belts to four enlisted men, who, because of the utter confusion and disorder brought about by the torpedoing, had become hysterical. . . . They helped save the lives of many of the troops."
—John F. Garey

"I made for the life raft to which I was assigned and . . . passed four chaplains. . . . One of them possessed a life jacket and the other three did not. As I passed I no-

ticed the chaplain with the life jacket remove his jacket and give it to a soldier . . . who did not have a life jacket. I overheard the soldier say, 'Thank you, Chaplain.' "
—Joseph D. Haymore

"I saw Chaplain Fox on deck, and am quite sure [I] heard [a fellow soldier exclaim] something to this effect: 'My God, I forgot my life preserver.' . . . I heard someone, whom I'm quite positive was Chaplain Fox, say in reply, 'Here, take mine.' "
—Nace F. Darnell

"They were singing songs, hymns. I knew they couldn't get off. The next time I looked, it was like slipping away under water."   —James A. Ward (not under oath)

APPENDIX 2

FATE OF PASSENGERS AND CREW
OF THE *DORCHESTER*

ARMY SURVIVORS

Aliano, George N.

Anzur, Frank G.

Archer, Joseph G.

Arnett, Henry H.

Basalay, John

Beam, Otto

Bednar, William B.

Belisle, Henry R.

Bernstetter, Mike

Beyer, Louis C.

Blakely, Robert L.

Boeckholt, Walter

Bones, John W.

Bunkelman, William G.

Burris, Norman W.

Bush, Charles R.

Calandriello, Michael A.

Charbhneau, Joseph C.

Clark, Grady L.

Collins, George A.

Cox, Charles M.

Crouch, Warren C.

Crump, Columbus G.

Darnell, Nace F.

Davis, Ralph F.

Dedomenico, Ralph W.

Deeds, Jerome W.

DiMeo, Frank G.

Dionne, Edward J.

Dorn, William H.

Eardley, James

Epstein, Benjamin

Evans, George L.

Evans, Oswald R.

Fisher, John W.

Forley, Arvin

Fox, Thomas W.

Garey, John F.

Garris, George C.

Geoguen, Joseph Henry

Gohl, Walter

Goldsmith, Anvaha L.

Gormley, James R.

Graham, William R.

Gray, Ernest L.

Gregg, Johnnie B.

Guz, Bruno J.

Harraadon, Alden F.

Harslerode, Wilmet E.

Hassler, George F.

Haymore, Joseph D.

Heaten, Ernest Leroy

Hunter, Albert T.

Irvin, Thomas A.

Jackson, John M.

Jandura, Caml C.

Jennings, Roy L.

Jones, Joseph P.

Josytwo, Roy

Kant, Donald C.

Karg, Harold J.

Keenan, George

Kerr, Robert H.

King, George L.

Kirkpatrick, Weldon F.

Kohn, Joe

Kramer, William W.

Labadie, David J.

Labux, Joseph J.

Larey, Weldon C.

Lemoine, Victor G.

Linaweaver, Kenzel L.

Locacono, Armando

Lumsden, Charles E.

Macli, Charles

MacNeill, Charles A.

Mahoney, William R.

Majsztrik, Andrew J.

Matson, Samuel A.

McAtamney, James W.

McClure, Roscoe

McHale, Richard T.

McLean, Marshall B.

Miller, Walter

Mursch, Eugene A.

Myers, Thomas W., Jr.

Naydyhor, Anthony J.

Nebel, Ralph

Nicolaus, Marvin C.

Nieman, Fred G.

Obee, Eugene C.

O'Brien, John P.

Ochse, Warren R.

Pantall, William J.

Panter, Roy E.

Perkins, James E.

Petri, Homer L.

Phelps, Albert N.

Poche, Felix A.

Ponath, Leonard W.

Povlak, Anthony J.

Rasmaita, Raymond J.

Reed, J. S.

Reynolds, Edward B.

Russell, Robert O.

Sanders, Theodore J.

Scott, Russell L.

Seiler, Ernest H.

Shackley, Leo R.

Shaw, Robert K.

Sheiffele, Kenneth F.

Slanker, Merle D.

Stamlen, Joseph F.

Statler, Maynard W.

Stiner, Woodward P.

St. Johns, Emile

Talvitie, Theodore T.

Thomas, Leander P.

Thompson, Milford H.

Towlen, Leonard J.

Turpin, George D.

Veidenheimer, Pete P., Jr.

Vickers, Ralph A.

Vona, Joseph J.

Wagner, George B.

Wall, Hollis, Jr.

Walter, Thomas L.

Walton, Charles

Ward, James A.

Warish, Michael

Weaver, Nevin C.

Webb, Burton D.

Wiener, Marcus

Williams, Robert C.

Young, Lowell H.

ARMY DEAD

Ace, Walter H.

Adams, Earl L.

Adkins, Leonard E.

Alesi, Alfred H.

Alvarez, Alejandro M.

Anderson, Albert L.

Anderson, Bruce

Angel, Bertie F.

Angerman, Herbert G.

Appleton, Wilfred E.

Aragona, John S.

Argyro, James B.

Armijo, Ermilo T.

Ashby, Theodore F.

Ayres, Elijah H., Jr.

Bailey, Thomas J., Jr.

Ballard, Fred

Barlow, Joel R.

Bartrug, Ralph J.

Bates, John B.

Becerra, Angelo

Beckman, Harold F.

Beevers, DeWitte E.

Bennett, Donald M.

Bevelacque, John F.

Bird, Lafayette L.

Bisconti, Francis J.

Blackwood, John

Blalock, Fred H.

Bokal, Edward R.

Bon, Michael

Bonlie, Melvin O.

Bontjes, Andy

Boyd, Melvin T.

Boyle, Hugh J.

Bradley, William M.

Braniff, Willard J.

Bricker, Norman

Brighton, Emmett J.

Brinsky, William J.

Broadwell, William A.

Brohm, Norbert M.

Brookshire, David C.

Brown, Eldon R.

Brown, Hansel

Brown, Harold M.

Brown, McIntosh

Brubaker, Harry

Brush, Edward

Buckhahn, Leroy F.

Budner, Walter C.

Bulgrin, Billy N.

Burd, Raymond V.

Burge, Jay L.

Burns, Clinton F.

Bye, Anthony E.

Cannon, William T., Jr.

Carson, Edward P.

Carter, Charles A.

Carter, Hubert W.

Carter, James H.

Caruso, Joseph P.

Cashen, John T.

Casper, Ralph N.

Chechile, Michael

Christian, Norman L.

Clarno, Malcolm W.

Clayton, Albert L.

Clemmons, John V.

Cline, Charles W.

Clute, Willis A.

Cochran, Ernest W.

Collins, John A.

Colwill, Leo L.

Commentz, Richard A.

Corcoran, James E., Jr.

Cornett, Vernal L.

Coughlin, Robert R.

Crane, William C.

Crockett, Homer L.

Crossland, William H.

Crotty, Bill B.

Cundy, John L.

Cunning, George D.

Dalrymple, George H.

Dametsch, Anton

Damm, Richard P.

Danjou, Emile L.

DeCrow, Joseph C.

Dekeyser, Albert

Demack, Anthony J.

Demeo, Pasqual A.

DeMunch, Virgil J.

Denmark, Harry T.

DeVuono, Carl J.

Diaz, John N.

Dickman, Charles

Dobies, Theodore R.

Dooner, John J.

Dowell, William R.

Dudley, Joseph E.

Dufort, Latimer G.

Duhl, Joseph A.

Dupray, Hubert F.

Dusseau, Lawrence D.

Eichwald, Howard W.

Eliopoulos, George

Elmaleh, Jacole D. A.

Estell, Garold R.

Ethier, Leo R.

Everett, Donald J.

Farbstein, Joseph

Feoley, Joseph E.

Ferrara, John G.

Fiedler, Daniel G.

Fischer, Claude E.

Fitt, John R.

Fitzgerald, Ray A.

Foot, Arthur F.

Fox, George L.

Franceschi, Germano

Freed, Irwin

Freeman, Joseph

Frese, Fred J.

Fricke, Glenn H.

Fromm, Dan F.

Frucelli, Vincent

Gaff, Homer F.

Gagliardi, Joseph P.

Gallagher, John F.

Gannon, Thomas M.

Garafana, Michael

Garlich, Edwin G.

Gassdorf, William K.

Gennrich, Frederick J.

Gill, Charles W.

Gillihet, Frank

Giltner, Robert P.

Goldman, Harry A.

Gonos, William

Goode, Alexander D.

Goodwin, Robert L.

Gordon, T. J.

Goss, William P.

Govorchin, John L.

Graham, Gordon

Grandinetti, George V.

Greenwood, Lee R.

Grimes, Denzle B.

Guidios, Jerome V.

Gusmerotti, Joseph P.

Hagans, Albert C.

Hallmark, Orville E.

Hamilton, Charles F.

Harmon, William E.

Harper, Frank N.

Hart, Gordon S.

Hartensveld, Orie J.

Hartzheim, William M.

Hayes, Robert K.

Hayman, Alfred C.

Heavel, Roland G.

Hensley, Jack V.

Henson, Robert H.

Hickey, Richard T.

Hicks, Harvie G.

Hightree, Randall G.

Hilliard, Daniel F.

Hillman, Kenneth L.

Hinchey, Thomas J.

Hinkle, Edmond B.

Hitson, Charles A.

Hochsprung, Norman C.

Hogan, Loy C.

Hogewood, Henry H.

Holland, Delmer D.

Hollers, Donald P.

Hollister, Kingsley S.

Honaker, Thomas H., Jr.

Horton, Louis C.

Hoslar, Wilber E.

Howard, Herbert W.

Hudson, John P.

Hughston, William M., Jr.

Hull, Rovello S.

Humble, Willard C.

Hunter, John T., Jr.

Hutchinson, John H.

Inks, Arthur E.

Jackson, Jack J.

Jacobs, Errol M.

Jacobson, Donald H.

Jatz, Fred P.

Johnson, Francis L.

Johnson, Hoyt H.

Johnson, Russel E.

Johnson, Vilus C.

Joines, Presley S.

Jones, Arnold G.

Jones, John L.

Jones, Ralph L.

Joyce, William J.

Juvinall, Leslie E.

Kagy, Fred L.

Kalman, Israel I.

Katzoff, Sidney H.

Kay, Arnold C.

Keller, Russell E.

Kelley, George B.

Kistler, Robert

Klein, Thomas H.

Kline, Charles E.

Klogetvedt, John C.

Knowles, McColley W. F.

Kolody, Paul

Kormos, Charles

Kozub, John A.

Kranson, Laurence A.

Krecker, Preston S., Jr.

Ksenyak, Stefan

Kupinski, Walter J.

Lafferty, Lee M.

Laird, Truman R.

Lallier, John A., Jr.

Landrum, Robert

Landscoot, Lloyd F.

Lang, Edward H.

Lassiter, Ernest C.

Lawrence, William J., Jr.

Ledford, William G.

Lehman, Raymond J.

Lehr, Lawrence W.

Lemanski, Casimer

Lemmer, Richard L.

Lewis, Albert F.

Lewis, Carl

Lewis, Irvin

Logan, William A.

Lohr, Charles F.

Long, William L.

Lord, Jesse M.

Loucks, William K.

Luisi, Rocco

Luthy, David M.

Lutkiewicz, Frank L.

MacFarlane, Hubert W.

Mahoney, Everett C.

Majofsky, Edward C.

Malecki, Albert J.

Malinowski, Edwin

Malone, Fred B.

Manning, John W.

Marino, John G.

Marshall, Richard J., Jr.

Martin, Guy H.

Matthews, William C.

Mauk, Raymond H.

May, Paul

Maycrovich, John S., Jr.

Maye, Paul R.

Mayer, Erwin K.

McAlister, Edgar L.

McAteer, Nowell C.

McCaffrey, Francis E.

McCann, Wilburn

McCanty, Oliver D.

McCarthy, William N.

McCloud, Linwood B.

McCoy, Ernest G.

McDowell, Hillary L.

McIntyre, Alvin E.

McIntyre, Clarence E.

McManus, Charles A., Jr.

Mertes, John G.

Metzger, Frederick

Meyerhoffer, Matthew J.

Michaud, Rosaire R.

Mikolosko, George

Miles, David S.

Miller, Clifford

Miller, William P.

Mincieli, Nicholas F.

Mizak, Joseph A.

Moeller, Ernest J.

Monaghan, Aloysius

Montalbano, James S.

Moran, Glenn J.

Morehead, Emmet H.

Morley, James L.

Morton, John D.

Mullin, Charles L.

Murphy, Kerney R.

Nash, James M.

Nau, Harold L.

Neese, Charles B., Jr.

Neuses, Joseph F.

Niehaus, Bernhard E.

Nimmo, Glenys O.

Nix, William E.

Nolen, Thomas E.

Novello, Charles L.

Nussear, Lawrence R.

Oberg, Harold E.

O'Connor, Daniel E.

O'Donnell, John J.

Oppenheimer, Morton

Oren, Clifford J.

Orlomoski, William E.

Ostrow, Edgar J.

Outten, Alvin G.

Pack, Charles L.

Paczosa, Harold G.

Paine, James R.

Palm, Stanley V.

Parent, William W.

Parsons, George W.

Pearsall, Richard H.

Peffers, William K.

Peiser, Budd

Pennepacker, James E.

Percy, Francis B.

Perdue, Robert S.

Peters, Arthur E., Jr.

Pettit, Albert

Pfohlman, Thomas G.

Phelps, Lloyd E.

Phillips, Walter E.

Pittman, Robert M.

Plemons, George D.

Poling, Clark V.

Pomelek, Leo J.

Potts, Charles P.

Prellwitz, Harold G.

Rankin, Paul L., Jr.

Rasche, Silas P.

Rathbone, Jack

Reeder, Martin L.

Rees, William G.

Reynolds, William C.

Ricks, Carson L.

Ritchie, Edward G.

Robinette, Mervin M.

Robinson, Marshall K.

Roccuzzo, Salvatore R.

Rooney, Philip H.

Roum, William

Rowdon, James A.

Rowe, Joseph F.

Ryan, James M.

Sabin, Walter R.

Sack, Ervin R.

Sanford, Ralph H.

Savant, John

Savidge, Elwood D.

Schefbauer, Joseph S.

Scheibel, Joseph A.

Schreibman, Harry

Serby, William A.

Shea, James J.

Sherbondy, Harry J.

Sherman, Jacob

Sherman, Robert H.

Shornak, Joseph F.

Silkey, Leonard F.

Silver, Henry

Silzle, Richard W.

Sitkowski, Chester E.

Spoonamore, William E.

Stack, Charles R.

Stelzman, Conrad J., Jr.

Stonage, Charles H.

Suder, Harold R.

Sutton, William J., Jr.

Tarbet, Thomas D.

Telck, John F.

Titsworth, A. C.

Todd, Vernon

Tonali, Ernest P.

Trobaugh, George D.

Turney, Kenneth E.

Vannaular, Ralph E.

Vernalis, Anthony

Vintera, Charles M.

Visconti, Febo

Vosse, John W.

Vreeland, George L.

Walker, Fred W.

Walsh, Michael P.

Washington, John P.

Webb, Asher B.

Wells, William S.

Westbrook, Huey M.

Whipple, Malcolm E.

Wilczenski, Chester T.

Willis, Aubrey C.

Wilson, Earl W.

Wright, Virgil

Wuestenberg, Clarence

Yarbrough, Glenn D.

Yee, Sam M.

Yingling, James, Jr.

Zelmanowitz, Milton

Zerden, Glenn

Ziverk, Johnnie, Jr.

NAVY SURVIVORS

Arpaia, William H.

Booth, Paul H.

Ciccia, Charles B.

McCoy, Winfield

McMinn, William J.

McVey, Edward J.

Nowinski, Michael J.

Stricklin, Willie F.

Summers, Roy N.

NAVY DEAD

Digiantommaso, Thomas J.

Estes, Don

Mangafreda, Joseph

McDonnal, William H.

Patterson, Daniel F., Jr.

Riggs, John R.

Stewart, Harold H.

Streicher, Richard B.

Strzykowski, John

Sutton, Garland A.

Swanson, Carl B.

Taylor, Ralph L.

Weaver, George W.

Williams, Robert R.

MERCHANT MARINE SURVIVORS

Alejandro, Juan R.

Beach, Harold W.

Bebber, Fred F.

Benkler, Frank A.

Berry, John D.

Buhn, Frank A.

Caulley, James F.

Clark, Wilbur M.

Dix, Samuel W.

Dore, Eugene N.

Evelyn, Lewis V.

Goodridge, Irwin C.

Janes, Nicholas N.

Jann, William L.

Kunickas, Chester F.

Lamey, Frank L.

Moffett, Hugh

Moran, Louis

Nehl, August H.

O'Keeffe, Daniel J.

Pazitka, Joseph

Rivera, Francisco

Rolita, Manuel P.

Tetreault, Donat E.

Van Clief, Allaire W.

White, Irwin Jr.

Williams, Charles

Zuniga, Timothy P.

MERCHANT MARINE DEAD

Ackermann, Ira E.

Barbara, Pasquale

Barends, Arnulfo

Barrios, Alejandro

Baylis, Graham W.

Bertolotti, Joseph

Bidgood, Frederick

Borkowicz, Wladyslaw J.

Brady, Kenneth

Brown, Gilbert F.

Browne, Hiram

Burgos, Louis

Caradeuc, Raymond J.

Colon, Adolph, Jr.

Corrales, Thomas

Cottrell, Joseph F.

Danielsen, Hans J.

Davies, Charles

Davila, Daniel

Day, Emmette C.

Delliano, Santiago

Dembofsky, Nathan

Dembofsky, William

De Rosa, Jerry

Diaz, Anthony

Duffy, George F.

England, Arnold W.

Figueroa, Enrique

Fishman, Morris S.

Flores, Mariano T.

Florez, Luis

Gamboa, Cruz

Gavin, Edward J.

Griesmann, Frank P.

Guissa, Antonio D.

Gunther, Emilio

Haahti, Wilja

Halsey, Samuel H.

Hanafin, William

Hector, Philip

Hederman, William E.

Hill, Carl G.

Ignacio, Nacho

Kaminski, Constanti

Klein, Gerald H.

Knutsen, Knute

Kuchavick, Victor J.

Lang, Charles G.

Lindstrom, Walter E.

Lisk, Cecil W.

Loeble, Charles I.

Logan, John H.

Lopes, Antonio J.

Lopes, Diamantino M.

Lopes, Miguel A.

Lopez, Ramon E.

MacPherson, Roy C.

Marin, Arturo

Matias, Catalino

Maxwell, John F.

McEachron, Willie

McGill, William J.

McTeague, Neal F.

Mearns, Robert

Median, Antonio

Merritt, Charles H.

Mido, J. R.

Mills, John E.

Monge, Alejandro
Newman, Edward
Nilsson, Bonde
Nitti, Daniel D.
Ocasio, Thomas
Olmo, Jose A.
O'Rourke, James J.
Overdick, Walter
Parks, Edward
Patalive, Frank J.
Paulsen, Frederick H.
Pella, Juan
Raymond, Richard T.
Rayner, Louis
Reinosa, Ignacio
Ritter, James
Roberts, Melvin E.
Robins, George

Rosario, Lorenzo E.
Schmoker, Richard J.
Schnauder, Ferdinand, Jr.
Seeger, Eugene
Seibel, John A.
Silberg, Martin
Slawson, Paul
Soto, Nicolas B.
Swogger, Herman W.
Tessler, Martin
Thomas, Paul H.
Toledo, Jose
Torres, Henry
Travisso, Guillermo
Tuckett, George
Tyler, Samuel T.
Wright, Norris L.
Yakonis, Anthony C.

COAST GUARD SURVIVORS
(Aboard *Dorchester*)

Birmingham, Thomas J.
Looney, Arthur J.
Peno, John O.

Phillips, James W.
Phillips, Roland Z.
Sepers, Leonard

COAST GUARD DEAD
(Aboard *Dorchester*)

Bell, Joseph B
Buerdsel, Joseph D.
Courtney, Phillip
Ellsworth, Harold J.
Fase, Marcus
Garrido, Victoriano B.
Gifford, Elliot T.

Hope, Paul F.
Kelley, William J.
Kretz, William J.
Lambert, William J.
Lee, Robert
MacDonald, George J.
McClain, James A.

McHugh, Walter F.

Mount, Willard

Olszewski, Joseph S.

Paterson, William G.

Phillips, Robert J.

Pitts, John A.

Smith, Alvin A.

Stokes, Franklin L.

Struder, James A.

Wicks, Eugene

Williams, Clarence V.

Zechini, Peter T.

CIVILIAN SURVIVORS

Allen, William E.

Bisgaard, Tony (Danish)

Bodeen, Gilbert W.

Bojesen, Knut (Danish)

Carriero, Samuel J.

Edmunds, William E.

Ferrary, William J.

Flink, Gunnar A.

Forsmark, Harold G.

Geschwind, David

Gillette, Donald E.

Gorton, Milan G.

Grimshaw, James R.

Gunthner, Emil G.

Hadan, Lee

Haij, Carl L.

Hamilton, Anthony J.

Haran, Patrick J.

Harrison, Archibald J.

Hoatson, James

Hull, William E., Jr.

Jorgensen, Paul

Kaar, Hagor W.

Kappers, Cornelius

Kelly, George N.

Kilroy, Thomas F.

Knudsen, Knut (Danish)

Landolina, Alexander

McCrosson, John

McGivney, J. P.

Mershon, George N.

Overvag, Alfred

Perez, Robert F.

Polachino, Dante

Reilly, Philip

Robinson, Joseph

Ross, Andrew L.

Schiavone, Martin

Sienkiewicz, Henry

Stenman, Eiler E.

Sytsma, Jack

Taylor, Blair J.

Vegas, Lawrence F.

Wachtel, Louis

Weaver, Walter L.

Zogg, Edward

CIVILIAN DEAD

Adrian, Joseph

Albach, Thomas J.

Albert, Leonard S.

Alvarez, Abraham

Andersen, Alex C. (Danish)

Andreasen, Holger H. (Danish)

Archer, Robert

Bailey, John W.

Barron, Harry

Berentsen, Arnfelth E.

Bitter, Henry H.

Blick, Gustaf A.

Boye, Johannes S. (Danish)

Brandt, Mervin H.

Brennan, John W.

Broderick, Nicholas

Brodsky, Harry M.

Buckheit, Jacob A.

Buckingham, Arthur J.

Burke, Francis J.

Burke, William F.

Carlson, Carl G.

Carrow, Norman F.

Cavaliere, Raymond A.

Centanni, Angelo

Clark, Arthur K.

Colin, Henry H.

Cornell, Gosta V.

Crater, Lloyd L.

Cunningham, John F.

Currey, Charles William

Daly, Eugene A.

Daniels, Lester W. J.

Daniels, Vincent J.

Dickel, Charles W.

Dierkes, Henry H.

Doering, Charles L.

Domanski, Frank

Dorrington, James

Doyle, James E.

Enquist, Henrik J. (Danish)

Evers, Huston N.

Fagerlie, Johannes

Finnegan, Thomas J.

Foster, William E.

Frederiksen, Aksel G. (Danish)

Fyfe, Thomas

Getz, William

Girton, Orville P.

Globnik, Louis

Gott, Charles M.

Grubman, Charles S.

Hagelberg, Otto A.

Haggerty, John L.

Handler, Lawrence C.

Hansen, Olaf (Danish)

Harris, Charles F.

Hegg, Harry L.

Herr, John E.

Holden, Thomas E.

Holle, Edward E.

Holt, Albert L.

Hommes, Walter

Hutchinson, Walter W.

Jackson, Reuben

Jacobsen, Finn

Jones, Albert T.

Jorgensen, Gunnar (Danish)

Kane, Frank
Kelly, William B.
Kleberg, Knud B. (Danish)
Knutsen, Knut A.
Kock, Johannes D. (Danish)
Kostoff, Herman H.
Kramer, Morris
Larsen, Richard B. (Danish)
Laureanti, Joseph M.
Lewis, George H.
Ludwig, Frank J.
Luning, Alexander
Luning, Henry J. C.
MacEwen, Wellington A.
Maier, John C.
Markowski, Benjamin
Mascia, Frank
Mensch, Andrew G.
Molino, Charles
Nichols, William S.
Obst, Harold L.
Olsen, Joseph W.
Paul, David
Pearson, Sven
Pegram, Homer L.
Peters, Charles E.
Petersen, Einar R. (Danish)
Peterson, William A.

Petricca, Norbert J.
Quinn, James J.
Raffe, Sam
Reed, William P.
Reilly, John J.
Roberts, Guy T.
Rodman, William
Rude, Vernon E.
Schutz, Richard W.
Seni, James J.
Smith, Ernest A.
Smith, Raymond W.
Snoek, Johannes W.
Sorensen, Andry M. (Danish)
Stonebanks, John, Jr.
Stray, Arthur S.
Swanwick, William E.
Taylor, William
Thomaen, Helge K. (Danish)
Thuren, Henry G.
Townsend, Canniff, Jr.
Vanderlaan, Richard
Van Etten, George E.
Voce, Frank W.
Weber, Frederick
Weinmann, Arthur
Wynne, Bernard T.
Youngman, Samuel

INDEX

celebrity of, 22--23, 33, 86, 88
and Chapel of the Four Chaplains,
    187--88
sermons of, 91--92
son's courtship and, 89
son's death and, 182
son's education and, 89--90
World War I service of, 84--85
Poling, Elizabeth Jung "Betty," 25--27,
    91--93
correspondence between husband and,
    36, 79
generosity of, 92
husband's courtship of, 89
husband's death and, 182
husband's eccentricities and, 91--92
husband's last visit with, 35--36
husband's posthumous honors and, 184
wedding of, 91
Poling, Eve Corey, 183
Poling, Jane, 84--85
Poling, Lillian Diebold Heingartner,
    85--86
Poling, Mary, 84--85
Poling, Rachel, 85--86
Poling, Susan (mother), 81, 83--85
Poling, Susan "Thumper" (daughter), 25,
    182--83
Povlak, Anthony J., 222
Prause, Robert H., 159
Protestants, Protestantism, 38
    Poling's ministry and, 22
    troopship assignments and, 32--33

Quakers, 80--81, 87
Queen Mary, 7, 32

Reagan, William, 87
Rednour, Forrest O., 159, 162, 179
Revolutionary War, 15, 24, 86--87
Roman Catholics, Roman Catholicism,
    22, 37--38, 44
    conservative, 57
    Dorchester and, 73
    Fox's abandonment of, 16
    Fox's childhood and, 41
    in St. John's, 79
    troopship assignments and, 32--33

U-boat sighting and, 114--15
Warish and, 37
Washington's education and, 105--9
Roosevelt, Franklin D., 64
Röser, Kurt, 98--99, 186--87
    and torpedo attack on *Dorchester,* 118,
    121, 176--77
Rutgers University, 88

St. Genevieve's Church, 109
St. John's:
    departure of *Dorchester* from, 95--96,
    99, 173
    docking of *Dorchester* at, 75, 78--79, 95,
    153
    and sinking of *Escanaba,* 178--79
St. Paul's Evangelical Lutheran Church, 71
St. Rose's, 105--6
St. Stephen's Church:
    Washington honored by, 185
    Washington's position as priest at, 28,
    109--10, 185
St. Venantius Church, 109
Schenectady, N.Y., 25--27, 36, 182
    Poling honored in, 185
    Poling's ministry in, 25--26, 90--92
Schwoebel, Anna Washington, 105--6,
    184
"Screening Instructions for Escort of
    Convoy Operations," 135--36
Secret Service, U.S., 99
September 11, 2001, terrorism on, x
Seton Hall University, 106--7
Seymour Johnson Field, 20--22
South Africa, 186
Soviet Union, Red Army of, 75
Staten Island Edison Company, 46
Strait of Belle Isle, 5, 7
Sugihara, Chiune, 186
Sullivan, Edwin, 110
Summers, Roy:
    abandon-ship order and, 123
    childhood of, 122
    civilian life of, 189
    religious beliefs of, 114, 155, 169
    and rescuing survivors of *Dorchester,*
    130, 137--38, 147--48, 151--52,
    154--55, 163, 169
    in storm, 101

247

PHOTO · JAMES KRIEGSMAN

DAN KURZMAN, a onetime foreign correspondent for *The Washington Post*, was the author of seventeen books, including *Fatal Voyage: The Sinking of the USS Indianapolis*; *Left to Die: The Tragedy of the USS Juneau*; and *Genesis 1948: The First Arab-Israeli War*. He was the recipient of the George Polk Memorial Award, the Overseas Press Club's Cornelius Ryan Award for the Best Book on Foreign Affairs (twice), the National Jewish Book Award, and the Newspaper Guild's Front Page Award.

Kurzman reported from almost every country in Europe, Asia, Africa, the Middle East, and Latin America. Before joining *The Washington Post*, he served as Paris correspondent for the International News Service, as Jerusalem correspondent for NBC News, and as Tokyo bureau chief of the McGraw-Hill News Service.

Dan Kurzman died in 2010.

A B O U T   T H E   T Y P E

This book was set in Requiem, a typeface designed by the Hoefler Type Foundry. It is a modern typeface inspired by inscriptional capitals in Ludovico Vicentino degli Arrighi's 1523 writing manual. *Il modo de temperare le penne.* An original lowercase, a set of figures, and an italic in the "chancery" style that Arrighi helped popularize were created to make this adaptation of a classical design into a complete font family.

Printed in the United States
by Baker & Taylor Publisher Services